A Republic of Men

A Republic of Men

The American Founders, Gendered Language, and Patriarchal Politics

Mark E. Kann

NEW YORK UNIVERSITY PRESS
New York and London

NEW YORK UNIVERSITY PRESS
New York and London

Library of Congress Cataloging-in-Publication Data
Kann, Mark E.
A republic of men : the American founders, gendered language, and patriarchal politics / Mark E. Kann.
p. cm.
Includes bibliographical references (p.)and index.
ISBN 0-8147-4713-2 (cloth : acid-free paper) :
ISBN 0-8147-4714 0 (pbk. : acid-free paper)
1. Political culture—United States—History—18th century.
2. Political science—United States—History—18th century.
3. Men—United States—History—18th century.
4. Patriarchy—United States—History—18th century.
5. Sex role—United States—History—18th century.
6. Social role—United States—History—18th century. I. Title.
JK54K26 1998
305.32'0973'09033—dc21 97-45399
CIP

New York University Press books are printed on acid-free paper, and their binding materials are chosen for strength and durability.

Manufactured in the United States of America

10 9 8 7 6 5 4 3 2 1

For my family

Contents

Preface ix

Introduction 1
1 The Culture of Manhood 5
2 The Grammar of Manhood 30
3 The Bachelor and Other Disorderly Men 52
4 The Family Man and Citizenship 79
5 The Better Sort and Leadership 105
6 The Heroic Man and National Destiny 130
7 The Founders' Gendered Legacy 155

Notes 179
Bibliography 219
Index 231
About the Author 238

Preface

I started this book in 1986. After doing some initial research, I began to write an introductory chapter meant to create a context for examining the American founders' construction of gender and politics. My idea was to explore the gendered basis of seventeenth-century English political theory and the gendered evolution of nineteenth-century American culture. Building on the past and anticipating the future, I would then focus the main analysis on how the founders inherited, adapted, altered, and bequeathed patriarchal politics during the late eighteenth century. Alas, the best laid plans . . . By the time I had drafted the first chapter and divided it in two, and then again several times, my introductory chapter had become a book. *On the Man Question: Gender and Civic Virtue in America* was published in 1991.

At that point, I focused directly on the writings and speeches of the American founders. I was intrigued by their language. Many of them were obsessed with democratic disorder in the ranks of men. They developed and deployed a "grammar of manhood" that provided informal rules for stigmatizing disorderly men, justifying citizenship for deserving men, and elevating exceptional men to positions of leadership and political authority. Importantly, the terms they used to stigmatize disorderly men (e.g., *effeminacy*), characterize citizenship (e.g., *manly freedom*), and legitimize political leadership (e.g., *civic fatherhood*) precluded women from participating in what became a republic of men. I decided to focus this book on how the founders' gendered language and concepts shaped their patriarchal politics.

I presented aspects of my research in a series of conference papers that explored the founders' gendered language and politics. Early comments from Shane Phelan, Christine Di Stefano, and especially Pauline Schloesser encouraged me to broaden my focus and refine my analysis. Later remarks by Kirstie McClure and Kathy Ferguson were important to the revision process. Booth Fowler, Judith Grant, and Robin Romans read rough drafts of several chapters, persuading me to temper some claims and investigate others. Michael Kimmel's reading of the full first draft provided a useful sense of what was still missing, while Harry Brod's superb critique of the entire manuscript guided me through the next round of research and revisions. Kevin White's thorough and informed reading of the penultimate draft was the basis for a final set of revisions. I thank all of these scholars for their time, energy, interest, and insights.

Two aspects of this research have been previously published. "Manhood, Immortality, and Politics during the American Founding," *Journal of Men's Studies* 5, 2 (November 1996), weaves together a number of loose threads to show how the founders relied on the idea of immortality to temper individualism and promote public order. "The Bachelor and Other Disorderly Men," *Journal of Men's Studies* 6, 1 (August 1997), explores the founders' portrait of male marginality and examines its relationship to family, citizenship, and political leadership. I am immensely grateful to *Journal of Men's Studies* editor James Doyle for his wisdom, collegiality, and flexibility.

I am tempted to spell out in detail how important my wife and son have been to the thinking that went into this book, the process of writing and rewriting it, and the fact that it is now completed. Instead, let me simply say, Kathy and Simon, I love you.

Introduction

The American founders aspired to create a republic of men. Their problem was that a democratic distemper infected the men of their time, resulting in disorderly conduct that threatened the republic's birth, health, and longevity. The founders addressed this problem by employing hegemonic norms of manhood to stigmatize and bring into line disorderly men, reward responsible men with citizenship, and empower exceptional men with positions of leadership and authority. One result was that their republic presupposed and perpetuated women's exclusion from politics. My thesis is that the founders employed a "grammar of manhood" to encourage American men to reform themselves, to restore order to the hierarchical ranks of men, and to foster social stability, political legitimacy, and patriarchal power.

The American founders' political aspirations were framed by manhood in two ways. First, the founders sought liberty, equality, and citizenship for American males. They inherited and accepted patriarchal laws, institutions, and values that portrayed politics as an exclusive male enterprise that precluded women's participation in public life. Theorists such as Louis Hartz and historians such as Bernard Bailyn have presumed that early American political thought was a discourse among men about men. More recently, scholars such as Linda Kerber and Joan Hoff have exhumed the founders' gendered language to demonstrate that they defined male citizenship in opposition to womanhood. The founders' original intent, then, was to create and sustain a republic based on male governance and female subordination.

Second, the founders made political distinctions among men. Most obviously, they elevated white males to rights-bearing citizens and at the same time devalued African males as dependents and Indian males as aliens. They also debated the implications of distinguishing propertied and unpropertied males. The English freeholder tradition reserved citizenship for men of substantial property because they alone were trusted to be independent and interested in the public good. But some American leaders suggested that a young man's coming of age could be a sufficient qualification for citizenship and that other factors, such as time of residence, family status, occupation, and future prospects, might be taken into account. Ultimately, the founders intended to establish a republic of men based on *some* men's rights and authority.

But which men? Simply asking the question suggests that the founders' rhetoric of liberty and equality should not be taken at face value. Certainly, the founders committed themselves to the democratic proposition that all men were created free and equal and could not be governed without their own consent. Simultaneously, they did not believe that "all men," or even "all white men" or "all white Protestant men," could be trusted with equal liberty or equal citizenship or equal authority. They could not imagine a "rankless republic." Most founders thought the majority of males were passionate creatures who converted liberty into license, perverted equality into leveling, and subverted republican order. Many were obsessed with democratic disorder in the ranks of men and sought to control it.

Whether America's disorderly males could be trusted with citizenship depended, in part, on whether they measured up to contemporary standards of manhood. Were they able to combine independence and self-restraint? Could they reconcile family responsibility with fraternal civility? Did they demonstrate a capacity to exercise rights but defer to legitimate leaders? There were no easy answers, particularly as the meanings of manhood shifted during the founding era. The ideal of the traditional patriarch was destabilized by significant changes in gender relationships. Americans debated, for example, whether a mature man ruled his family with an iron fist or a velvet glove. Disputed images of manhood were further complicated by nuances of class, religion, race, and region. After the Revolution, evangelicals identified manhood with restored patriarchal prerogative whereas artisans equated manhood with "the assertion of the autonomous individual over and above the patriarchal pretensions of the merchant elite."[1] America's culture of manhood was a complex, diverse, and contested arena.

Nevertheless, the subtext of American manhood was remarkably stable. Americans agreed that manhood demanded economic and political independence, or "manly freedom." They marked out pathways to manhood that commonly passed through marriage and fatherhood. John Witherspoon spoke for his contemporaries when he linked manhood to tempering the passions of "the single life," recognizing "the necessity of marriage," and becoming a father who "subdues selfishness" in parenting his children. Americans also defined manhood in opposition to womanhood. Being a man meant governing female dependents and exhibiting the manly virtue and merit that controlled alleged female vices such as deceit and corruption. The consensual core of early American manhood was the conviction that young males should mature into independent family patriarchs who governed female dependents.[2]

Like most elites, the American founders drew on cultural complexities and consensual norms to establish and maintain their hegemony. In particular, they employed a "grammar of manhood" to promote public quiescence, encourage popular consent, justify leadership, and stabilize political authority. They used gendered language to stigmatize disorderly males and democrats as effeminate and childish, to encourage them to settle into family responsibility and sober citizenship, to foster fraternal trust between citizens and their representatives, and to legitimize the extralegal prerogative of exceptional leaders. The founders' grammar of manhood functioned as the conservative core of early American liberalism. It was not planned or systematic, but it was sufficiently coherent and compelling to communicate criteria for excluding some males, including others, and elevating a few to political prominence and power.

At times, the founders were self-conscious about relating manhood to politics. Thomas Paine published *Common Sense* to awaken Americans from "unmanly slumbers" and shame men into defending the liberty earned by forefathers, enjoyed by families, and owed to posterity. Stanley Griswold condensed a call for men's self-discipline against political factionalism by making a plain but pertinent plea: "Oh Americans! Be men." Most of the time, however, the founders were not self-conscious about using gendered language to explain the political world. They simply found it natural and appropriate, for example, to applaud "this manly, this heroic, and truly patriotic spirit" of American militiamen and to condemn the "effeminate and delicate soldiers" of the British army.[3] Self-conscious or not, nearly all founders relied on the grammar of manhood to convey the message that manly courage in the struggle for liberty and manly self-restraint in the exercise of liberty were the essence of republican citizenship. Women need not apply.

Chapter 1 explores the culture of manhood in eighteenth-century America by identifying shifting and stable elements in gender relations that linked the language of manhood to politics. Chapter 2 examines the founders' grammar of manhood—the hegemonic norms, language, and rules they employed to promote public quiescence and justify leadership. Chapters 3–6 focus on how the founders applied the grammar of manhood to reform disorderly men, restore order in the hierarchical ranks of men, and legitimize political leadership and authority. Chapter 3 looks at "the Bachelor" and other disorderly men who provoked the founders' exclusionary tendencies. Chapter 4 discusses "the Family Man" as a symbol of male maturity in the service of citizenship. Chapter 5 considers the founders' commitment to "the Better Sort" of men as leaders and lawmakers. Chapter 6 analyzes the figure of "the Heroic Man," whose exceptional manhood and leadership abilities qualified him to exercise an extralegal prerogative to resolve crises and procreate a promising future for posterity. Chapter 7 concludes by considering how the founders' hegemonic norms continue to order men's relations, restrain democracy, and devalue women's place in modern American politics.

1 The Culture of Manhood

Judith Sargent Murray once instructed her readers, "Let every American play the man for his country."[1] The phrase was a common one. Writers and speakers employed it to motivate young males to quit their disorderly ways, measure up to standards of manhood, and fulfill their duties as citizens. What did "play the man" mean? How did manhood relate to politics? In the last half of the eighteenth century, the American culture of manhood was a complex discursive arena composed of contested ideals and consensual norms that the American founders molded into a relatively coherent "grammar of manhood" that defined citizenship and legitimized leadership in the new republic.

The Traditional Patriarch

Early America's dominant ideal of manhood was the traditional patriarch who devoted himself to governing his family and serving his community. E. Anthony Rotundo describes the traditional patriarch as "a towering figure . . . the family's unquestioned ruler." He exhibited exemplary self-control and little visible emotion. He might express "approval or disapproval in place of affection or anger" and govern family dependents through "persuasion and sympathy," but he also could issue edicts and enforce his will with coercive power and corporal punishment. The traditional patriarch governed his "little commonwealth" by supervising his wife's piety and productivity, and by managing his sons' education and children's marriages to perpetuate his family line. Though his authority was nearly absolute, a family father was accountable to church officials and civic leaders, who sought to ensure the "good order in the home" they thought essential to social harmony and the public good.[2]

American culture encouraged young males to discipline desire, marry early, sire legitimate offspring, and mature into traditional patriarchs. Protestant clergy counseled youth on marital duty as an alternative to sexual promiscuity or priestly chastity. During the Great Awakening, Susan Juster reports, Congregational ministers worried that New Light spiritual individualism, disregard for authority, and emotionalism fostered "a kind of sexual anarchy," "a potential for sexual libertinism," and "a sexualized climate" subversive of family stability and public order. The proper way to transform male lust into virtue was to channel it into monogamous marriage and sublimate it into family responsibility. Secular wisdom also urged young men into marriage. A Virginian communicated common sense on the subject in 1779 by stating, "No man who has health, youth, and vigor on his side can when arrived to the age of manhood do without a woman." In turn, marriage focused male passion on family duty. Nancy Cott observes, "Marriage was seen as a relationship in which the husband agreed to provide food, clothing, and shelter for his wife, and she agreed to return frugal management, and obedient service." Fundamentally, "to 'act like a man' meant to support one's wife."[3]

Not all young males could act like a man. Mary Noyes Silliman counseled her sons to "lay a foundation in subsistence" before contemplating marriage. That was especially difficult when fathers withheld the land and patrimony that sons needed to support a family, or when fathers had little or no realty to transmit to their sons. Still, few writers saw economic want as prohibitive. Benjamin Franklin argued that any poor, hardworking young man could acquire enough land to start a family. George Washington applauded the opening of the Ohio Valley as an opportunity for "the poor, the needy, and the oppressed" to own land and start families. Thomas Jefferson justified the Louisiana Purchase, in part, as enabling "everyone who will labor to marry young and to raise a family of any size." The choice of marriage was a different matter for servants, apprentices, and slaves, who needed their masters' permission to marry; but masters such as Thomas Jefferson approved of dependent marriages as a means to tame male passions and make male slaves more obedient and reliable.[4]

The reputed "taming effect" of marriage threatened to subject young men to the manipulative powers of potentially domineering women. John Gregory's popular advice book *A Father's Legacy to His Daughter* admonished against women's tendency to abuse their power "over the hearts of men," and *Pennsylvania Magazine* sounded an alert against "bad wives [who] flatter and tyrannize over men of sense." Alas, marriage exposed men to female tyranny. One counterresponse was to define manhood as tyranny over women. American fiction embodied figures such as Hannah Webster Foster's Peter Sanford, a coxcomb who saw overcoming obstacles to the sexual conquest of an innocent girl as "the glory of a rake," and Judith Sargent Murray's Sinisterus Courtland, a rogue who squandered his patrimony, fell into debt, and tried "to extricate himself by . . . deluding some woman whose expectations were tolerable into an affair of the heart."[5] A fictive war of the sexes was waged by seductive coquettes and deceitful libertines.

Mainstream culture condemned both the coquette and the libertine but condoned the notion that men needed to restrain disorderly women. The preferred means of restraint were parental education and marital supervision. Laurel Thatcher Ulrich writes that colonial parents sought to instill in their daughters virtues such as "prayerfulness, industry, charity, [and] modesty." At an appropriate age, young women were to marry and submit to their husbands' authority. A well-bred wife did not tyrannize over her husband; nor did a manly husband fear "bondage" from his wife. Benjamin Franklin asserted that "every man that really is a man" would be "master of his own family." If he married a "difficult girl," he still was expected to "subdue even the most restless spirits" and transform an unruly spouse into a virtuous "helpmeet" who practiced piety, gave birth, nursed infants, educated children, cooked, healed, manufactured, managed servants, grew food, tended livestock, traded in the marketplace, worked in the family shop, took in boarders, or engaged in paid employment. The precise nature and degree of a husband's authority varied by religion, race, ethnicity, class, and region, but the legitimacy of his family sovereignty was everywhere secured by law and custom.[6]

A major motive for young men to marry was to procreate legitimate sons. John Demos explains that the traditional patriarch sired, raised, and educated sons to continue his "accomplishments, indeed his very character, into the future." The Reverend John Robinson noted that grandfathers often were "more affectionate towards their children's children than to their immediates as seeing themselves further propagated in them, and by their means proceeding to a further degree of eternity, which all desire naturally, if not in themselves, yet in their posterity." A concerned father made sacrifices to provision and protect sons and, in turn, expected to achieve a sense of immortality through his children. Contemporary testamentary practices indicated that northern men tried to extend family dynasties for one generation and southern men hoped to perpetuate them even longer. The conviction that fathers were deeply devoted to their posterity suggested that they had an enduring stake in the community that justified citizenship. Accordingly, New York artisans proposed in the 1760s that "every man who honestly supports a family by useful employment" should have the right to vote and hold office.[7]

The traditional patriarch's performance as husband and father was his main contribution to the community. Men with marital responsibilities disciplined their passions; husbands who were masters of a household restrained women's disorderly conduct; and responsible fathers produced sons likely to mature into trustworthy citizens. Also, the traditional patriarch represented his household in the various hierarchies that ordered the larger society. This meant, among other things, that he recognized, respected, and deferred to his superiors—the "fathers" and "tender parents" of his communal family.[8]

Destabilizing Traditional Patriarchy

The ideal of the traditional patriarch was destabilized between 1750 and 1800 when, Jay Fliegelman suggests, Americans began to surrender "an older patriarchal family authority" in favor of "more affectionate and equalitarian" family relationships.[9] English Whig ideology and disputed gender relations, a gap between American patriarchal ideals and actual gender relations, and dynamic economic change contributed to a weakening of the traditional patriarch as the dominant ideal of manhood. The result was not the elimination of the old ideal but the emergence of several alternative ideals.

England transmitted to America a mixed image of manhood. On the one hand, seventeenth- and eighteenth-century Englishmen legitimized the traditional patriarch and authorized him to rule family dependents with almost "absolute authority." He managed a wife whose lot was "perpetual pregnancy" to multiply her husband's person "by propagation." He supervised his sons' upbringing to ensure they would mature into responsible stewards of the family dynasty. The exemplary patriarch spoke with an upper-class accent, but his authority trickled down so that even "lower-class household rulers" were considered more manly and mature than "peers who were still in service and lacked families of their own." English writers agreed that a "well-ordered family," with an "orderly head" and "orderly members," was "the basis of the entire social order."[10]

On the other hand, the Whig attack on absolute kingship generated doubts about all absolute authority. Algernon Sidney, James Tyrrell, and John Locke vested familial authority in the traditional patriarch but they also sought to limit paternal power to prevent domestic tyranny. They experimented with the idea of marriage as a negotiable contract that could be terminated in divorce; they emphasized a husband's duties toward his wife; and they declared adult sons to be fully free and equal men. Also, they allowed for occasional state intervention to prevent and punish patriarchal abuses and even contemplated instances when female sovereignty and filial rebellion were justified.[11]

Popular pamphleteers pushed further in this direction. Mary Astell compared tyrannical husbands to tyrannical kings and suggested that wives in families deserved the same rights that Whigs claimed for men in politics. Other writers complained of "foolish, passionate, stingy, sottish" husbands who thought themselves "free from all restraints." They needed to be less authoritarian and more respectful and loving toward their wives. In the changing family, writes Lawrence Stone, "The authority of husbands over wives and of parents over children declined as greater autonomy was granted to or assumed by all members of the family unit. There were the beginnings of a trend toward greater legal and educational equality between the sexes. . . . Although the economic dependence of these women on their husbands increased, they were granted greater status and decision-making power within the family."[12] This emerging companionate ideal suggested a new model of husband-wife relations, plus a new understanding of father-son relations.

The Whig notion that fathers and adult sons were equals weakened paternal authority. Fathers had only a few years to leave an imprint on sons before the latter became autonomous men. Unfortunately, that imprint was often one of neglect and abuse. James Harrington reported that "innumerable children come to owe their utter perdition" to fathers who ignored them and thereby exposed them to excessive maternal indulgence. John Locke was particularly appalled by fathers whose poor parenting skills "weaken and effeminate" their sons. He proposed a theory of psychological fatherhood to strengthen intergenerational bonds, so that a father could train a son to mature into a proper heir and an "affectionate friend when he is a man." The traditional patriarch's strict authority over his sons was gradually transformed into mere influence over them.[13]

Gordon Schochet concludes that the Whig "rejection of absolute fatherly authority" was more symptomatic "of what was coming rather than . . . [of] what had already taken place." What was coming finally arrived when Americans adapted Whig rhetoric to local conditions. In 1764, James Otis, Jr., resurrected a century-old line of questioning: "Are not women born as free as men? Would it not be infamous to assert that the ladies are all slaves by nature?" A decade later, Thomas Paine denounced men who abused patriarchal authority to play the "tyrant" and keep women "in a state of dependence" akin to slavery. He urged men to give more recognition and respect to women. The next year, Abigail Adams called it indisputable that men had been "naturally tyrannical" to women. She wanted husbands to "give up the harsh title of master for the more tender and endearing one of friend" and to treat wives not as "vassals" but as "under your protection."[14]

In America as in England, Whig rhetoric generated skepticism of vast authority.

Whig rhetoric also called attention to a gap between the ideal of the traditional patriarch and the everyday reality of gender relations. Kenneth Lockridge agrees that traditional patriarchs were expected to control "all things in their households." However, even within a context of domination and subordination, women were historical agents with "substantial power." They had leverage over men during courtship as well as in their roles as mothers, household managers, laborers, religious activists, and widows who controlled family estates and minor children. The extent of women's agency grew during the Revolution, when women assumed de facto family sovereignty, ran farms and shops, participated in America's political and military life, and thereby blurred the boundaries between the masculine and feminine. For many men, women's enlarged influence made them appear to be especially dangerous, destructive, and disorderly creatures.[15]

The gap between the patriarchal ideal and family reality expanded as republican values seeped into domestic culture. Criticism of husbands' arbitrary power and abusive treatment of wives was common in eighteenth-century America. In 1743, for example, a poet castigated "the tyrant husband" who imposed "fatal bondage" on his wife. In 1759, Annis Boudinot Stockton declared, "Oh men behave like men," to insist that husbands stop degrading their wives and instead cherish their virtues. The Revolution's attack on tyranny in favor of benevolence weakened traditional patriarchal authority and strengthened companionate norms in marriage. Judith Sargent Murray wrote that men "usurped an unmanly and unfounded superiority" over women when they ought to strive for "mutual esteem, mutual friendship, mutual confidence, begirt about by mutual forbearance." A husband's respect for his wife was "as tender as it is manly," implying that it was not the stern patriarch but the loving husband who epitomized true manhood.[16]

The dominant ideal was also undermined by economic trends that impaired paternal power. The traditional patriarch monopolized control of land and command of his children's destinies. However, population growth, economic expansion, and commercial development destroyed this monopoly. Even affluent fathers suffered a diminished capacity to transmit land to sons when their settlements became densely populated. In Dedham, Massachusetts, for example, intensified land use fostered family dispersion. As wealth became more unevenly distributed, poor fathers without land to distribute or bequeath discovered they had little economic clout. They could not "control their sons by promising the gift of a farm later in life." Finally, young men had options. Some settled western lands to achieve "what only total independence would recognize, the right to shape their own communities." Others sought their fortunes in towns and cities where commerce opened up new opportunities for income. Many fathers became what scholars call "enlightened paternalists" or "friendly paternalists" who relied on Locke's "subtle, psychological means" to maintain a grip on their posterity.[17]

The traditional patriarch's authority was further eroded by an emerging separation of home and workplace. As men began to leave home to spend their days at separate workplaces, they gradually became part-time husbands and fathers who depended on their wives to manage their households and parent their children. Americans came to believe that men's days in the marketplace "depleted" virtue whereas women and children's time in the domestic sphere "renewed" it. With fathers and sons occupying different spatial and ethical worlds, fathers began to lose the capacity to guide their sons into manhood. Some critics questioned whether fathers tainted by social vices should educate their sons, and most agreed that mothers were increasingly responsible for promoting and protecting their sons' virtue. Eventually, fathers' parental authority was transferred to mothers.[18]

Some Americans reacted to the destabilization of the traditional ideal with what Lockridge labels "patriarchal rage." A youthful Jefferson filled his commonplace book with quotations indicating a misogynist hatred for women allied to an ongoing fantasy "that men could reproduce without women." Jefferson's youthful rage matured into "the subtle and perverse misogyny of the new democratic age" manifested in the nascent doctrine of separate spheres which, Nancy Cott argues, was a means "to shore up manhood (by differentiating it from womanhood) at a time when the traditional concomitants and supports of manhood . . . were being undermined and transformed." New England shoemakers put the doctrine into effect in the 1780s when they began to set up shops outside their homes, take male apprentices into their shops to teach them the entire production process, and recruit female relatives to perform limited functions from within their homes. Artisans reinforced their authority over production in "men's sphere" and reaffirmed their prerogative to confine females, control their knowledge, and harness their labor in "women's sphere." Some women reacted to persistent patriarchy by opposing marriage. Grace Galloway confided to her journal, "Never get tied to a man / for when once you are yoked / Tis all a mere joke / of seeing your freedom again."[19]

Alternative Ideals

The great authority of the traditional patriarch seemed to be at odds with the more egalitarian ethic of republicanism, but the reality was more complex. R. W. K. Hinton remarks that patriarchal fathers could not fully rule their families as long as they were subjected to the king's superior authority.[20] Thus, when rebellious Americans attacked the monarchy, denounced centralized power, and weakened external controls on paternal governance, they made it easier for family heads to exercise authority with minimal external intervention. American law continued to support men's patriarchal powers in their families well beyond the eighteenth century. Nevertheless, the destabilization of the traditional ideal diminished its dominance, and the Revolution stimulated the development of new gender discourses and alternative models of manhood.

One alternative was what Michael Kimmel calls the "aristocratic manhood" of the "the genteel patriarch." A worthy man was someone who adhered to a British upper-class code of honor, cultivated manly sensibilities, relied on inherited wealth or rent on land to support his lifestyle, sired legitimate male heirs to perpetuate his family dynasty, and promoted civic order through philanthropy and public service. An American did not need a title to achieve aristocratic manhood, but he found it immensely helpful to be born into a family that was sufficiently wealthy and cultivated to provide him a proper liberal education, lessons in "manners, taste, and character," and sufficient land and patrimony to become an independent man who established his own family, dispensed patronage, and wielded local authority.[21]

Richard Bushman points out that one paradox of the Revolution was that patriots associated aristocracy with corruption but still sought to capture "aristocratic culture for use in republican society." Men of middling means bought books to teach themselves the details of genteel speech and conduct; they purchased homes and objects that testified to their refined status; and they sought social respectability by admission to the ranks of polite society and participation in public leadership. Even "the rustic," wrote John Perkins, could appreciate and emulate "the gentle manner and obliging behavior of the well-bred and polite." Often, men who pursued the aristocratic ideal saw women as fellow travelers on the road to refinement. Timothy Dwight stated that refinement "raised both men and women above the brutes . . . to make them kindly, cheerful, and modest."[22]

However, the attraction of aristocratic manhood was limited. Men who cultivated their sensibilities were vulnerable to charges of effeminacy. Americans made a fine distinction between manly gentility and unmanly servitude to fad and fashion. G. J. Barker-Benfield reports that men could take refinement only so far, "or it would become effeminacy." That was why a grandfather who noticed his grandson's too great affection for his mother worried lest the boy's "affection should overcome his manhood." Furthermore, male refinement meant keeping up appearances, which could be deceiving. Popular literature portrayed the licentious libertine as a man with "a polished exterior" that masked an "unmanly ambition of conquering the defenseless," while political commentators portrayed the demonic demagogue as a man who pretended refinement to seduce and manipulate the brutish masses.[23] An American male might seek aristocratic manhood for himself but still distrusted its corrupting influence on others.

Another alternative was "republican manhood." This ideal devalued family background, breeding, wealth, and manners to emphasize manly virtue, sociability, and civic-mindedness. The exemplar of republican manhood was the independent farmer who worked his land to ensure his family's subsistence and security as well as his sons' patrimony, established kinlike relations with neighbors, and participated in public activities, including militia service. An allied exemplar was the master artisan who owned his shop, passed on trade skills to his sons, earned respect as a useful contributor to the community, and joined social and political organizations committed to fostering the public good. The republican farmer or craftsman mostly went about his own business and allowed local elites to conduct public affairs. However, he staked his manly independence on his willingness to challenge upper-class corruption and elite domination when necessary. For example, Philadelphia artisans generally deferred to merchant and professional leaders but, at crucial moments, organized against them.[24]

Fictional representations of republican manhood emphasized virtue and independence. In Royall Tyler's play "The Contrast," Colonel Manly was a model of honesty, courage, and commitment. He respected his ancestors, emulated the "illustrious Washington" by fighting in the Revolution, and defended liberty for posterity. Manly had an aide but he was no "servant." The aide affirmed, "I am a true blue son of liberty. . . . Father said that I should come as Colonel Manly's waiter . . . but no man shall master me." A republican man sought happiness with a republican woman. He kept company with worthy women; admired their virtues more than their beauty; respected their reason, education, and skills; married one out of mutual affection; and then relied on his republican wife to keep him virtuous and raise patriotic children. Judith Sargent Murray contended that a republican man found fulfillment in a companionable family organized by "the united efforts of male and female."[25]

This ideal was suited to a republican age, but it still failed to become dominant. Male misogyny persisted and periodically resurfaced to favor the traditional patriarch, for example, in post-Revolution evangelical churches. Also, many people doubted that most men could or would live up to republican standards of manly virtue. Caroline Robbins reminds us that republicanism was generally quite elitist, assuming the necessity of a propertied ruling class to control the "scum" who made up the democratic masses. Finally, the republican ideal may have been born to obsolescence. Gordon Wood, Joyce Appleby, and John Diggins argue that early America's republican rhetoric was accompanied by a more powerful liberal individualism and materialism that guided men's actual conduct. Writers may have felt driven to idealize republican manhood because they sensed its imminent demise.[26]

The third alternative to the traditional patriarch was "self-made manhood." This ideal associated manhood with individualism, materialism, and an entrepreneurial spirit. The new man-on-the-make repressed carnality, avoided alcohol and gambling, and sublimated his desires into competition for accumulation. He did not oppose the other ideals of manhood so much as harness them to his own economic ends. He learned that a reputation for good manners and sober morality could facilitate commercial transactions and business success. Indeed, Americans who exemplified self-made manhood eventually transformed aristocratic sensibilities and republican morality into the highly prized "bourgeois respectability" of nineteenth-century America.[27]

The self-made man was not an isolated, selfish individual. He was a married man who competed in the marketplace to provision and protect his family. He was like George Mason, who explained to his son that he speculated in frontier property not for himself but to ensure his family's comfort for years to come. Furthermore, the self-made man headed a family partnership. He managed any property his wife brought into the marriage, supervised her paid and unpaid labor during the marriage, detailed her role in transmitting family property to the next generation, and sometimes organized and sold his family's labor at home or in factories. Finally, the self-made man was sociable. He belonged to social clubs and fraternal organizations that combined self-improvement efforts and fraternal camaraderie. These groups often encouraged entrepreneurship but usually kept it within the bounds of civility.[28]

Two recent histories of American manhood declare the "triumph of the self-made man" who cultivated "self-improvement, self-control, self-interest, and self-advancement" in the early republic. In fact, the ideal of self-made manhood was the most controversial alternative. Writers, ministers, and politicians equated self-interest to selfishness and factionalism; they attacked materialism as a spur to greed, gambling, profligacy, luxury, conflict, crime, and violence. Commentators who recognized men's grasping nature as an immutable reality rarely idealized it; instead, they tried to cushion its destructive impact. Certainly, the idea that men should be free to make economic decisions to achieve comfort without political restraint was popularized by Jeffersonians in the 1790s but, as Louis Hartz has argued, it was not until the mid-nineteenth century that American culture was able "to electrify the democratic individual with a passion for great achievement and produce a personality type that was . . . the hero of Horatio Alger."[29]

America's mainstream culture of manhood was further complicated by economic, religious, and regional variations of the traditional ideal and its alternatives. Farmers, artisans, gentlemen, Baptists, Congregationalists, northern commercial men, southern planters, and various fraternal groups relied on selective aspects of manhood to isolate dissenters, forge solidarity in their own ranks, build influential coalitions, and defeat opposing interests. Simultaneously, a libertine counterculture cast doubt on all major variations of manhood, while the uncertain gender status of African and Indian males added confusion to the mix. No one knew with confidence whether one alternative or another would predominate, what syntheses might emerge, or if America's multiple masculinities pointed in any discernible direction. The contested old ideal endured alongside the competing newer ones.[30] The chief limit on the cultural diversity of manhood was a general consensus that three norms were central to all manly ideals.

One consensual norm was that manhood required the economic and political independence sometimes known as "manly freedom." A traditional patriarch relied on rents; a male in search of aristocratic manhood was likely to have a profession; a republican farmer worked his land, a craftsman his shop; and a self-made man acquired and invested capital. An independent man was self-supporting. He determined the nature and pace of his labor and kept free of others' patronage and government relief. He could afford to have his own conscience and demanded the liberty to exercise his conscientious will in public. He claimed a right to resist any government that threatened to rob him of liberty and property, and he felt entitled to participate in public deliberations and decision making. A "man" was an independent agent of his personal and public destiny.[31]

The second consensual norm was that a mature man was a family man. A traditional patriarch governed a family estate, assisted by his wife and perpetuated by his sons; an aspirant to aristocratic manhood established a respectable family dynasty by wedding a genteel lady and teaching proper manners to his children; a republican farmer or artisan called on his wife to contribute to family welfare and passed on his land and skills to his sons; a self-made man entered into a lifetime partnership with his wife to build a family business and produce sons to sustain and enlarge it. The ubiquitous belief that every man should mature into the head of a family was predicated on the expectation that married men were relatively responsible and trustworthy men. For most Americans, manhood, marriage, and stability were nearly synonymous.

The third consensual norm was that manhood opposed womanhood. Joan Gundersen suggests that Americans used "a system of negative reference" to define manhood. An independent man was someone who was not a dependent woman or a slave to "effeminacy." Americans also defined a mature man as someone who controlled women. Many years after the Revolution, Americans could still describe a married man as a "king in his family." Critics of tyrannical husbands rarely questioned their authority over women but simply demanded that they conduct themselves with greater civility toward women. Even Judith Sargent Murray's argument for "Equality of the Sexes" conceded male "superiority" to the extent that man was naturally meant to be woman's "protector" and woman was naturally suited to transact "domestick affairs."[32]

Manhood as an Oppositional Concept

Scholars have demonstrated that Western culture commonly defined manhood in opposition to womanhood. Nancy Hartsock writes that classical Greek theorists associated manhood with wisdom, virtue, and citizenship but tied womanhood to "dangerous, disorderly, and irrational forces" in conflict with truth and the public good. Hanna Pitkin reads Machiavelli's republicanism as a story about male protagonists who seek manhood by conquering *Fortuna*, a symbol for treacherous women and antagonistic female forces such as sexuality, dependence, seduction, manipulation, fury, mystery, and chance. Men strive for independence, but *Fortuna* "threatens a man's self-control, his mastery of his own passions." Men who overcome destructive female forces achieve the liberty and civic virtue that constitute manhood and citizenship; those who fail suffer personal instability, social disorder, and political chaos. As such, "The feminine constitutes the other . . . opposed to manhood and autonomy in all their senses: to maleness, to adulthood, to humanness, and to politics." Carole Pateman provides a complementary reading of modern liberal theory as a tale about men who forge a sexual contract to subordinate women and insulate political society against "the disorder of women," whose "bodily natures and sexual passions" threaten to subvert the rule of law.[33]

Similarly, late-eighteenth-century Americans assessed male worth in opposition to female disorders. Carroll Smith-Rosenberg argues that Americans equated manhood to self-control, productivity, virtue, and independence but linked womanhood (a "negative other") to seduction, deceit, luxury, and dependence. Linda Kerber dissects Americans' "gender-specific" citizenship to reveal concepts of ownership, military service, suffrage, and civic virtue that wed public life to male prerogative over disorderly women. Ruth Bloch states that Americans reproduced gender domination by urging patriots to seek manly "glory" and conquer female vices such as "idleness, luxury, dependence." Philip Greven suggests that Americans construed the Revolution as a choice between republican "manliness" and monarchic "femininity" and, Susan Juster adds, they carried on the Revolution "against, not merely without, women." Joan Gundersen, Christine Stansell, and Judith Shklar all agree that patriots "heightened and reinforced" their claim to independence by contrasting it to female dependence. Joan Hoff contends that the framers institutionalized male rights, interests, and opportunities in a market society regulated by a "masculine system of justice" and "the masculinity of the Constitution." Joyce Appleby summarizes the result: "The liberal hero was male." His proper companion, Jan Lewis concludes, was the "republican wife" who managed her family's moral reclamation and civic education.[34]

Scholars of American manhood generally agree that late-eighteenth- and nineteenth-century Americans perpetuated gender opposition. Rotundo identifies the liberal language of the founding era with "the male self," and Kimmel pinpoints "femininity" as the "negative pole" against which men defined themselves. David Pugh argues that the Sons of Liberty displaced their anxieties onto malignant "female qualities" such as "smothering materialism and effeminate inaction," while Michael Rogin suggests that the Jacksonian Era's male mystique was part of men's struggle "to rescue sons from maternal power." Joe Dubbert characterizes the nineteenth century as an era when male "domination, supremacy, and control" in public life stood in opposition to women's moralism in private life. Finally, Kimmel and Peter Filene ascribe a late-nineteenth-century "crisis of masculinity" to male fears that women were making boys effeminate.[35]

Remarkably, the academic accord that Americans defined manhood against womanhood is supported by a wealth of cultural evidence but a dearth of direct political evidence. One can review thousands of pages of founding-era political documents that dwell on virtually every aspect of men's relations without encountering more than a rare reference to women's existence. Political discourse was male-centered, as if men were doing what came naturally when they presumed to monopolize power and ignore women's potential or presence as public persons. Christine Stansell points out that female figures were omnipresent in literature but "almost invisible" in politics. *The Federalist Papers* was typical. It spoke volumes about male power and politics but provided only two tertiary comments about women. When writers and speakers actually injected women into political discourse, they usually did so to make a point about men. For example, John Adams discussed women's exclusion from suffrage to show that unpropertied men also should be excluded. Anna Jónasdóttir's insight into Hobbes and Locke also applies to Adams and his contemporaries: "Women are used as a device of argument only to be deftly shuffled out of sight once they have served their purpose."[36]

Still, gender opposition did have a substantial indirect influence on political discourse. To begin, it shaped the philosophical foundations of American political thought. Genevieve Lloyd observes that "the maleness of reason" was deeply embedded in Western political thought. Conceptions of manhood and reason "have been formed within structures of dominance" that declared "the Man of Reason" superior to women. Carole Pateman analyzes early modern political theory to expose male thinkers' belief that only "men possess the capacities required for citizenship, in particular, they are able to use their reason to sublimate their passions" and "internalize the universal rules of socio-political order." Male theorists believed that women, in contrast, were driven by passions that clouded their reason, subverted their commitment to universal justice, and legitimized their exclusion from politics.[37]

We can read the indirect influence of gender opposition between the lines of writings that populated the state of nature with rational men who voluntarily chose to enter civil society and establish a government of law. American authors usually assumed that women's inability to harness reason and discipline passion precluded them from participation in political life. Women were nowhere to be found in most states of nature. Theophilus Parsons was unusual because he was explicit about why political manhood required female exclusion. Parsons emphasized the importance of wisdom, learning, and discretion in politics, and favored a presumption that all males over twenty-one years had ample intelligence to participate. Simultaneously, he favored the rule that all women be viewed "as not having sufficient discretion," and he disqualified them from politics. True, he argued, women had "no deficiency in their mental powers." However, it was dangerous for them to develop reason and practice politics lest "promiscuous intercourse with the world" ruin "the natural tenderness and delicacy of their minds, their retired mode of life, and various domestic duties."[38] Political manhood meant ruling women for their own good.

Gender opposition was also embedded in the psychodynamics of early American political thought. Christine Di Stefano argues that modern political theorists constructed "configurations of masculinity" as misogynist attempts to achieve "clean and ultimate release from the (m)other." Male thinkers desired women but feared dependence on them. They projected their "irresolute masculinity" into political theories that thickened the connection between political manhood and female subordination. Similarly, Kenneth Lockridge argues that eighteenth-century American males constructed images of manhood based on contempt for women. Men desired women for sexual pleasure and reproduction but feared their engulfing sexuality and malignant power. Reacting as if "patriarchy is in imminent danger of becoming matriarchy," they expressed insecurity and rage by forging a misogynistic public identity based on intimidation and control of women.[39] American men had powerful unconscious passions and gendered assumptions that infused patriarchal meaning into public phrases such as "All men are created equal."

We can glimpse male misogyny in the common usage of the term *effeminacy*. Linda Kerber suggests that Americans equated "effeminacy" to "timidity, dependence, and foppishness." For example, Samuel Adams opposed "effeminate" refinements that seduced men into the self-indulgence and corruption associated with disorderly women. Samuel Williams criticized profligate men for creating "an emaciated feeble race, degraded by effeminacy and weakness," that was "unmanly" and "incapable of manly exertions." Only men who mastered female vices could ward off tyranny and establish a republic. However, not all uses of *effeminacy* conveyed gender opposition or misogyny. John Adams hinted at gender similarity when criticizing both "my own sex" and "American ladies" for "luxury, dissipations, and effeminacy." And Mercy Otis Warren was not expressing misogyny toward women when criticizing General William Howe for enjoying "effeminate and reprehensible pleasures . . . in the arms of a handsome adulteress" rather than doing his civic duty.[40]

We can also detect gender opposition in founding-era metaphors. Speakers and writers often defined political manhood as a matter of controlling symbolic female figures who were typically blamed for public disorder. The figures included "Fortune" (a coy woman who needed to be tamed), "Fancy" (an enchantress), "Trade" (a lady who needed to be courted), and "Popularity" (an adulteress). Some oppositional metaphors conveyed a mixed message. Thomas Paine portrayed the Revolution as the struggle of a maturing American male against a grasping British mother, and as a conflict pitting patriots defending manly freedom against corrupt governors hoping to seduce them back into female dependence. Paine also portrayed the Revolution in terms of all-male rivalry. He considered it a filial revolt against a despotic royal father, as well as the case of a wealthy ward fighting off a covetous guardian. Political manhood opposed womanhood, but it also opposed male tyranny and avarice, and an assortment of male failings.[41]

Quite often, Americans defined political manhood in opposition to African slavery. Judith Shklar suggests that a white male's sense of personal dignity, social worth, and citizenship was largely a function of distinguishing himself "from slaves and occasionally from women." She emphasizes that citizenship was mostly conceived as a denial of slavery. White males measured their public worth by their distance from slave status. The main marker of that distance was the right to vote, which functioned as "a certificate of full membership in society" that had a "capacity to confer a minimum of social dignity." Men without the ballot saw themselves and were seen by other men as second-class citizens approaching "the dreaded condition of the slave."[42]

Northern writers regularly suggested that political manhood required opposition to slavery. James Dana argued that "our liberty as men, citizens, and Christians" demanded that "we set ourselves to banish all slavish principles" and "unite to abolish slavery." Southern writers often suggested that white political manhood was strengthened by its juxtaposition to slavery. David Ramsay wrote that white men's "spirit of liberty" was nurtured by daily reminders of the degradation of slavery; Timothy Ford believed that white men felt stimulated to defend liberty "to avoid being confounded with the blacks"; John Taylor added that white men's affection for liberty was heightened by "the sight of slavery." If white manhood contrasted with slavery, what was the gender identity of male slaves? Enslaved black males had no clear gender identity. They were mostly seen as outsiders lacking the manly reason to discipline their passions and the manly freedom to provision and protect their families. J. Hector St. John de Crèvecoeur's "American Farmer" was typical: he abhorred slavery but could not imagine including African slaves among the mix of immigrants who could "become men" within the new race "called Americans."[43]

Often, Americans defined manhood in opposition to boyhood. A mature man was a self-supporting adult who defended liberty, fulfilled family responsibilities, and governed women. His opposite was the "boy," "libertine," or "bachelor of age" who was lustful, impulsive, and avaricious rather than disciplined; self-centered instead of family-oriented; and socially destructive, not politically constructive. This contrast was standard fare in political discourse. For example, Noah Webster portrayed the French Revolution as a contest between the mature males who originally fought for "liberty and the rights of men" and later Jacobin rebels who united "the littleness of boys" with "the barbarity of Goths." Activists criticized political opponents by likening them to "giddy youth" or by patronizing them as "restless, vigorous, luxurious youth prematurely emancipated from the authority of a parent."[44] The idiom of male rivalry was potent because Americans believed that a "man" deserved the rights of men, but a "boy" needed to be governed.

Sometimes, manhood was not an oppositional concept but a conjuncture of female and male characteristics. American culture considered both men and women to be disorderly creatures, disposed to seduce and be seduced. Writers criticized women for manipulating male passions and men for preying on female innocence. They worried about young women being corrupted by rogues and naive male citizens being abused by demagogues. Also, both sexes seemed to share many vices. Benjamin Franklin noted women's intemperance and men's "more frequent" intemperance, as well as women's fickleness and men's "wavering and inconstant" ways. Overall, however, commentators thought men were the more disruptive sex. The coquette's vices mainly threatened her own well-being. Hannah Webster Foster's novel *The Coquette* tells of a "young, gay, volatile" girl who rejected a virtuous suitor for "a designing libertine" only to suffer a premature death. By contrast, the libertine epitomized what Alexander Hamilton called men's "ambitious, vindictive, and rapacious" nature which imperiled female innocence, family integrity, the bonds of society, and legitimate political authority.[45]

A disorderly female subdued passion and achieved womanhood by way of marriage, submission to a husband, and motherhood. A disorderly male subdued passion and achieved manhood by way of marriage, family responsibility, and fatherhood. America's ideal couple produced order and procreated the future. But men claimed superior procreative powers: they sired children, women only carried them. Jefferson's fantasy of men reproducing without women was reflected in Joel Barlow's satirical poem "The Hasty Pudding," where a farmer's vitality (and virility) was confirmed by the fact that "Ten sturdy freeman sprung from him." Men also procreated culture, society, and the nation. Carole Pateman remarks that modern male thinkers claimed "the procreative powers of both a mother and a father" and took credit for "masculine creation of (giving birth to) social and political order."[46] In early America's male fantasies, female disorders and procreative powers were inferior; in early America's patriarchal politics, disorderly men were the primary problem, procreative men the primary problem solvers.

Disorderly Men

The destabilization of the traditional patriarch, the emergence of alternative ideals, and the instability of gender relations disrupted the lives of American men. Satires mocking married men as both brutal tyrants and effeminate slaves became commonplace. Family men's expectations that they should rule dependents were disappointed in some degree by wives' agency and sons' mobility. Some men reacted with an antimarital ideology; others channeled misogyny into revitalizing the traditional ideal; many experimented with the new alternatives; and most muddled through the confusion. Commentators worried that gender turbulence eroded men's commitment to family life and intensified male licentiousness. They warned that men who failed to marry, refused family responsibility, or forswore legitimate fatherhood lacked proper self-restraint, engaged in destructive vices, and often lured sober men into depravity. The specter of masses of disorderly men causing chaos became more terrifying to civic leaders when the revolutionary rhetoric of liberty and equality weakened traditional restraints on male conduct and strengthened men's claims to individual rights against authority.

In 1766, Jonathan Mayhew congratulated colonists for defending liberty against the Stamp Act but quickly condemned them for "riotous and felonious proceedings" compounded by cloaking their "rapacious violences with the pretext of zeal for liberty." Mayhew warned that some American men had lost "all sense of religion, virtue, and good order" and caused a "state of general disorder approaching so near to anarchy" that they almost brought on "more dreadful scenes of blood and slaughter." For the next forty years, public officials were haunted by visions of disorderly men indulging democratic desire as an excuse for venting passion and renewing earlier scenes of bloodshed and slaughter. It was not until 1805 that Thomas Jefferson was ready to declare a "union of sentiment now manifested so generally as auguring harmony and happiness to our future course." Even then, Fisher Ames warned that only "grown children" were so foolish as to believe that men's licentiousness, factionalism, and mobbish conduct had been cured.[47]

Why were men so apt to transform claims to liberty and equality into disorderly conduct? A frequent explanation was that males were inherently passionate, lustful, impulsive, greedy, manipulative, unpredictable creatures. That is, they were just like women. Benjamin Franklin highlighted men's passionate nature in a satire about "Celia Single," who sought to set straight the public record in a letter to the editor:

> I have several times in your paper seen severe reflections upon us women for idleness and extravagance, but I do not remember to have once seen any such animadversions upon the men. If I were disposed to be censorious, I could furnish you with instances enough. I might mention Mr. Billiard who spends more than he earns at the green table . . . Mr. Finikin who has seven different suits of fine clothes and wears a change every day while his wife and children sit at home half naked . . . Mr. Crownhim who is always dreaming over the checkerboard . . . Mr. T'Otherpot the tavern-hunter.[48]

Franklin spent a lifetime satirizing male vices to mark out the common failings of men and women. And Jefferson entertained the radical proposition that men were more enslaved by ardor and ignorance than women. His correspondence with Maria Cosway proclaimed the dominion of a man's "heart" over his "head," and his educational plan for his daughter assumed a "fourteen to one" chance that she would marry "a blockhead" and be forced to manage her own family.[49] Note that Franklin and Jefferson were optimists about male virtue and reason compared to misanthropes such as Alexander Hamilton and Noah Webster.

A related explanation was that male passions were particularly troublesome at a time when traditional restraints on male conduct were crumbling. Colonial America had been dominated by two ranks of men who, according to Gordon Wood, "had different psyches, different emotional makeups, different natures." *Gentlemen* were "great-souled" men "driven by passions that ordinary people could never comprehend, by pride, by honor, and by 'a prospect of an immortality in the memories of all the worthy to the end of time.'" *Commoners* were mainly farmers whose lives were shaped by the need to extract a living from the land to provision their families. What commoners most wanted "was sons to whom they could pass on their land and who would continue the family name."[50] These two ranks were bound together in equality and inequality. They shared responsibilities as family fathers who supported, protected, and managed dependents; they were freeholders with the historical rights and responsibilities of Englishmen; and they were driven by a shared desire to produce a memorable patrimony for posterity. Still, gentlemen were superiors, commoners inferiors; gentlemen cultured, commoners coarse; gentlemen patrons, commoners patronized; gentlemen militia officers, commoners rank-and-file militiamen; gentlemen governors, commoners governed. Colonial men existed within traditional, complex hierarchies constructed of personal ties, mutual obligations, cultural rituals, and the politics of preference and deference.

However, America's hierarchical bonds were comparatively weak. Gentlemen had no formal titles, special legal status, or inherited political privileges. They relied on family name, education, talent, wealth, generosity, and reputation to achieve personal honor, social dignity, and political authority. Meanwhile, commoners' subordinate status was compromised by America's abundance of land, its opportunities for socioeconomic mobility, and the rapid population growth that encouraged young men to seek opportunity on the frontier or in the city. American colonists sustained a fragile balance between male hierarchy and social fluidity until their opposition to the Stamp Act overspilled the boundaries of political protest. Thereafter, Bernard Bailyn suggests, "Defiance to constituted authority leaped like a spark from one flammable area to another, growing in heat as it went."[51] Any systematic effort to impose order on the ranks of men by subordinating some men and elevating others was sure to provoke public consternation.

On the one hand, Americans were enthusiasts for liberty. Indeed, they claimed *exceptional* liberty against hierarchical authority. James Otis, Jr., argued in 1764, "The colonists are entitled to as ample rights, liberties, and privileges as the subjects of the mother country and, in some respects, to more." Why more? American farmers and English freeholders were born with identical natural and constitutional rights; but American men merited exceptional liberty because they had carved a new world out of the wilderness while Englishmen wallowed in old-world corruption. In particular, Americans demanded extraordinary "natural, inherent, and inseparable rights as men and citizens" to individual liberty against royal governors and to local political autonomy against parliamentary authority. Anyone who appeared to deprive American men of their exceptional liberty stood accused of seeking to emasculate and enslave them.[52]

On the other hand, many leaders feared that this enthusiasm for liberty generated what David Ramsay called "undecided claims and doubtful rights" that were likely to be abused by disorderly men, who excelled at "disturbing the freest governments that were ever devised." Disturbances often took the form of mob action. John Adams complained in 1774, "These private mobs I do and will detest. . . . these tarring and featherings, this breaking open of houses by rude and insolent rabble . . . in pursuance of private prejudices and passions must be discountenanced." George Washington was outraged in July

1776 when a celebration of independence ended with soldiers toppling a statue of George III. His "General Orders" stated, "Though the General doubts not the persons who pulled down and mutilated the statue . . . were actuated by zeal in the public cause, yet it has so much the appearance of riot and want of order . . . that he disapproves the manner and directs in the future these things shall be . . . left to be executed by proper authority."[53] Leaders worried that most men recognized no proper authority.

How could men reconcile democratic desire and political authority? Ideally, men showed self-restraint in the exercise of liberty and voluntarily obeyed their chosen leaders. However, John Adams felt that patriots' demands for liberty were so excessive that self-restraint and obedience were doubtful. In 1776, he used Abigail's plea to remember the ladies as an occasion to express his fear that Americans' revolutionary claims jeopardized all authority: "We have been told that our struggle has loosened the bonds of government everywhere; that children and apprentices were disobedient; that schools and colleges were grown turbulent; that Indians slighted their guardians, and Negroes grew insolent to their masters." Decades later, Adams argued that claims to liberty had become so extreme that men refused to defer to superior authority or even recognize their superiors. "Some years ago," he explained, "a writer unfortunately made use of the term *better sort.* Instantly, a popular clamor was raised and an odium excited which remains to this day to such a degree that no man dares to employ that expression at the bar, in conversation, in a newspaper, or pamphlet, no, nor in the pulpit."[54] Critics lambasted Adams for saying aloud what many leaders quietly believed: American men were too disorderly to be trusted with liberty unless they learned to temper democratic passions and defer to the better sort.

American intellectuals were brilliant at making abstract distinctions between liberty and license to persuade men to temper passion and defer to authority. But their philosophical analyses had a little impact on men's willingness to exercise self-restraint or obey government. Abstract political language had become so slippery that it was as easily used against as in favor of authority. Terence Ball, J. G. A. Pocock, and Joyce Appleby point out that concepts such as "liberty" and "equality" or "republic" and "democracy" were contested, revised, and recoined during the founding era. Most intellectuals did little to clarify their language. They were part of what Jay Fliegelman identifies as an "elocutionary revolution" that encouraged speakers and writers to de-emphasize the clarity, logic, and evidence that appealed to men's minds and instead to emphasize the theatricality, metaphor, imagery, myth, and body language that moved men's passions. Political leaders seeking to counteract democratic disorders needed to employ language and concepts that appealed to men's passions, indeed, to their very identities as males.[55]

The Politics of Coercion and Consent

The American founders encompassed several generations of thinkers, speakers, writers, ministers, activists, soldiers, and statesmen who conceived and contributed to the struggle for independence and the creation of the Republic. They included local and national political elites who opposed the old regime and constructed new ones. Though a diverse lot, the founders shared an enduring and sometimes obsessive fear that disorderly men would generate chaos in society, endanger hard-won liberty, and imperil the Republic. They hoped to fend off democratic disorders by stabilizing gender relations and by promoting hegemonic norms to stigmatize disorderly men and reward stable men.

First, the founders stabilized gender relations by depoliticizing opposition between men and women and by reinforcing the ideal of the traditional patriarch. They mostly restricted gender turbulence to the cultural sphere and thereby fostered fraternal politics. They regularly discussed and debated men's liberty, equality, citizenship, and leadership without mentioning women; they often heaped honors on patriotic men who fought the Revolution without giving much recognition to patriotic women who participated in it. When the war ended, "Women disappeared from the public eye."[56] Thereafter, the founders framed a new republic without considering women's place in it or experiencing much pressure to question women's exclusion from it. They could perpetuate women's subordination because republican and liberal ideology invited them to do so, male misogyny and uncertainty gave them an incentive to do so, and their political priorities urged them to do so.

Republican ideology equated absolute kingship with absolute corruption. Republican thinkers were much less critical of family patriarchs, whose power was ostensibly limited by law and softened by affection. As such, their criticism of monarchy did not necessarily apply to domestic patriarchy. Liberal ideology widened the chasm between politics and family life by separating public and paternal power. It made the language of liberty and equality appropriate for the public sphere but allowed a traditional idiom of natural hierarchy to persist in the domestic sphere. The founders took advantage of these ideological openings to defy political tyranny and depoliticize men's authority in their families. Revolutionaries fought against monarchy, not family patriarchy. Legislators disputed aristocratic laws, not patriarchal laws. Governors forfeited royal prerogative over men, but fathers and husbands maintained patriarchal prerogative over women's bodies, behavior, and property. The result was that misogynists remained free to vent patriarchal rage against women, and ambivalent males were cued to resolve uncertainties about manhood in favor of the traditional patriarch, who retained the coercive authority "to intimidate, not to accommodate" women.[57]

Simultaneously, the founders' political priorities urged them to keep women off the public agenda. Most founders feared that disorderly men threatened to destroy liberty by unleashing the twin evils of mob anarchy and demagogic tyranny. Accordingly, they focused much of their intellectual and political energy on encouraging men to defend liberty and show great restraint when exercising it. The founders would have had to compromise their focus on male mobilization and quiescence to debate women's rights or deal with prejudices regarding public women. Politicizing gender certainly would have meant deepening male discontents, while admitting women to political discourse would have invited the sexual improprieties and political corruption often associated with the "public woman."[58] The founders focused on restoring order among men; they relied on still powerful family patriarchs to subdue disorderly women.

Historical possibilities for democratizing family life did not translate into enhanced prospects for political equality. Women were mostly eliminated from political discourse and politics—but they were not forgotten. Some founders sensed that women's exclusion fortified fraternal unity among otherwise disorderly males. Carole Pateman explains that men's monopoly of citizenship and leadership provided them "a common interest *as men*" in sharing power over women. Meanwhile, most founders believed that men were more apt to defend liberty and exercise it with self-restraint when courting, betrothed, or wed to respectable women. Noah Webster calculated that a man's best defense against "a dissipated life" was a fondness for "ladies of character."[59] In sum, the founders appealed to men's patriarchal interests and fraternal instincts by reaffirming their coercive power over women, reinforcing women's exclusion from politics, and recruiting virtuous women to encourage men's good behavior.

Second, the founders enlisted Christian morality, republican virtue, liberal self-interest, and public education along with women's benign influence in the cause of taming men's passions, encouraging male responsibility, ensuring their orderly conduct, and promoting mass compliance to legitimate authority. They also framed innovative political institutions to neutralize men's passions and cushion the consequences of their disorderly conduct. And like most elites, the founders sought to establish hegemony and secure stability by soliciting men's consent and quiescence.

Historically, Antonio Gramsci observes, elites not only "request" consent but "educate it." They establish hegemony by raising "the great mass of the population to a particular cultural and moral level." They use cultural norms to perform "a positive educative function" by promoting ways of thinking, speaking, and acting conducive to mass compliance; and they operate coercive institutions to discharge "a negative educative function" by penalizing subversive ideas, words, and deeds. Hegemony is "protected by the armor of coercion." Elites' attempt to establish hegemony is not always a self-conscious, systematic effort to make culture function as an instrument of mass subordination. Raymond Williams suggests that hegemony is more of "a lived, social process" in which elites organize the various and shifting "meanings and values" that saturate people's lives. Hegemony is never static because it is continually "renewed, recreated, defended, and modified," as well as "resisted, limited, altered, challenged."[60]

R. W. Connell adds that the struggle for hegemony often involves the culture of manhood. Male elites promote a "hegemonic masculinity" that deploys norms of manhood to justify dominant authority and encourage mass deference to it. Elites also foster "conservative" or "complicit masculinities" that urge men to accept and benefit from dominant male norms and institutions; and they identify, stigmatize, and punish "subordinated" or "marginal masculinities" that potentially undermine political stability. Unlike ideologies that appeal to men's minds, hegemonic masculinity taps into the deepest recesses of men's psychosexual, social, and political identities. Many scholars believe that one of men's strongest motives has involved male rivalry. Men have found it exhilarating to be elevated above other men; and they have felt degraded when treated "as a boy and not a man."[61] By controlling the criteria for male elevation and degradation, elites who join hegemony to manhood significantly strengthen their ability to secure men's consent and quiescence.

That is what American founders did. They promoted hegemonic masculinity as part of their effort to restrain disorderly male passions, temper men's democratic desires, restore fraternal order, and reconstitute political authority. They advanced a coherent conception and language of manhood based on the consensual norms that enjoined males to establish independence, start families, and govern dependents to achieve manhood and procreate new generations. They stigmatized, sanctioned, and reformed disorderly men, whose marginal masculinity associated them with dependency, effeminacy, immaturity, and sterility. They rewarded the complicit masculinity of men who conformed to consensual norms by recognizing their social merit and citizenship. And they promised immortal fame along with social status and political authority to extraordinary men who, like themselves, procreated a new nation and glorious future for humankind.

The founders also appropriated aspects of America's contested ideals of manhood to stabilize and fine-tune the male pecking order of the new republic. For example, they attacked the self-interested manhood of males who failed to settle into family life, but they generally applauded the self-interested manhood of married men who worked to protect and provision their families. Moreover, they emphasized the ideal of republican manhood when defining citizenship but drew more heavily on images of aristocratic manhood and traditional patriarchy to legitimize the political authority and prerogative of national leaders. The founders rarely debated the alternative ideals of manhood, but they habitually relied on them to educate the consent of the governed.

Judith Sargent Murray's call for every American "to play the man for his country" conveyed two implicit but unmistakable messages. First, greater sexual equality may have been conceivable for the home, but men were to be the sole arbiters of the nation's political fate. Second, all men may have been born free and equal, but each male had to measure up to standards of manhood to earn citizenship or merit leadership status. Murray's language was not unusual. Indeed, it was a representative sample of the "grammar of manhood" that the founders used to promote hegemonic norms of manhood, secure men's consent, define citizenship, and legitimize political authority.

2

The Grammar of Manhood

The American founders coupled the concept of manhood to the language of liberty. Benjamin Franklin proclaimed that his grandfather's essay on liberty was written with "manly freedom" and Thomas Paine explained that *Common Sense* was meant to prepare the way for "manly principles of independence." John Adams praised his Puritan ancestors for their "manly assertion of . . . rights" and "manly pertinacious spirit" against tyranny while Thomas Jefferson applauded his American brethren for demonstrating "manly firmness" and "manly spirit" by renouncing British authority and declaring independent nationhood.[1] Manhood modified liberty and thereby injected an element of masculine merit into the rhetoric of early American citizenship.

One reason the founders joined manhood to liberty was to motivate males to be warriors in the struggle against Great Britain. They delivered the message that men who trumpeted the glories of liberty and triumphed over its enemies merited the honor and respect due to manhood as well as the rights and responsibilities of citizenship. Thomas Paine and Abigail Adams sent a complementary message to men who opposed the patriot cause or did not join it. Paine wrote that any male who lent credence to Tory propaganda was "an apostate from the order of manhood." Adams declared that men who did "not fight and defend their own particular spot . . . deserve the slavery and subjection which awaits them."[2] The unmistakable implication was that those men who failed to measure up to martial manhood were unworthy of liberty and citizenship.

A second reason the founders joined manhood and liberty was to promote an ethic of self-restraint. Patrick Henry applauded the "manly fortitude" that encouraged men to sacrifice popularity for moral integrity while James Otis, Jr., honored "manly sentiments" that enjoined men to sacrifice "health, ease, estate, or even life" for freedom. Paine gloried in the "manly and martial spirit" that disciplined soldiers and Benjamin Franklin cheered the "manly constancy" that kept men calm in the midst of hardship. George Washington called for "manly conduct" to transform demobilized soldiers into self-disciplined citizens and others pleaded for "manly reflection" to inhibit licentiousness, "manly graces" to cure conflict, "manly confidence" to bind citizens to officials, and "manly reverence" to foster obedience to the U.S. Constitution and its "manly government."[3] Men who engaged in licentious conduct and democratic excess deserved to be marginalized, stigmatized, ostracized, and even deprived of liberty, while those who exhibited manly self-restraint earned the freedom to practice responsible citizenship and promote the public good.

The founders promoted the idea that men should be enthusiastic in the cause of liberty but restrained in the exercise of liberty by elaborating a grammar of manhood. Their grammar drew on hegemonic norms of manhood to encourage disorderly men to conform to a standard of manly conduct conducive to individual self-restraint, good citizenship, and public order. Their grammar of manhood also articulated consensual criteria for sorting out the ranks of men, restoring order to them, and legitimizing leadership authority in the new republic. The founders' main motivation for deploying the grammar of manhood was to encourage men to discipline democratic desire; a crucial consequence of their use of it was to develop and disseminate ideas of citizenship and leadership that precluded women from political participation.

Manhood in Time

George Washington saw the American Revolution as a test of whether Americans could "act like men and prove themselves worthy of the blessings of freedom." What did it mean to act like men? The founders drew on consensual norms embedded in the culture of manhood to emphasize male independence and family responsibility in opposition to female dependence and slavery. They sang "The Liberty Song" in praise of "worthy forefathers" who "bequeathed us their liberty," and they committed themselves to protect and perpetuate liberty "for our children." When "each manly breast" was "call'd to bleed" in defense of liberty, those who answered the call made themselves "dear to every free-born mind" and eligible for "deathless fame," while those who exhibited fear or lethargy deserved to be "stripp'd of their freedom," "robb'd of their right," and shamed by patriotic "Daughters of Liberty." To act like men, concludes Philip Greven, meant to inherit, defend, and transmit the liberty that enabled citizens to be "self-assertive and self-willed in public," not dependent, effeminate, or enslaved.[4] The founders elaborated this hegemonic vision of manhood in an autobiographical story about procreative men giving bloody birth to a new people, land, fraternity, leadership, and nation.

The founders' saga was based on the ancient assertion that fertile males procreated children. Gerda Lerner recalls that the Bible told of man generating woman from his rib and planting the active seed of life "in the passive receptacle of woman's womb." Anna Jónasdóttir adds that Greek philosophers elevated the status of the male seed by asserting that "light and beautiful male seminal fluid" was the source of humanity's higher sensibilities and the conduit of civilization from generation to generation. Seventeenth-century Englishmen idealized male fecundity. For example, satirist Richard Ames fought the battle of the sexes in a fantasy about a homosocial Eden where men could "procreate like trees, and without women's aid—promote and propagate our species." Carole Pateman observes that Hobbes and Locke fought the battle against divine kingship in fantasies about states of nature that attributed to men the "generative power" to create "new physical life" as well as "new political societies." Whether such claims stemmed from male identification with God the Creator, unconscious fears of women's power to give birth, or men's desire to avoid dependence on women, Western thinkers have defined manhood as much in terms of procreation as of virtue or reason.[5]

The American founders reaffirmed myths of male procreativity each time they invoked the state of nature to justify their claims to liberty. Reflecting the misogynist fantasies of Thomas Jefferson and Joel Barlow as well as Richard Ames, they constructed all-male states of nature which assumed that men could reproduce the species without women. John Leland was unusual because he was explicit. His state of nature began, "Suppose a man to remove to a desolate island and take a peaceable possession of it. . . . In the process of time from this man's loins ten sons are grown to manhood." Occasionally the founders populated nature with men, women, and children. Almost immediately, however, they made the women and children perish. Here is John Adams's disappearance act: "When a number of men, women, and children are simply congregated together, there is no political authority among them. . . . To leave women and children out of the question for the present, the men will all be free, equal, and independent of each other."[6] Adams left women out of the question for the future too because his main concern was to stabilize relationships among men.

The emblem of stable male relationships was the blood bond that joined procreative fathers to their sons and grandsons. George Washington explained that men had a divine duty to engage in the "agreeable amusement of fulfilling the first and great commandment, increase and multiply." Men especially hoped for sons who would transmit their bloodline along with their family name, estate, and social standing into the next generation. Better yet, they wanted grandsons to perpetuate their families for several generations. One grandfather referred to his grandchildren as "Our life, while we live!—Our hopes, when dead."[7] A family patriarch could expect to achieve personal dignity, social recognition, and symbolic immortality by siring respectful, resourceful heirs. He assumed a paternal obligation to protect, provision, educate, and provide patrimony for his sons and grandsons. In turn, his male offspring acquired a filial obligation to respect their father and, eventually, to honor him by siring, protecting, provisioning, educating, and providing patrimony for yet another generation. The ultimate goal of procreative manhood was to propagate, preserve, and prolong family dynasties.

Intergenerational blood bonds played a pivotal part in patriot politics. Colonial leaders constructed heroic histories of America's first "fathers" to encourage filial opposition to the British. Jonathan Mayhew applauded colonial ancestors as courageous men who refused to be victimized by old-world tyranny. They were hardy "adventurers" who uprooted their families, ventured their fortunes, and risked their lives by hazarding an Atlantic voyage, investing "their money, their toil, their blood" in the land, and joining together in agricultural platoons and military brigades to provision and protect their families against hostile forces. These accomplished ancestors earned "their rights or their dearly purchased privileges, call them which you will." Pamphleteers such as Thomas Fitch called them "the purchase of their ancestors . . . [the] reward of the merit and services of their forefathers . . . the best inheritance they left to their children." John Adams proclaimed, "Our fathers . . . earned and bought their liberty."[8]

If "our fathers" fulfilled their part of the intergenerational bargain by purchasing liberty for their offspring, how did sons and grandsons who inherited liberty as a birthright demonstrate their manly merit? Sheldon Wolin reminds us that a birthright may carry with it "an inherited obligation to use it, take care of it, pass it on, and hopefully improve it." The founders argued that each generation had an obligation to protect, nurture, and enhance ancestral liberty in order to transmit it to the next generation and the next. Indeed, only men who acted to defend and extend liberty truly deserved it. Accordingly, Mercy Otis Warren told the story of the Boston Tea Party as a parable of patriots who proved themselves worthy sons of liberty. Governor Thomas Hutchinson imperiled ancestral liberty when he attempted to enforce the tea tax by using stealth and deception to "disarm his countrymen of the manly resolution that was their principal forte." Fortunately, Bostonians demonstrated manly resolution by their "extraordinary exertions" in defense of liberty.[9] The patriots proved themselves their fathers' equals; they inherited but also merited liberty.

The founders called on the dictum that each male generation was obligated to prove its worth as leverage for recruiting colonists to the cause of liberty. In 1768, Silas Downer instructed Americans "manfully to oppose every invasion of our rights" so as to preserve and deserve their fathers' legacy:

> Our fathers fought and found freedom in the wilderness; they clothed themselves in the skins of wild beasts and lodged under trees among bushes; but in that state they were happy because they were free. Should these our noble ancestors arise from the dead and find their posterity trucking away that liberty . . . , they would return to the grave with a holy indignation against us. . . . We cannot, we will not, betray the trust reposed in us by our ancestors by giving up the least of our liberties.[10]

The same year, Daniel Shute contrasted "the first renowned settlers" to a modern generation of "degenerate offspring" that was guilty of "prostitution of patrimonial privileges" and "criminal want of philanthropy" because its members were loath to defend liberty "for millions yet unborn." In 1773, John Allen asked colonists to recall "the right of liberty which their forefathers bought with their blood" as motivation for their own struggles. Again in 1775, Moses Mather challenged Americans to measure up to their heroic fathers, who earned liberty "at their own risk and expense and by their own sword and prowess."[11] Most founders presumed that worthy men would not be willing to suffer the personal shame and social disgrace associated with squandering their fathers' legacy or forfeiting their sons' liberty.

The Revolution amplified the voice of heroic fathers commanding their sons to preserve and pass on liberty. Thomas Jefferson ushered in the Revolution by declaring, "Honor, justice, and humanity forbid us to surrender that freedom which we received from our gallant ancestors and which our innocent posterity have a right to receive from us." Samuel Cooper encouraged American men to maintain support for the Revolution by memorializing "our venerable fathers" as men marked "by all the manly virtues and by an unquenchable love of liberty," and also as men who "call on us . . . to perpetuate the honor of their liberty."[12] One reason the founders developed what Douglass Adair sees as "an almost obsessive desire for fame" was that they felt pressured to measure up to the reputations of their pioneering ancestors. That they did measure up was evident a few decades later, when they themselves were remembered as gallant ancestors. Stanley Griswold, for example, attacked factionalism in turn-of-the-century Connecticut by asking,

"Where are our fathers? Where are our former men of dignity, our Huntingtons, Shermans, Johnsons, and Stiles who in their day appeared like men, gave exaltation to our character, and never descended to a mean thing? It appears to me . . . we are dwindled and more disposed to act like children than men." Griswold's injunction was "Let the spirit of our fathers come upon us. Be men."[13]

American males who obeyed Griswold's injunction to "be men" could expect a triple reward. First, they robbed mortality of its finality. Benjamin Franklin asked, "What old bachelor can die without regret or remorse when he reflects upon his death bed that the inestimable blessing of life and being has been communicated by father and son through all generations from Adam down to him but in him it stops and is extinguished?" Men who met their intergenerational obligations could live on through their sons and in the memory of their sons. Second, men who defended liberty for their families could expect to be praised by Spartan women who urged them to fight and then honored their heroism. Judith Sargent Murray told the story of "Artemisia, wife of Mausolus," who "rendered herself illustrious" by building the Mausoleum to honor and immortalize her brave husband. Third, men who honored family obligations and defended liberty merited fraternal trust. They were reputed to be stable individuals who restrained their passions, checked their impulses, and earned their neighbors' respect and cooperation. Conversely, men outside intergenerational time were temporal itinerants who deserved their neighbors' distrust. That was Franklin's supposition, for example, when he suggested that royal governors could not be trusted to be other than arbitrary because they ruled America without having American fathers to venerate or American sons to protect. They come and go but "leave no family behind them."[14]

A fundamental rule in the founders' grammar of manhood was that worthy men situated themselves in intergenerational time. They respected their birthright of liberty and proved themselves worthy of it by procreating and nurturing sons and by defending and extending liberty to new generations. They thereby achieved personal honor, social reputation, and the symbolic immortality associated with enduring family dynasties. In contrast, men who existed outside intergenerational time were not worthy of their birthright; nor were they likely to be trusted by other men. Instead, they were presumed to be selfish individuals who recognized no obligations to the past or future. They lived in the present where they unleashed lust, played out passion, and indulged impulse to disgrace their fathers' memory and procreate nothing better than bastards.

Manhood and Space

The next episode in the founders' story of America concerned fertile men giving birth to a new land. American men could procreate children and pass on liberty only if they cultivated sufficient land to support their offspring and sustain their independence. Property was a precondition for families and freedom. Benjamin Franklin believed that an abundance of land was America's greatest resource. Young men were not afraid to marry early or raise large families because they could acquire enough land to provision their offspring and be confident that, when their children were grown, there would be "more land to be had at rates equally easy." Thomas Jefferson agreed. That was why he thought "the immense extent of uncultivated and fertile lands" called Louisiana was crucial to America's future.[15] In general, the founders equated abundant land, early marriage, large families, rapid population growth, and economic prosperity with the national strength that guaranteed men's liberty and security.

What made the founders' story about men and land unique was the extent to which they injected manhood into real estate. John Locke made a mixture of men's labor and land the source of property value and ownership. The Americans, however, concocted a mixture of men's blood and land. They portrayed America's "fathers" as procreative pioneers and fertile farmers who impregnated a virgin continent with their blood to give birth to a new land and prosperity. Franklin asserted that America's European settlers were men who "purchased or conquered the territory at the expense of their own private treasure and blood." Jefferson described early settlers as men whose "own blood was spilt in acquiring lands for their settlement." A metaphoric measure of property value was the volume of blood that Americans spilled to acquire, defend, and bequeath it. George Duffield considered the continent extremely valuable because "America's choicest blood had flowed in liberal streams" during the Revolution and thus America's "soil [was] made fat with the blood of her children."[16]

"Fat soil" was more than an economic instrumentality. The founders saw fertile land as a field for manhood. It was the landscape for what Washington called "the manly employment of agriculture." What was "manly" about it? Agriculture tested men's physical and mental abilities to survive and thrive in nature, endure hardship and adversity, recognize and reap the rewards of opportunity. It was the economic basis of manly independence. Agriculture also beckoned men to procreate prosperity to prolong their family dynasties. Thus, eastern men often tried to solve the problem of too many sons and too little land by speculating in western property to ensure future family access to farmland. For John Taylor, agriculture was the vocation of worthy men who dared to "subdue sterility" and convert "a wilderness into a paradise" able to support manly freedom and family heirs.[17] Fathers and farmers alike procreated the future.

The founders regularly linked the image of the republican farmer to manly virtues such as simplicity, benevolence, friendship, and patriotism. Jefferson went further by endowing men's relationship to the land with religious meaning: "Those who labor in the earth are the chosen people of God . . . [in] whose breasts he has made his peculiar deposit for substantial and genuine virtue. It is the focus in which he keeps alive that sacred fire, which otherwise might escape from the earth." He complemented his pastoral idyll with a contrasting image of American males cast out of paradise. His list of fallen men included unsettled, dependent Americans such as urban laborers, immigrants, itinerants, strangers, emancipated slaves, and nomadic Indians who survived by hunting. None of these men practiced the "agricultural and domestic arts" that fostered "improvement of the mind and morals"; none invested themselves in a particular piece of land or a settled community; none were stable men of character. Rather, they were among the perpetual migrants that John Taylor would blame for having fled "their natal spot" for new climates, only to fuel America's social and political decay.[18]

Most founders believed that a worthy man was someone who occupied a fixed place in continental space. Leaders such as Washington, Adams, and Jefferson broadcast this belief each time they announced their yearning to exit the public stage and retire, respectively, to Mount Vernon, Braintree, and Monticello. Certainly, these declarations were politically expedient. It was wise for ambitious men to protest public service as a sacrifice of their personal desire for a simple agrarian life. Garry Wills suggests that Washington's repeated pleas to forgo high office for farming constituted a major factor in his immense popularity. Still, more than politics was involved in the founders' oft-expressed yearnings for a life on the land. They agreed with contemporaries that a man's dignity and dynastic aspirations required him to settle down in one place—under his vine and fig tree—to enjoy his freedom, family, and farm.[19]

The linkage between manhood and settled space played a part in the conflict leading up to the Revolution. Early on, American colonists complained that they were unjustly stigmatized when the British treated them as itinerants who had ripped up their European roots to wander the New World. One colonial author asked fellow Americans to compare themselves to their English brethren: "Are you not of the same stock? Was the blood of your ancestors polluted by a change of soil? Were they freemen in England and did they become slaves by a six-weeks voyage to America? Does not the sun shine as bright, our blood run as warm? Is not our honor and virtue as pure, our liberty as valuable, our property as dear, our lives as precious here as in England?"[20] The colonists denied their itinerancy and instead portrayed themselves as patriotic men who extended the British Empire, tamed a continent, and fixed a place for themselves and their families in the New World. That made them worthy men who deserved the rights of Englishmen.

The irony of the British stigma, according to Daniel Dulany, was that America's most worthy men—those who successfully settled a piece of land and fixed a place for their families in the New World—were effectively precluded from citizenship. A citizen had to vote in person in Great Britain. Therefore, an American freeholder could exercise a citizen's suffrage only "upon the supposition of his ceasing to be an inhabitant of America and becoming a resident of Great Britain."[21] The result was that America's most notable men and their offspring were refused the manly dignity of political independence and full citizenship. This refusal encouraged many of America's wealthiest and most influential colonists to express their sense of alienation by joining and leading escalating colonial protests against British authority.

The founders' concern for the relationship between manhood and space resurfaced at the Constitutional Convention in a debate over immigrant eligibility for U.S. Senate seats. James Madison supported immigrant eligibility by arguing that meritorious men who migrated to America and settled there "would feel the mortification of being marked with suspicious incapacitations though they should not covet the public honors." James Wilson's supporting argument concluded, "To be appointed to a place may be a matter of indifference. To be incapable of being appointed is a circumstance grating and mortifying." The founders presumed that men who settled a place for themselves in America deserved full citizenship; and such men were justly aroused to anger when denied the right to vote or run for office, regardless of whether they intended to exercise suffrage or stand for election. Judith Shklar reminds us that civic indignity is important because men who feel "dishonored" and "scorned" can cause significant disorder.[22]

Concerns about manhood, space, and citizenship were tied to women's economic contributions. The law of coverture granted husbands control over family property, whether or not wives brought that property into the marriage. Without economic independence, married women were thought to lack the unencumbered mind and independent will essential to citizenship. They were "civilly dead." Nonetheless, women contributed to the property and wealth that supported men's independence and citizenship. Women worked family space. They kept gardens and livestock, manufactured items for the household and marketplace, took in boarders, prepared and preserved food, assumed responsibility for childbearing and rearing, conducted welfare activities, and often transmitted family property from generation to generation. In practice, Robert Gross suggests, husbands and wives "were partners in a common enterprise, although, in the end, only one was chairman of the board."[23] Alas, only the "chairman of the board" could achieve manhood and merit citizenship.

The second rule in the founders' grammar of manhood was that meritorious men mixed their blood with the land to acquire and settle space for themselves and their families. Their ownership of property was a fixed foundation for maintaining liberty and independence, governing other family members, taming nature, and claiming citizenship. Worthy men might migrate—from Europe to America or from a father's farm to the wilderness—if their goal was to acquire and settle new land. At times, the durability of intergenerational dynasties depended on younger sons claiming and clearing new land. As Michael Lienesch puts it, "Movement through time would invariably be influenced by movement across space." Conversely, the founders doubted the merit of men who failed to establish a fixed place for themselves. They were "strangers" who wandered the land, suspects who threatened to disrupt decent society. Caleb Lownes, who administered Philadelphia's prisons in the 1790s, announced that the city streets were safe—except for the crimes perpetrated by "strangers . . . on their way to the westward."[24]

Manhood and Fraternity

The founders told a tale about fathers and farmers who sought to transform a continent of strangers into the fraternity known as civil society.[25] They assumed that the organic bonds joining American men to their sons and estates were sufficiently strong to motivate relatives and neighbors to protect their communities. That assumption was borne out by the eight father-son teams that manned the local militia to fight the British at Lexington, and by the complex kinship network of fathers and sons, uncles and nephews, brothers, cousins, and in-laws that mustered at Concord. When America's parochial protests escalated into a continental revolution, the founders faced the more formidable challenge of forging unity among American men from diverse and distant communities. How could these strangers learn to trust each other? Would they cooperate in war and then contribute to a harmonious peace and shared prosperity?

The founders generally characterized men as social creatures. True, most men were selfish, but they also wanted to be respected by other men. They earned that respect by measuring up to consensual norms of manhood, most dramatically, by defending and extending manly liberty. Accordingly, colonial leaders called on Americans to enlist in the struggle against Great Britain to merit manhood and earn continental respect. Samuel Adams challenged Bostonians: "If you are men, behave like men." Moses Mather rallied opposition to Britain by imploring Americans "to nobly play the man for our country." Men who served with honor deserved public acclaim. Thus, Oxenbridge Thatcher complimented Virginia legislators for their resolutions against the Stamp Act by declaring, "Oh, yes. They are men!" Samuel Sherwood congratulated his courageous countrymen by praising "this manly, this heroic, and truly patriotic spirit which is gradually kindling up in every freeman's breast." By 1775, more and more American men were heeding the fraternal call to "fight manfully for their country."[26]

The founders' injunctions to "behave like men" and "play the man" and "fight manfully" had contingent meanings. Initially, such phrases suggested that American men should be reluctant to take up arms against their British brethren. James Otis, Jr., advised colonists to protest the Stamp Act but also to recognize Parliament's authority and exhibit "loyalty, patience, meekness, and forbearance under any hardships," insofar as these traits were "consistent with the character of men." John Dickinson counseled Americans to exercise self-restraint in their protests and to remember that the British were still brethren "by religion, liberty, laws, affections, relations, language, and commerce." He also warned patriots to avert the bloody consequences of separation: "Torn from the body to which we are united, . . . we must bleed at every vein." Worthy men restrained martial ardor to balance claims of liberty against established loyalties. Thomas Jefferson exemplified this disciplined ardor in 1774 when he expressed outrage at British tyranny but continued to plead with the king to reaffirm "fraternal love and harmony."[27]

With the onset of armed hostilities in the mid-1770s, patriot leaders began to urge men to war against their treacherous British brethren. George Washington condemned the British for subverting "the laws and constitution of Great Britain itself, in the establishment of which some of the best blood of the kingdom has been spilt." John Witherspoon expressed disgust that men who were "the same in blood, in language, and in religion should notwithstanding butcher one another with unrelenting rage." Joseph Warren saw separation as a forgone conclusion and issued a call to arms: "Our all is at stake. . . . An hour lost may deluge your country in blood and entail perpetual slavery upon the few of your posterity who survive the carnage." Thomas Paine announced that the time for talk was done. His message to the pitiful men who pined for peace rather than arming for war was, "You are unworthy of the name of husband, father, friend, and lover and . . . you have the heart of a coward and the spirit of a sycophant."[28]

The founders used consensual norms of manhood to judge men's conduct during the war. For example, they argued that British peace overtures that promised to restore fraternal harmony at the price of American men's liberty were deceitful seductions that meritorious men must reject. Paine called Lord Howe's proposals "cruel and unmanly." Abigail Adams suggested that Americans who favored peace without independence had "neither the spirit nor the feeling of men." Meanwhile, Jefferson attacked the British for destroying the trans-Atlantic bonds of brotherhood by committing fratricide and then compounding their treachery by using "Scotch and foreign mercenaries to invade and deluge us in blood." Washington often mentioned Britain's use of mercenaries. He refused several proposals to talk peace with the explanation, "I am satisfied that no [peace] commissioners were ever designed except Hessians and other foreigners." The proper response to Britain's unmanly conduct, he argued, was for Americans to engage in a "vigorous and manly exertion" consistent with "our character as men."[29] Overall, the founders prided themselves on having vindicated their character as men in dealing with Great Britain. They sought liberty but respected British authority. Their fraternal loyalty to Britain faltered only when fratricide and mercenary activity made unity impossible. Finally, they declared independence, raised a respectable army to defend liberty, and refused peace without honor.

When the founders declared independence, they initiated a process of procreating a distinctive American fraternity. War catalyzed the process. Wilson Carey McWilliams suggests that men are usually encouraged during a struggle against a common enemy to set aside small differences and "find solidarity" with one another. That was David Ramsay's explanation for early national unity: "A sense of common danger extinguished selfish passions [and] local attachments were sacrificed on the altar of patriotism." But fraternities forged in battle are fragile. They depend on the presence of a common enemy or danger rather than on shared values and visions. Jefferson made a similar point during the Revolution. He predicted that from the conclusion of the war onward, American men were likely to forget the struggle for liberty and equality and "forget themselves but in the sole faculty of making money."[30] The founders' fear that wartime fraternity would falter lent urgency to their efforts to fortify American unity.

The exigencies of revolution and nationhood burst open the issue of membership in American society. What qualified a man to fit in? How early did he have to join the patriot cause? Did he have to serve for the duration? Could loyalists who switched sides be trusted? Were neutrals, the ambivalent, opportunists, and pacifists eligible? Should Catholics be admitted if priests and papists used their "influence in the next world" to turn "the superstitious multitude" against the Revolution? What about clergymen and laymen who were deemed slaves to superstition and avarice? Were they so different from those spiritual souls who participated in "an intercourse of humane, generous kindness and grateful attachment and fidelity which like the vital fluid diffuses cheerful health through the whole political body"?[31] Did ethnicity affect membership? James Winthrop felt that ethnic homogeneity in New England "preserved their religion and morals [and] that manly virtue which is equally fitted for rendering them respectable in war and industrious in peace," but mixed blood in Pennsylvania cost that state its "religion and good morals." Questions also arose about America's backwoodsmen. Were they Americans or "a mongrel half-breed, half civilized, half savage?" And how did race factor in? "A Constant Customer" was surprised "that a people who profess to be so fond of freedom . . . can see such numbers of their fellow men, made of the same blood, not only in bondage but kept so even by them." However, a South Carolinian denied that whites and blacks were "of the same blood." He equated emancipation to miscegenation and proclaimed, "Let every spark of honest pride concur to save us from the infamy of such a mongrel coalition."[32]

The issue of fraternal blood bonds resurfaced in the debate over the Constitution. James Madison invoked "the kindred blood which flows in the veins of American citizens" and "the mingled blood which they have shed" to build continental support for a national government. In contrast, "Cato" stressed the local scope of men's bonds, arguing that America was made of families and fraternities loosely knit together "to provide for the safety of [their] posterity." He argued that the Constitution promoted an artificial unity that would see Americans "traveling through seas of blood." Competing images of fraternity and fratricide resurfaced in the 1790s. Madison proposed the Bill of Rights to invite antifederalists into the national fraternity; but Peres Fobes warned that excessive liberty incited men to practice the licentiousness and factionalism that "create jealousies, infuse suspicions, weaken public confidence, kindle and augment the flames of such contention as may desolate a country and crimson it with blood."[33] Transforming a land of strangers into a band of blood brothers proved a daunting challenge.

Several factors fostered fraternal unity despite disagreement and diversity. The founders mostly agreed on what it meant to be a worthy man in search of fraternity. Such a man disciplined his passions, impulses, and avarice to win other men's respect and establish fraternal membership. He continually earned his membership by exhibiting manly virtues such as the courage, integrity, and civility that attracted other men's trust and friendship. He also recognized manly merit and deferred to meritorious leaders. Noah Webster suggested that the only alternative to men's self-discipline, fraternal solidarity, and deference to manly leaders was the chaos and violence of Jacobin France. The founders also agreed that the search for national unity was a male endeavor. Men *as men* shared responsibility for defending liberty, provisioning and protecting families, fitting into fraternal society, and shaping public life. Women could encourage men to fit into fraternal society and compensate for men's failure to do so, but they could not transcend their political marginality. Jefferson's attitude was typical. He applauded American women for having "the good sense to value domestic happiness" rather than to "wrinkle their foreheads with politics," and he condemned Parisian "Amazons" for hunting social pleasures and fomenting political riots rather than minding their nurseries.[34]

The third rule in the founders' grammar of manhood was that worthy men were social creatures who sought to fit into fraternal society. They respected established loyalties and disregarded minor disputes. When necessary, however, they created new fraternities of self-disciplined, meritorious men. In time of war, they invited strangers to demonstrate manly worth by joining the fraternity of battle against enemies who threatened their liberty, property, and posterity. In peacetime, they sought to sustain fraternal bonds and guard them against the corrosive acids of individualism and avarice. Unworthy men came in three varieties: men alleged to have different blood; selfish egotists and social isolates whose only loyalty was to themselves; and misguided mobs, fratricidal factions, and demagogues who menaced the public good. Most founders thought that America's social stability depended on persuading the bulk of American men to provide fraternal support for worthy leaders who, in turn, would tame the disorderly passions and counteract the democratic distemper of aliens, egotists, isolates, mobs, factions, and demagogues.

Manhood and Leadership

Could American men procreate a national fraternity without fostering fratricide? The founders agreed that American men were disorderly creatures prone to bloody violence; but they disputed the implications of men's penchant for bloodshed. Jefferson found redeeming value in the bloody violence of Shays's Rebellion. He wrote Ezra Stiles, "What country can preserve its liberties if its rulers are not warned from time to time that this people persevere in the spirit of resistance? . . . What signify a few lives lost in a century or two?" But Washington considered Shays's Rebellion unmitigated evil. He exclaimed, "What, gracious God, is man! that there should be such inconsistency and perfidiousness in his conduct? It is but the other day that we were shedding blood to obtain the constitutions under which we now live . . . and now we are unsheathing the sword to overturn them."[35] These contrasting views were not wholly contradictory. The founders' grammar used "blood" both as a metaphoric testing ground for manhood in search of fraternity and as a symbol of disorderly manhood in need of fraternal leadership.

Jefferson returned to the relationship between the struggle for liberty and lost lives in 1793, when reflecting on a bloody turn of events in the French Revolution:

> In the struggle which was necessary, many guilty persons fell without the forms of trial, and with them some innocent. These I deplore as much as anybody. . . . But I deplore them as I should have done had they fallen in battle. It was necessary to use the arm of the people, a machine not quite so blind as balls and bombs, but blind to a certain degree. A few of their cordial friends met at their hands the fate of enemies. But time and truth will rescue and embalm their memories, while their posterity will be enjoying the very liberty for which they would never have hesitated to offer up their lives. The liberty of the whole earth was depending on the issue of the contest, and was ever such a prize won with so little innocent blood?[36]

Jefferson took the long view. He saw revolutionary abuses as deplorable but necessary for achieving lasting liberty, implying that men must endure self-sacrifice and bloodshed in fraternal solidarity with future generations. Jefferson's perspective highlights two major motifs in the founders' birthing story of America.

First, the founders conceived of blood as a medium for testing men's membership in society. A man had to invest, risk, give, and take blood to procreate and participate in fraternal society. Crèvecoeur's American Farmer stated that immigrants who invested their blood in American soil received the title of freemen and the opportunity to "provide for their progeny . . . the most holy, the most powerful, the most earnest wish he can possibly form, as well as the most consolatory prospect when he dies." The payoff was "a new race of men, whose labors and posterity will one day cause great changes in the world." Washington moved from Crèvecoeur's fraternity of farmers to his own fraternity of soldiers. Following the winter of want at Valley Forge, he paid homage to farmers as men whose labors guaranteed that soldiers' starvation and suffering would soon end. Meanwhile, "American soldiers will despise repining at such trifling strokes of adversity, trifling indeed when compared to the transcendent prize which will undoubtedly crown their patience and perseverance, glory and freedom, peace and plenty to themselves and the community . . . the admiration of the world, the love of their country, and the gratitude of posterity." Bloodshed and starvation were minor matters to worthy men who willingly paid the price for "being immortalized" as benefactors of posterity.[37]

Second, the founders suggested that historical necessity challenged Americans to transcend mundane manhood and engage in self-sacrifice to achieve fame. Madison invoked historical necessity to dismiss antifederalist claims that the Constitutional Convention abused its authority: "Which was the more important, which the less important? Which the end, which the means? Let the most scrupulous expositors of delegated powers, let the most inveterate objectors against those exercised by the convention answer these questions. Let them declare whether it was of most importance to the happiness of the people of America that the Articles of Confederation should be disregarded, and an adequate government be provided; or that an adequate government should be omitted, and the Articles of Confederation preserved." Alexander Hamilton added that necessity sometimes demanded that a representative oppose the will of the people to achieve the public good: "Instances might be cited in which conduct of this kind has saved the people from very fatal consequences of their own mistakes and has procured lasting monuments of their gratitude to the men who had courage and magnanimity enough to serve them at the period of their displeasure."[38] Necessity, expediency, exigency, and fortune were opportunities for great men to assert a manly prerogative, regardless of law or adverse public opinion, in the expectation that, eventually, they would be vindicated by the timeless fraternity called posterity.

Many founders believed that most American men had the potential to be farmers and fighters who invested, risked, and shed blood to secure liberty and earn membership in society. It was this potential that Jefferson honored in his remarks on Shays's Rebellion and the French Revolution. However, most founders feared that the male majority was not qualified to recognize necessity, address it, or meet its challenges. Consider George Washington's reaction to the 1783 "Newburgh Addresses," by which his officers threatened a military takeover if they did not receive their due compensation. Washington warned the officers not to assert a dangerous prerogative that would "open the flood gates to civil discord and deluge our rising empire in blood."[39] If the "gentlemen" of Washington's officer corps could participate in an anarchic plot, it was even more likely that common citizens and soldiers could be seduced by demagogues into factional bloodshed. Washington's sharp reaction to Shays's Rebellion expressed his fear that disorderly men might destroy American liberty and fraternity.

John Adams hoped that most men were "too economical of their blood" to join mobs or follow demagogues; he hoped that most men would become habituated to deferring to the "better sort" of men. However, recognizing the better sort and distinguishing worthy leaders was a controversial matter. Approaching the presidential election of 1800, for example, Alexander Hamilton condemned candidate Jefferson as a dangerous demagogue. Hamilton argued that the possibility of "an atheist in religion and a fanatic in politics" assuming "the helm of the state" constituted a crisis that made it necessary for leaders not to be "overscrupulous" about "a strict adherence to ordinary rules" to prevent Jefferson's election. He implied that a few exceptional men were needed to wield nation-saving prerogative. Jefferson won the election only to demonstrate that he, too, was not overscrupulous about adhering to ordinary rules. When he was president, Gary Schmitt observes, Jefferson advanced a "doctrine of extra-constitutional executive prerogative" in the name of domestic order and national security.[40]

Why would ordinary American men who were skeptical of authority become loyal followers of powerful national leaders? One reason was that men and leaders were bound together by the living memory of the revolutionary fraternity of battle. Annual Fourth of July sermons and orations reminded men of their noble struggle, and fraternal groups such as the Society of Cincinnati and the Freemasons provided settings for veterans to sustain their military ties. Another reason was that men and leaders were united by consensual norms of manhood. They agreed that men ought to strive for independence, head families, and fit into fraternal society. Moreover, they believed that individuals who excelled at manly virtues, such as self-sacrifice in the service of independence and the public good, deserved to be recognized, admired, and elevated to national leadership status. That was why William Emerson praised Washington as "a man among men" as well as "a hero among heroes [and] a statesman among statesmen."[41]

Still, the founders felt that unity between men and leaders was always fragile. Individuals risked their manly independence whenever they conformed to group norms or deferred to authority. The founders tried to minimize the risk by portraying leaders as manly men, citizens' choice, hesitant public servants, and benign governors. Hopefully, most men would trust officeholders who exhibited manly merit and acted the part of affectionate father figures. Another problem was that women potentially subverted men's attachment to fraternal society and leadership. Wives might keep husbands from militia musters that were excuses for drinking and gambling. Or women might urge men to stay at home to support and protect them rather than do their civic duty as soldiers by marching off to war. One reason the founders felt justified in perpetuating patriarchal power was to defeat women's efforts to resolve conflicts between domesticity and fraternity in favor of parochial family interests regardless of the public good.[42]

A fourth rule in the founders' grammar of manhood was that worthy men fit into a civic fraternity led by meritorious men. Worthy men were independent farmers and citizen soldiers who suffered pain, risked blood, and underwent self-sacrifice to earn membership in fraternal society. They were also modest men who recognized the need for leadership to address the crises of modernity, deferred to manly leaders, and sometimes consented to leadership prerogative in the service of posterity. Unworthy men were selfish men who demanded the liberty to indulge their passions, viewed others as instruments to fulfill their personal goals, and supported demagogues who pandered to public opinion, fostered factionalism, and sought power to do infamous deeds. Like men isolated in intergenerational time and continental space, those outside the flow of fraternal society and leadership threatened ruin to the republic of men.

Manhood and the Republic

The final chapter in the founders' autobiographical story was the one that Abraham Lincoln resurrected in his Gettysburg Address. That was the episode in which our fathers "brought forth," "conceived," and "consecrated" a "new nation." The founders saw themselves as more than virtuous men restoring republican rights or rational men negotiating a social contract; they also portrayed themselves as fertile men who procreated an organic republic. One prerevolutionary expression of their belief in political animation was John Tucker's 1771 portrait of an ideal American polity:

> The political state would be like a body in full health. The constitutional laws, preserved inviolate, would like strong bones and sinews support and steady the regular frame. Supreme and subordinate rulers duly performing their proper functions would be like the greater and lesser arteries, keeping up their proper tone and vibrations; and justice, fidelity, and every social virtue would, like the vital fluid, run without obstruction and reach, refresh, and invigorate the most minute and distant parts. While the multitude of subjects, yielding in their various places and relations a ready and cheerful obedience would, like the numerous yet connected veins, convey back again the recurrent blood to the great fountain of it and the whole frame be vigorous, easy, and happy.[43]

The founders depicted themselves as life-givers who, by 1776, had committed themselves to giving birth to a new republic. However, the creation of political life presumed the possibility of political death. American dreams of political fatherhood were premised on Britain's political degeneration, and the founders knew that their republic was vulnerable to the same fate. Though some founders imagined linear progress, most agreed, "It is with states as it is with men, they have their infancy, their manhood, and their decline."[44]

Many founders spoke as if they were giving birth to a living, breathing, pulsating republic. During what Samuel Miller commemorated as "our country's natal hour," John Adams anticipated parturition in June 1776 by announcing that the "throes" of Congress soon "will usher in the birth of a fine boy." Mercy Otis Warren saw a bright future for "an infant nation at once arisen to the vigor of manhood," but others feared for the Republic's health. In 1782, a Bostonian worried, "How humiliating would it be to have our independence, just brought to birth, fail for want of strength to be delivered." A year later, Washington likened the states to "young heirs come a little prematurely perhaps to a large inheritance." But Warren remained optimistic. She was joyful that the "young republic . . . had rapidly passed through the grades of youth and puberty and was fast arriving to the age of maturity." By 1788, "An Old State Soldier" was arguing that the best way to ensure the continuing health and development of "that tender infant, Independence" was to support ratification of the U.S. Constitution.[45]

The imagery of an infant nation seeking the maturity of manhood pervaded the ratification debates. Jeremiah Hill likened the "glory of this young empire" guided by a new Constitution to a "fair, healthy, promising boy rising to maturity." Simeon Baldwin summed up federalist optimism by recalling the "effusions of genius [that] distinguished the infancy of this nation." He awaited with delight "what we may expect when she [*sic*] shall ripen into manhood!" Mercy Otis Warren, for her part, turned federalist imagery on its head when contrasting the "manly exertions" of revolutionary patriots and the "manly feelings" of antifederalists to the childish federalists who resembled "a restless, vigorous youth, prematurely emancipated from the authority of a parent, but without the experience necessary to direct him with dignity and discretion."[46]

Movement toward national manhood was debated for another decade. In 1790s, Judith Sargent Murray observed "the budding life" of an "infant constitution" invigorated by "luminous rays of manly hope," but warned that factionalism was "murdering in the cradle so promising an offspring" and bringing forth in its place "hell-born anarchy." Bishop James Madison praised the United States for its "progress from infancy to manhood" but Peres Fobes recalled, "We saw a nation born in a day [and] felt the pangs and pleasures of the parturition of a new empire" only to have it infected by male licentiousness. Jonathan Maxey added that America's democratic politics had become "a capricious offspring of a moment, perpetually exposed to destruction from the varying whim of popular frenzy or the daring strides of licentious ambition." In the early nineteenth century, Noah Webster compared the unstable new republic to young men who have "more courage than foresight and more enthusiasm than correct judgment." Fisher Ames complained that the U.S. Constitution was conceived "with all the bloom of youth and splendor of innocence . . . gifted with immortality," only to fall prey to "licentiousness, that inbred malady of democracies that deforms their infancy with gray hairs and decrepitude."[47]

Many founders saw themselves as participants in what Hannah Arendt calls "natality," the action of founding and sustaining political bodies in anticipation of an influx of new generations. Their self-portraits depicted men of exceptional merit who procreated a new nation, protected its infancy from democratic excess, nurtured it to mature manhood, shielded it from death, and, by way of exemplary thinking, innovative constitutions, and a federal republic, improved the future for all posterity. To borrow Nancy Hartsock's language, they regarded themselves as "pregnant in soul." They certainly ranked themselves among history's great nation builders and felt they deserved the respect shown by men who called them "fathers of their country." In effect, the founders expropriated the idea of natality from women. They did not give much weight to female reproductive powers. Judith Sargent Murray understood that women's public standing would not result from their biological powers but instead invested hope in their cultural productivity. Women needed to emulate "manly fires" of wisdom, develop the "fertile brain of the female," and exhibit their "creative faculty" to achieve a public presence. Nevertheless, the founders did not include creative women in politics as founding mothers, republican citizens, or national leaders. Often, they even failed to consider women as noteworthy subjects or significant spectators.[48]

The final rule in the founders' grammar of manhood was that exceptional or heroic men contributed to the birth and nurturance of a republic. They were the fathers of the country and the future. They invested their fame in the fate of the public and posterity, rather than solely in their own families and estates. Unworthy men were sterile men or destructive men. They felt no connection between themselves and future generations; they were innocent of dreams of distinction; or they were licentious men who imperiled national birth, retarded political maturation, and endangered the newborn republic. The most worthy men sought a fame borne of procreating a glorious future, whereas the most unworthy males acquired infamy by sapping other men's political potency.

Order in the Ranks of Men

The Boston colonists who resisted royal authority set a lasting precedent when they "chose to hazard the consequences of returning back to the state of nature rather than quietly submit to unjust and arbitrary measures."[49] Henceforth, most founders feared, American men exhibited a propensity to claim unlimited rights and hazard disorderly conduct whenever they opposed public measures, even those enacted and administered by their own representatives. The founders developed and deployed the grammar of manhood to encourage American males to engage in self-sacrifice in defense of liberty and to exhibit self-restraint in the exercise of liberty, to support and consent to deserving leadership, and thereby to promote order in the ranks of men.

The founders' grammar of manhood consisted of hegemonic norms and rules meant to move the hearts of men. Its main message was that a male worthy of self-esteem, social respect, and civic dignity achieved manly independence, family status, and governance of women by fulfilling intergenerational obligations, fixing a settled place for himself and his heirs, fitting into fraternal society, recognizing and deferring to worthy leaders, and helping to father a new nation. This message was steeped in blood. Manhood was a matter of blood bonds between fathers and sons, the investment of blood in land and liberty, the kindred blood that defined fraternal society, the innocent blood that linked ancestral sacrifice to future happiness, the risking and shedding of blood that tested citizens and leaders, the bloody birth of the body politic, and the factional bloodletting that imperiled the Republic's survival.[50]

The grammar of manhood offered little direct guidance regarding male-female relations. However, the founders assumed that women motivated men to risk their blood and defend liberty, bore their children, contributed to family provision and comfort, and supported men's fraternal relations and nation-building ambitions. Ongoing patriarchal domination ensured women's assistance in American men's procreative mission to shape the course of history. The founders saw themselves as autonomous historical agents, the fathers of a new people, land, society, and republic destined to change the world for the better. They inflated the value of their natality, in part, by devaluing female sexuality. They instituted a new republic in which the prior identification of women with bloody childbirth and menstruation would gradually give way to the Victorian era's bloodless images of female passionlessness and political innocence.[51]

The founders communicated challenging standards—and they were convinced that many males did not measure up to everyday expectations about manly courage and self-restraint. Cowards and libertines betrayed ancestors and offspring, transformed liberty to license, engaged in deceitful and criminal conduct, and fueled the factionalism that mobilized mobs and leveled republics. Worse, the example of a few licentious men threatened to awaken within America's more sober family men dormant passions, impulses, and interests that threatened to destroy social harmony and political legitimacy. The founders generally believed that only the most mindless democrat would advocate the rights of man and citizen for disorderly males who acted like children. They did not deserve the rights of men. Nor could they be trusted to participate in politics. Like women, they needed to be governed to ensure public order.

3

The Bachelor and Other Disorderly Men

The founders used the stock figure of the Bachelor to identify the lowest rung of manhood. The Bachelor symbolized the dangers of democracy and the corruption of patriarchy. He was the male who failed to invest liberty in responsibility, only to foster disorder in the ranks of men. He refused to assume the family obligations of the traditional patriarch or participate in the benevolent governance of women and other dependents, as required by republican manhood. Sometimes he exhibited the manners of aristocratic manhood to mask his lustful desires, and often he wore the guise of self-made manhood to justify his selfishness. The Bachelor broke all the rules in the grammar of manhood. He was unsettled in intergenerational time and continental space, unfit for fraternal society and estranged from its natural leaders, and destructive of republican virtues and institutions. The founders associated him with the promiscuity, licentiousness, sex crimes, itinerancy, pauperism, frontier lawlessness, racial taboos, and martial violence that destroyed families, fostered social anarchy, and invited political tyranny.

American leaders applied the grammar of manhood to stigmatize, ridicule, degrade, and humiliate the Bachelor by portraying him as a man-child who did not merit the rights of men, fraternal respect, or civic standing. Their informal but influential message was that immature males were not free and equal men so much as overgrown children who should be excluded from public discourse, citizenship, and authority. Males who heeded the message might avoid exclusion by conforming to consensual norms of manhood and settling into family responsibilities and community respectability. Those who ignored the message exposed themselves to a coercive criminal justice system designed to control and penalize but also to rehabilitate males identified with subordinated masculinities. When James Winthrop wrote that "it is necessary that the sober and industrious . . . should be defended from the rapacity and violence of the vicious and idle," he was asserting polite society's demand to be protected against the Bachelor and other disorderly men.[1]

The English Bachelor and Redcoat

Late-seventeenth-century England hosted a debate on liberty and disorder. The Bachelor represented disorder. Mary Astell expressed a common viewpoint: "He who lives single that he may indulge licentiousness and give up himself to the conduct of wild and ungovernable desires . . . can never justify his own conduct nor clear it from the imputation of wickedness and folly." The Bachelor's wickedness was manifested in his unrestrained sexuality. He seduced women but refused to recognize his offspring. Aphra Behn wrote, "The roving youth in every shade / Has left some sighing and abandon'd Maid / For tis a fatal lesson he has learn'd / After fruition ne're to be concern'd." Critics attacked "the compleat beau" who produced ruined women and bastard children, cursed "predatory males" for leveraging lust into drinking, gambling, and crime, and linked the libertine to gangs such as the "Roysters, Hectors, Bucks, Bravados, Blades, [and] Bloods" that wreaked havoc in towns. Critics also condemned the Bachelor for spreading an antimarital gospel that equated bachelorhood to freedom and marriage to slavery. For instance, Robert Gould warned men who valued their liberty to steer clear of the "wild, rocky matrimonial sea."[2]

Writers stigmatized the Bachelor as more slave than man. The Bachelor was a slave to lust, impulse, and avarice. He lacked self-restraint, rationality, and virtue, and lived by his "appetites" in a "lapsed state of mankind." He suffered an "inconstancy" that rendered his word meaningless, his behavior frivolous, and his actions erratic. Women could not trust him to be other than a rogue, and men did not expect him to be a trustworthy neighbor. He also was a slave to "unnatural" proclivities associated with the effeminate "fop" who dwelled on appearances, haunted sporting, gambling, and prostitution houses, and cleaved to the latest fashion in "Gallic lust." One satirist wrote, "Far much more time men trifling waste / E'er their soft bodies can be drest / The looking glass hangs before / And each o' th' legs requires an hour." Critics often condemned the fop's abnormal sexuality. One pamphleteer announced, "The world is changed I know not how / For men kiss men, not women now . . . / A most unmanly trick / One man to lick the other's cheek."[3] The Bachelor's lust drew him alternately to the prostitute's parlor and to a comrade's chamber.

Some writers saw the Bachelor as seditious. He failed to father legitimate sons to replenish the ranks of freeholders dedicated to defending liberty: "A bachelor of age has broken the laws of nature [and] contributes little or nothing to the support of our freedoms. The money he pays in taxes is inconsiderable to the supplies given by others in children, which are an addition to the native strength of the kingdom. . . . A bachelor can, in no sense, be esteemed a good Englishman."[4] The Bachelor was isolated in time. Having squandered any patrimony and sired no legitimate children, he was estranged from the intergenerational bonds of family and nation. The Bachelor was also unsettled in space. He wandered the English countryside and cities in search of pleasure, threatened other men's families and property, and claimed rights without responsibilities.

What should be done with this parasite? Proposed solutions included preventive education and political remediation. John Locke's *Some Thoughts Concerning Education* was a primer for fathers to teach sons self-discipline and social civility in anticipation of manhood, marriage, and citizenship. Others recommended sanctions. Magistrates should arrest "strumpets and harlots" who made "the lewder sort of men out of love with matrimony," and legislators should enact "compulsive laws" to force bachelors to marry. One satirist suggested that a twenty-four-year-old bachelor should be taxed to defray costs resulting from his failure to procreate freeholders, and a twenty-five-year-old bachelor "ought to be reckoned superannuated and grown an old boy and not fit to be trusted with what he had, as not knowing the use and benefit of riches." Regardless of actual age, "a bachelor is a minor" who "ought to be under the government of the parish."[5]

Critics hoped to hasten the Bachelor's progress to marriage by reforming male manners and female morality. Locke's protégé, the third earl of Shaftesbury (Anthony Ashley Cooper), praised the "man of sensibility" who claimed "manly liberty" to unite "a mind subordinated to reason, a temper humanized and fitted to all natural affections . . . with constant security, tranquillity, [and] equanimity." Unlike flatterers, seducers, and bullies, the genteel man knew that marriage to a good woman wed virtue to happiness.[6] Others emphasized women's morality. David Hume saw male lust as an immutable reality. What prompted men to accept the "restraint" of marriage and "undergo cheerfully all the fatigues and expenses to which it subjects men" was their egotistical desire to clone themselves by siring legitimate sons. Men could satisfy that desire only if they could find faithful wives. Accordingly, the Bachelor was more likely to choose marriage when female fidelity was fortified.[7]

Where education and remediation failed, the Bachelor was apt to embroil himself in family feuds, gambling debts, and crime. He often escaped harm's way by being sent to or enlisting in England's standing army. John Trenchard complained, "Our prisons are so many storehouses to replenish [the king's] troops." Trenchard considered the marginal males who composed the army's rank-and-file redcoats to be rogues and mercenaries whose anarchist bent was commandeered by corrupt, aristocratic officers using draconian discipline to mold the army to the king's despotic will. Critics accused the officer corps of synthesizing libertinism and brutality into an instrument of monarchical tyranny.[8]

Observing the standing army in peacetime, William Prynne asked, "What do these soldiers do all day?" He answered, "These lusty men spend their time eating, drinking, whoring, sleeping and standing watch . . . make off with wives and daughters and leave not a few great bellies and bastards on the inhabitants of the country's charge." Trenchard noted that the army rendered "men useless to labor and almost propagation, together with a much greater destruction of them, by taking them from a laborious way of living to a loose idle life." That loose idle life encompassed "the insolence of the officers and the debaucheries that are committed both by them and their soldiers in all the towns they come in . . . and a numerous train of mischiefs besides, almost endless to enumerate." John Toland listed among redcoat mischiefs "frequent robberies, burglaries, rapes, rapines, murders, and barbarous cruelties." Andrew Fletcher accused libertine officers of "debauchery and wickedness" as well as "frauds, oppressions, and cruelties."[9]

If the Bachelor's wickedness was evident in his tendency to see a woman's ruin as "a step to reputation" as he built "his own honor on her infamy," the Redcoat's vices were manifested in his tendency to speak patriotism but practice selfishness. Toland noted, "If one . . . who would pass for a patriot has an interest separate from that of the public, he is no longer entitled to this denomination; but he is a real hypocrite that's ready to sacrifice the common good to his private gain." The idea that only "sober, industrious freemen" in the militia (as opposed to "ignorant, idle, and needy" redcoats) were sufficiently trustworthy to bear arms was the basis for a century-long attack on the standing army as an engine of anarchy and tyranny. That attack often returned to the Bachelor. Demobilized soldiers were mostly single males, many of whom traveled to London where they joined "loose fellows" engaged in antisocial activity and criminal behavior.[10]

Toland condemned the Bachelor and the Redcoat for being estranged from the deepest stirrings of manhood, the desire for symbolic immortality that inspired self-sacrifice from the procreative father, industrious freeholder, and patriotic militiaman. He wrote:

> All men would live somewhere eternally if they could, and they affect to become immortal even here on earth. To have their names perpetuated was the true spring of several great men's actions; and for that only end have they patiently undergone all manner of toil and danger. But this inclination never dis-

> covers itself so plainly as in the care men take of their posterity. Some are content to live beggars all their days that their children after them may be rich, for they look upon these as their own persons multiplied by propagation; whence some as had none themselves adopted the children of others to bear their names.[11]

English critics stigmatized the Bachelor and the Redcoat for sterility. They demonstrated no commitment to family, friends, or nation. They procreated nothing of public value. They were destructive children who lived solely in the present, where they generated social disorder and fostered political tyranny. Like minors, they needed to be governed.

America's Vilest Race of Men

The English introduced the Bachelor into American discourse as early as 1623, when Sir George Ferrars condemned Virginia colonizers as "unruly sparks, . . . poor gentlemen, broken tradesmen, rakes and libertines, footmen." Sir Edwin Sandys hoped to calm colonial disorders by sending women to America to marry these disorderly men and make them "more settled." Colonial administrators experimented with land incentives to encourage men to marry and penalties to discourage lengthy bachelorhood. Nonetheless, a 1708 missionary report criticized the inhabitants of Carolina as "the vilest race of men upon the earth . . . bankrupts, pirates, decayed libertines, sectaries, and enthusiasts . . . of large and loose principles."[12] These men did not measure up to manhood.

No American enjoyed ridiculing the Bachelor more than Benjamin Franklin. In "The Speech of Polly Baker," he told the story of a trial in which Polly stood accused of bearing bastard children. She defended herself with three arguments. First, she stated that it could not possibly be a crime to propagate the species and add subjects to the king's dominions. Second, she supported her own children who, therefore, were no burden to the community. Third, she had consented to a marriage proposal from the father of her first child, but he abandoned her and the child. Polly concluded that the Bachelor was the real culprit: "Take into your wise consideration the great and growing number of bachelors in the country, many of whom, from the mean fear of the expenses of a family, have never sincerely and honorably courted a woman in their lives; and by their manner of living leave unproduced (which is little better than murder) hundreds of their posterity to the thousandth generation. Is not this a greater offense against the public good than mine?" The Bachelor's selfishness was a crime against nature and nation that was magnified by what Robert Gross characterizes as an "epidemic" of premarital sex and children conceived out of wedlock in the last half of the eighteenth century.[13]

The founders also ridiculed the aged bachelor for promiscuity and irresponsibility. When Abigail Adams wrote John Adams that a canister from Philadelphia had not arrived, John replied that he had given it to Elbridge Gerry, "an old bachelor" wont to get distracted. Abigail speculated that "perhaps he finds it very hard to leave his mistress." She added to the fun a year later by telling John about an old Boston merchant, "a bachelor," accused of hoarding goods and price gouging. One hundred women "seized him by the neck and tossed him into the cart." Next, they broke into his warehouse and distributed his goods, while "a large concourse of men stood amazed, silent spectators of the whole transaction." John's light-hearted response was that "the women in Boston begin to think themselves able to serve their country."[14] The remarkable thing about this exchange is that both Adamses were consistently horrified by mob actions but responded here with humor, apparently because the "victim" was a bachelor who stood beneath men's contempt and, importantly, beyond the protection of law.

Early American fiction was filled with morality tales about selfish bachelors who schemed to conquer girls' chastity and acquire their family fortunes. Royall Tyler's "The Contrast" focused on young Mr. Dimple, who set his sights on the hearts and purse strings of several innocent girls. Tyler made it clear that Dimple was no man. Rather, he was a "depraved wretch whose only virtue is a polished exterior; who is actuated by the unmanly ambition of conquering the defenseless; whose heart, insensitive to the emotions of patriotism, dilates at the plaudits of every unthinking girl; whose laurels are the sighs and tears of the miserable victims of his specious behavior." Fortunately, the aptly named Colonel Manly saved the women by unmasking Dimple's deceptions and banishing him from polite society. Manly was a "good" bachelor, but he was atypical. He considered his "late soldiers" his family; he was so virtuous that women mistook him for a married man; and he still hoped to wed one of "his fair countrywomen." Most writers recognized that women could not count on a Colonel Manly to defend them. Joel Barlow suggested that women don the armor of virtue to protect themselves from "the powder'd coxcomb and the flaunting beau," and Judith Sargent Murray advised that women acquire a substantial education to set themselves "above the snares of the artful betrayer."[15]

Ideally, the identification of the Bachelor with unmanly conduct was sufficient to prompt most young men to discipline their sexuality as a means to achieve manhood. A young George Washington recognized the danger of sensuality and sought to live "retired from young women," that he might bury that "troublesome passion in the grave of oblivion or eternal forgetfulness." The older Washington warned young male relatives to beware of lust. He wrote a grandson that he had been told "of your devoting much time and paying much attention to a certain young lady" and counseled that "this is not the time for a boy of your age to enter into engagements which might end in sorrow and repentance." He cautioned other young men to avoid "scenes of dissipation and vice which too often present themselves to youth in every place and particularly in towns." Instead, they should keep company only with "the best kind." Similarly, James Madison warned a classmate to avoid improper company: "Pray do not suffer those impertinent fops that abound in every city to divert you from your business. . . . [Keep] them at a becoming distance." John Adams detested urban infestations of impertinent young men. He advised Americans to learn from the example of "the Covent Garden rake" who "will never be wise enough to take warning from the claps caught by his companions." Enslaved by passion, "three out of four" young men who were "poxed" became "even by their own sufferings more shameless instead of being penitent."[16] Venereal disease was the Bachelor's perverse badge of honor.

Unfortunately, the Bachelor's perversity was infectious. The libertine who bragged about his sexual conquests was likely to influence impressionable boys with misguided notions of manhood. A 1763 Boston article contrasted a sensible manhood based on "knowledge and civility" with a false masculinity constituted by "cavalier-like principles of honor" which declared that "boxing, clubs, or firearms are resorted to for deciding every quarrel about a girl, a game of cards, or any little accident that wine or folly or jealousy may suspect to be an affront." The author noted that a "delicate and manly way of thinking" was conducive "to the peace of society," whereas the Bachelor's false "gallantry" produced among the educated a "smooth-speaking class of people who mean to get their living out of others" and, in the lower ranks, "a disrespect to every personage in a civil character." The Bachelor's mischief had to be stopped lest it foster among young men the growth of upper-class corruption and lower-class chaos.[17]

Sometimes, the founders chastised the Bachelor by accusing him of effeminacy and luxury; often times, they degraded him for his unmanly selfishness and slavery to desire; most of the time, they humiliated him for being less than a man—for being a boy. Benjamin Franklin pointed out that the Bachelor often consorted with boys. He lured them into vice by filling their heads with visions of "gay living," distracted them from "the dull ways of getting money by working," and tempted them into little dishonesties, followed by "others a little more knavish," until a youngster became "a consummate rascal and villain." The Bachelor himself was but a grown boy, in that "a man's value" was diminished when he did not head a family. He was only "half a man." Labeling an adult male a "grown boy" or "half man" had consequences. A whole man had a presumptive claim to manly freedom and independence, but a boy was still a dependent minor in need of guidance and governance. Jeremiah Atwater likened libertines to boys who lacked "manliness of manner and personal independence" to legitimize disciplining them; another writer went so far as to recommend that "the whole power of government should be exerted to suppress them."[18]

The Bachelor within All Men

The Bachelor could not be wholly suppressed because he existed within all men. Most founders saw males as inherently passionate creatures whose sexual propensities were emblematic of their overall inability to resist temptation. Benjamin Rush typified men as self-absorbed individuals who engaged in the "solitary vice" of masturbation as well as the social vice of promiscuity. Benjamin Franklin thought young males were especially lustful creatures subject to "violent natural inclinations." They sought and enjoyed sex but failed to recognize or respect the obligations attendant to paternity. They also failed to demonstrate much concern for their own health, morality, wealth, and family prospects. Franklin confessed that the "hard-to-govern passion of youth" had hurried him "into intrigues with low women," and he employed Poor Richard's voice to warn young men, "Women and Wine / Game and Deceit / Make the wealth small / And the wants great."[19]

Thomas Jefferson agreed that nature embedded lust in men's constitution and that "the commerce of love" was indulged on "this unhallowed principle." Unfortunately, "intrigues of love [that] occupy the young" tended to "nourish and invigorate all our bad passions" rather than prepare men to achieve "conjugal love" and "domestic happiness." According to Bernard Bailyn, Jefferson viewed "sexual promiscuity [as] the ultimate corruption." He confessed to his own youthful indiscretions with "bad company" and urged young men to practice sexual self-denial. He warned a grandson to avoid "taverns, drinkers, smokers, idlers, and dissipated persons," especially loose women. He opposed sending a young man to polish his education in Europe, where he was likely to be "led by the strongest of all human passions into a spirit of female intrigue destructive of his own and others' happiness, or a passion for whores destructive of his own health." However, he praised a French mother who sought to save her seventeen-year-old son from European "excesses" by sending him to America, because education was "more masculine here and less exposed to seduction." George Washington made a finer domestic distinction. He advised one of his grandsons to transfer to a college in Massachusetts, where young men "are less prone to dissipation and debauchery than they are in colleges south of it."[20]

The founders feared that youthful debauchery had lifelong consequences. Thomas Paine stated that a young man who consorted with prostitutes was "unfitted to choose or judge of a wife." Jefferson added that such a youth "learns to consider fidelity to the marriage bed as an ungentlemanly practice." Sexual license in boyhood undermined a young man's chance for marital happiness. It either confirmed him in bachelorhood by exposing him to alternative sexual outlets or drew him into unworkable marriages. Charles Carroll fretted that few males restrained lust long enough to choose a proper spouse. He warned, "Beauty . . . affects our propensity to lust so strongly that it makes most matches, and most of those miserable." John Adams asserted, "The first want of man is his dinner, and the second his girl. . . . the second want is frequently so impetuous as to make men and women forget the first and rush into rash marriages, leaving both the first and second wants, their own as well as those of their children and grandchildren, to the chapter of accidents." To avoid this chapter of accidents, Noah Webster proposed that "a young man's best security against . . . dissipated life" was to cultivate "a fondness for the company and conversation of ladies of character."[21]

Young men who rushed into bad marriages could expect pain and humiliation. Many would experience misery in their family lives, lending credence to the libertine's definition of liberty as freedom from marriage. Others would betray their marriage vows and suffer the sting of public disapprobation. Jacob Rush condemned men's adultery as "a cruel breech of trust" that "tends directly to destroy families" and "tears up the very foundation of society." When men "abandon themselves to adulterous courses," they nullify the "solemnities of an oath" and foster a "universal depravity of morals" that "must utterly destroy society." Even youth who chose virtuous wives were adultery-prone. In 1797, Alexander Hamilton published a remarkable pamphlet to confess that "the ardor of passion" led him into an adulterous affair with Maria Reynolds. He apologized for the pain that he caused his wife ("a bosom eminently entitled to all my gratitude, fidelity, and love") but explained that public confession was his only defense "against a more heinous charge" of financial corruption made by Reynolds's husband. Hamilton suffered humiliation when critics attacked him as an faithless man "who had the cruelty publicly to wound and insult the feelings of his family." Still, his apology implied that all men have an ardor of passion, many give in to it, and most rely on virtuous wives to pardon them for it. Ruth Bloch reminds us that a common figure in early American fiction was "the adulterous husband redeemed by his faithful and forgiving wife."[22]

American civic leaders who denounced promiscuity wanted to do more than monitor male sexuality. They believed that men's "inability to control sexual impulse indicated a more dangerous inability to control all vicious impulses of the self." Authorities stigmatized male promiscuity to deter it and legitimize coercive controls on the men most closely associated with it. Colonial governments often required bachelors to live in family households, assuming that single males "lack someone . . . to hold them within the bounds of order." Connecticut fined bachelors who did not reside in family dwellings, and Maryland enacted punitive taxes on them. Meanwhile, magistrates and courts made bachelors liable for their sexual misdeeds. Especially in New England, governments prosecuted white bastardy cases to establish paternity, force fathers to support their illegitimate families, and "prevent fatherless children and unwed mothers from becoming town charges." Though this juridical quest for sexual purity and financial responsibility flagged by the mid–eighteenth century, leaders' suspicions of male desire persisted.[23]

Most founders saw male sexuality as a seedbed of disorder. They urged young man to channel sexual energy into monogamous marriage which, Mary Beth Norton notes, was conceived as an "indispensable duty" and "debt to society." Their efforts were abetted by writers who portrayed bachelorhood as painful and marriage as pleasurable. On the one hand, Judith Sargent Murray proclaimed, "The life of the bachelor is almost invariably gloomy." He was "alone in the universe." He confessed to himself, "No young props list their green heads for my support; not an individual of the rising generation is bound to me by the silken bands of attachment. . . . When I expire, my name will be extinct, and all remembrance of me will cease from the earth!" The Bachelor was "truly pitiable." On the other hand, Benjamin Rush proposed, men could achieve a sense of fulfillment in marriages founded on shared affection, mutual respect, and children. His letters to his betrothed, Julia Stockton, oozed republican romance. Rush decried his years as a selfish bachelor. He looked to Julia to "point out to me the duty and happiness of a life of piety and usefulness." He forswore the ostensible joys of bachelorhood "as nothing when set in competition with you" and pledged to earn Julia's eternal love by serving the poor and becoming a better patriot.[24] Colonial leaders often relied on coercion to prevent the Bachelor from infecting other men; the founding generation usually solicited men's consent to sexual self-discipline in anticipation of monogamous marriage.

Other Disorderly Men

Some men were unmoved by threats of coercion or pleas for self-discipline. They indulged their desires to criminal extremes. They were guilty of sex crimes such as rape and sodomy or engaged in lawless conduct associated with itinerancy, vagrancy, pauperism, and frontier anarchy. These disorderly men may have been relatively few in number, but their "seditious and disorganizing spirit" was thought "contagious." Nathanael Emmons contended that men infatuated with themselves were apt to reject all authority and "imagine that there is little or no criminality." A few disorderly men could be a "leaven of rebellion" that "poisoned the minds of many" and destroyed "the bands of society."[25]

In postrevolutionary New York City, young men joined "crowds of 'bloods' . . . who lounged on city sidewalks and, affecting the contemptuous stance of the aristocratic libertine, tossed provocative remarks at any single woman who passed." These "self-styled libertines" were known for their sexual aggression and their tendency to make contempt for women an "emblem of high style." Some went beyond provocative words to violent deeds, to be charged with "attempted rape" or "rape." The former charge referred to coercive sexual acts up to and including forcible penetration. The more serious latter charge involved penetration and ejaculation.[26] New York legislators wanted to penalize unbridled male sexuality, especially when it was apt to produce dependent bastards.

Marybeth Hamilton Arnold states that the founding generation condemned rape as "a horrid crime" that excited "universal abhorrence." Certainly, some American men blamed the victim. In one case, the defense attorney claimed his client, the accused rapist, had been seduced by a carnal thirteen-year-old girl. However, the founders mostly blamed male rapists for violence against innocent females. Josiah Quincy was outraged by the "brutal ravisher." John Adams attacked redcoats for having "debauched" Boston girls and David Ramsay cursed British and Hessian troops for "rapes and brutalities committed on women and even on very young girls." Criminologist William Bradford condemned rape as an unmanly crime that demanded manly vengeance: "Female innocence has strong claims upon our protection, and a desire to avenge its wrongs is natural to a generous and manly mind."[27] Penal codes commonly called for capital punishment.

Abhorrence of rape, laws forbidding it, and hanging for those convicted of it resulted in few prosecutions, convictions, or executions. American jurists seemed nearly as eager to coddle the criminal as to condemn the crime. William Penn tried to liberalize colonial Pennsylvania's rape law by reducing a first-time rapist's punishment to a fine and one year in prison and by reserving for the repeat offender a penalty of life imprisonment. Penn's reforms were vetoed by the Crown. After the Revolution, Pennsylvania led the nation in liberalizing English law. It eliminated the death penalty for rape and substituted a maximum penalty of property forfeiture and ten years imprisonment. Why condemn the crime but reduce the penalty? William Bradford explained that rape was rooted in "the sudden abuse of a natural passion" and "perpetrated in a frenzy of desire." It was an "atrocity" that should be punished. But because it was an atrocity rooted in natural passion rather than in the "incorrigibility of the criminal," the rapist did not suffer an "irreclaimable corruption" that demanded death. He could be rehabilitated. As Joel Barlow put it, "a wise and manly government" administered "a tender paternal correction."[28]

Bradford observed that judges and juries rarely convicted a man of rape when they knew the penalty would be death. No jury would convict a husband for forcibly exercising his sex right within marriage, and few jurists would hang a man for submitting to frenzied desire. One reason for leniency was the widespread belief that the injury to the rape victim was largely a matter of perception. Bradford wrote, "It cannot be denied that much of [rape's] atrocity resides in the imagination." Rape was thought most injurious when committed against a woman of high "rank" and "character," less so when the victim was a servant girl, and least harmful when it involved "the violation of a female slave." Because rape was often a class crime committed by high-status males against lower-class women, juries "frequently treat this charge so lightly as to acquit against positive and uncontradicted evidence."[29] Judges and juries were reluctant to impose lethal penalties on perpetrators. Nonetheless, antirape rhetoric and laws communicated the cultural message that men should exercise sexual self-restraint and deserved punishment when they failed to do so.

The founding generation allied sexual self-restraint to avoidance of same-sex relationships, which represented a "potential in the lustful nature of all men" and "a potential for disorder in the cosmos." During the eighteenth century, public perception transformed sodomy from a mortal sin against God into a passion "against the order of nature" and, therefore, an abuse of the natural laws that regulated "the peace, government, and dignity of the state." Why did private sexual acts have public meaning? John Winthrop's explanation was the enduring one. Like libertinism and masturbation, same-sex relations "tended to the frustrating of the ordinance of marriage and the hindering [of] the generation of mankind." The sodomist separated sex and pleasure from marriage and procreation to unleash passion and cause chaos. Jonathan Edwards, Jr., condemned ancient Greeks for glorifying "the most abominable practices openly" and ancient Cretans for encouraging sodomy "to prevent too great an increase of the people," because he believed that same-sex relations eroded men's commitment to family responsibilities.[30]

Sodomy, like rape, was a capital offense that was rarely prosecuted. Bradford wanted to eliminate the death penalty for "the crime against nature." After all, America was "a country where marriages take place so early, and the intercourse between the sexes is not difficult." With females abundant and accessible, no mature male had good reason to be drawn into a same-sex relationship. Indeed, "the wretch who perpetrates [sodomy] must be in a state of mind which may occasion us to doubt whether he be *Sui Juris* at the time; or whether he reflects on the punishment at all." Bradford saw sodomy as a manifestation of a sort of temporary insanity in a man enslaved by unnatural, excessive sexual appetites.[31] Because the insanity was temporary, a man convicted of sodomy could be rehabilitated.

If American leaders saw rapists and sodomists as sex criminals, they considered itinerants known as the "strolling poor" as suspects. The strolling poor were young men who roamed from town to town in search of work, land, or adventure. Townspeople greeted these strangers with grave distrust. After all, they were young, rootless, and unpredictable males—threats to daughters' virtue, wives' fidelity, men's property, and public coffers. Officials examined them for signs of drunkenness and poverty lest they become a source of disorder or a burden on the community. Villages often "warned out" itinerants. Magistrates gave these transients a few days to secure a sponsor, post a bond, or exit. Those who failed to sink roots or leave could be sent to the stocks or the whipping post. Many were escorted to their last known residence, where they might again be removed "until they reached the end of the line—usually their birth place."[32]

The stigma against transience was pervasive. Local leaders distrusted itinerant preachers who traveled from town to town, scorned established ministers and fixed houses of worship, and held religious services in open fields. Analogously, most founders feared the public's "transient impressions" and relied on elites to protect men against their fleeting fancies. Civic leaders especially despised transient vagrants and paupers who did not fit into orderly society. They were rootless men thought to wed moral deficiency to poverty. Benjamin Franklin was horrified that Great Britain exhibited the "unexampled barbarity" to "empty [its] jails into our settlements" and fill colonial America with "vagrants and idle persons" who "continue their evil practices [and] contribute greatly to corrupt the morals of the servants and the poorer people among whom they mix." After the Revolution, Raymond Mohl writes, civic spokesmen denounced the "idle, ignorant, immoral, impious, and vicious" paupers whose ranks included "immigrant wanderers, soldiers, sailors, prostitutes, peddlers, beggars, thieves, and rogues [and] the idle and profligate banditti," who "begged, stole, disturbed the peace, drank to excess, and . . . committed 'shameful enormities.'" These unsettled men were a significant source of disorder.[33]

The frontier version of vagrants and paupers was backwoodsmen. Crèvecoeur's American Farmer saw backwoodsmen as men driven by misfortune into the wilderness, where they roamed about with little or no government supervision. They tended to be intemperate, greedy, profligate, lawless men prone to conflict and violence. They survived by hunting, led "a licentious idle life" of "rapacity and injustice," and behaved "no better than carnivorous animals." George Washington called them "banditti" because they stole the "cream of the country" despite the fact that "officers and soldiers . . . fought and bled to obtain it." Washington also rebuked frontier "land jobbers, speculators, and monopolisers" as "avaricious men" whose "unrestrained conduct" caused conflict and promised "a great deal of bloodshed." White backwoodsmen and speculators met their anarchic match in American Indian peoples. Many founders admired Indian cultures but attacked Indian men as savages. Franklin stressed that they were "apt to get drunk" and become "very quarrelsome and disorderly," and Jefferson warned that their intemperate use of "spirituous liquors" often led to violence. While Franklin saw Indian alcoholism as part of "the design of Providence to extirpate these savages in order to make room for cultivators of the earth," Jefferson hoped that Indians would enter into "a state of agriculture."[34] Either way, the founders agreed that earth belonged to sober, settled farmers.

This juxtaposition of disorderly backwoodsmen and greedy speculators on the one hand and intemperate, itinerant Indians on the other made the frontier a dangerous place. Doreen Alvarez Saar reports that American leaders worried that the conjuncture of these peoples would produce a promiscuous mixing of European stock with the indigenous population. The result would be "a mongrel breed" that combined the vices of both populations and created a people "of unpleasant and immoral character." Founders such as Washington saw the frontier as combustible. Whites sold liquor to Indians, deceived and defrauded them, and stole their lands only to inflame the passions of Indians, who reacted like "wild beasts of the forest" by taking up "the hatchet." He hoped that white men would purchase Indian land. That way, "the gradual extension of our settlements will as certainly cause the savage as the wolf to retire, both being beasts of prey."[35] For many founders, disorderly white men were the primary problem on the frontier but the removal of Indians was the preferred solution. Their analysis of slaveholders and slaves was quite similar.

Slaveholders and Slaves

White male slaveholders faced daily sexual temptation. David Ramsay criticized them for engaging in "early, excessive, and enervating indulgences" with slave women. A South Carolina champion of slavery warned that white men's "inconsiderate debaucheries" with female slaves were producing a "jumble of colors" in the population. A Kentuckian opposed to slavery bemoaned the loss of "worth and dignity" among those "pernicious pests of society" who "gratify their lust" by raping slave women who might be "their own sisters or even their aunts." A Connecticut abolitionist attacked white males who "procreate slaves" only to degrade, tyrannize, and sell their own sons and, in the case of daughters, "force [them] to submit to . . . horrid and incestuous passion."[36] White males with easy access to female slaves regularly surrendered to carnality and incest.

Theodore Dwight worried that this surrender weakened white men's commitment to family responsibilities and sensibilities. White males compounded the sin of adultery with female slaves when they failed to exhibit "the protection, the support, and the affection of a father" toward their mixed-race children. Jefferson suggested that white self-indulgence tended to transform liberty into license: "The whole commerce between master and slave is a perpetual exercise of the most boisterous passions, the most unremitting despotism on the one part, and degrading submissions on the other. Our children see this and learn to imitate it." David Rice thought that master-slave relations undermined white manhood by allowing masters to forsake industry by relying on slave labor. After all, "To labor is to *slave*, to work is *to work like a Negro*, and this is disgraceful; it levels us with the meanest of the species." White idleness, in turn, beckoned kindred vices such as "gaming, theft, robbery, or forgery, for which [youth] often end their days in disgrace on the gallows." John Taylor disagreed. Slavery did not inspire "furious passions" among whites because slaves occupied an incomparable, distant, and lowly rank. Indeed, slavery invited white children to learn virtue and feel benevolence when "seeing the bad qualities in slaves." Taylor believed that slavery made liberty more precious to whites and pointed out that slave societies such as ancient Greece and Rome, as well as modern America, produced "more great and good patriots and citizens than probably all the rest of the world."[37]

Though the founders disputed the justice and impact of slavery, they uniformly denounced tendencies toward miscegenation. They saw whites as a distinct species. That was John Witherspoon's contention when he located the tragedy of the Revolution in the fact that men "who are the same in complexion, the same in blood . . . should, notwithstanding, butcher one another with unrelenting rage and glory in the deed." Most founders saw blacks as "outsiders" or "outcasts from humanity." They had difficulty imagining the two distinct species living together in freedom and harmony. Jefferson's well-known assertions about inherent racial differences and antagonisms were adopted by Jeffersonians such as Tunis Wortman, who argued that interracial mingling and marriage were tantamount to a "universal prostitution" that would produce "a motley and degenerate race of mulattos." Other founders ranted against "the infamy of such a mongrel coalition," condemned "the disgraceful and unnatural" evil of interracial unions, and proclaimed that a "free nation of black and white people [will] produce a body politic as monstrous and unnatural as a mongrel half white man and half negro."[38]

Why were the founders so fearful of race mixing? Many founders saw black males as oversexed creatures whose passions threatened to degrade the white race. Jefferson observed that black males were "more ardent after their female" but lacked "a tender delicate mixture of sentiment and sensation." He attributed this combination of black lust and coarseness to black inferiority in "body and mind" as well as in "imagination," where blacks were "dull, tasteless, and anomalous." Jefferson described black males as sexually promiscuous and culturally sterile. He wrote, "Never yet could I find that a black had uttered a thought above the level of plain narration; never see even an elementary trait of painting or sculpture." Frank Shuffelton remarks that Jefferson was blind to the richness of slaves' African cultures and to the creativity of black artisans in his own household.[39] This blindness allowed him and other founders to see black males as creatures without culture and to rank them on a scale of manly refinement well below licentious libertines.

While whites sometimes perceived black women to be "remarkable for their chastity and modesty," they almost always considered black males' lust to be immutable. Early New England rape narratives centered on black lust. A 1768 narrative titled *The Life and Dying Speech of Arthur* was typical. Arthur was a black slave who discarded piety and industry for a "licentious liberty" that included drinking, promiscuity, running away, theft, and the rape of a white woman, for which he was hanged. Daniel Williams suggests that Arthur's story helped solidify the stereotype of the African male as an "immoral, hypersexual black wildly pursuing women to satisfy his prodigal lusts." The stereotype was not new. In 1682, when Pennsylvania Quakers tried to eliminate the death penalty for rape in the belief that rapists could be rehabilitated, they wanted to retain hanging for black rapists, apparently because they believed black males were beyond redemption.[40]

One reason the founders thought black male slaves beyond redemption was that they could not assume patriarchal family responsibilities. Slave status meant that black males had little control when it came to starting families, keeping them together, preventing wives' victimization, or protecting children. Many male slaves lived in small households where they were isolated from potential brides. Slave traders sometimes forced slave husbands to separate from wives and children, and slaveholders wrote wills that distributed slave family members among dispersed heirs. Benjamin Rush pointed out that overseers often made slave husbands "prostitute their wives and mothers and daughters to gratify the brutal lust of a master." As a result, male slaves had little confidence "in the fidelity of their wives" and little certainty that their wives' offspring were their own, and they showed comparatively little regard "for their posterity." Even when male slaves were confident of their paternity, they could not "partake of those ineffable sensations with which nature inspires the hearts of fathers" because their "paternal fondness" was compromised by the knowledge that their children would always be "slaves like themselves."[41] Male slaves were in no position to achieve manly mastery in their own families.

Perhaps most founders opposed slavery and many stigmatized slaveholders for lust and brutality. Simultaneously, they saw black males as dangerous creatures who were not and never truly could be "men" because they lacked independence, self-discipline, family integrity, mastery of women, and concern for posterity. They were hypersexual, coarse beings who did not fit into polite society. Jefferson feared a race war fueled by white bigotry and black rage: "Deeply rooted prejudices entertained by the whites; ten thousand recollections by the blacks of the injuries they have sustained; new provocations; the real distinctions which nature has made; and many other circumstances divide us into parties; and produce convulsions which will probably never end but in the extermination of the one or the other race." John Taylor opposed slavery but detested the abolitionism that encouraged the "black sansculottes" to cut masters' throats. Jefferson, Taylor, and other founders felt that disorderly white males caused most problems associated with slavery, but they believed the removal of blacks to Africa was the primary cure for racial conflict.[42]

The Refuse of the Earth

The founders hoped disorderly white men could redeem themselves. The idea of "starting over" was embedded in the myth of an American Adam freed from old-world corruption to cultivate the New World's Edenic garden. It also was etched into the image of the prodigal son who put away the past and undertook a noble pilgrimage to posterity. Most founders held out the possibility of rebirth but they did not count on it. They were alarmed by men's "general sense of lawlessness" and by "disorders and deviances" that easily escalated into social chaos and political instability. Their grave concern for the dangers associated with disorderly soldiers highlighted the possibility that licentious males were less likely to be reformed than sober men were apt to be corrupted.[43]

Americans inherited from Whig ancestors a loathing for redcoats. The British quartered redcoats in the colonies after the French and Indian War. At first, many Americans welcomed the troops as protection against hostile Indians and as consumers of local goods. Kermit Hall observes that colonists soon grew contemptuous as "the bored troops" of idle youth "engaged in whoring and petty thievery." In 1768, Samuel Adams joined with others to start the *Journal of the Times*, a scandal sheet that attacked redcoat misdeeds. A. J. Langguth notes that a typical story reported that a local citizen "discovered a soldier in bed with his favorite granddaughter." Don Higginbotham highlights patriot press stories that decried "insults to city officials, assault, theft, and rape committed by Red Coats." Many Americans blamed redcoats for ruining America's finest young men. "This idle and dissipated army," wrote Mercy Otis Warren, "corrupted the students of Harvard College and the youth of the capital and its environs, who were allured to enter into their gambling parties and other scenes of licentiousness."[44]

Colonists considered redcoats "the refuse of the earth." Their officers were "effeminate and delicate soldiers who are nursed in the lap of luxury and whose greatest exertion is . . . tedious attendance on a masquerade or midnight ball." Benjamin Franklin attacked the British army as organized slavery. After all, "The sailor is often forced into service. . . . The soldier is generally bought." Redcoats were lost in time and space. They were "generally such as have neither property or families to fight for, and who have no principle either of honor, religion, public spirit, regard for liberty, or love of country to animate them." Many were young men "dragged up in ignorance of every gainful art and obliged to become soldiers or servants or thieves for a subsistence." Simeon Howard focused on their instability. Their sole "temporal interest" was "the promise of larger pay"; they "have no real estate in the dominions which they are to defend"; and "they become distinguished by their vices." The only reason to gather such men into an army, concluded Mercy Otis Warren, was to eradicate America's "manly spirit of freedom."[45]

Patriots advertised redcoat sex scandals and depravity to rally Americans to the cause of liberty. Warren counted up "the indiscriminate ravages of the Hessian and British soldiers" in coin of the "rape, misery, and despair" suffered by "wives and daughters pursued and ravished in the woods" while "unfortunate fathers in the stupor of grief beheld the misery of their female connections without being able to relieve . . . the shrieks of infant innocence subject to the brutal lust of British Grenadiers and Hessian Yaughers." Phillips Payson asked the rhetorical question, "Is it possible for us . . . to hear the cries and screeches of our ravished matrons and virgins . . . and think of returning to that cruel and bloody power which has done all these things?" Thomas Paine used hatred of redcoats and mercenaries to shame American men into service: "By perseverance and fortitude we have the prospect of a glorious issue; by cowardice and submission, the sad choice of . . . our homes turned into bawdy houses for Hessians, and a future race to provide for, whose fathers we shall doubt of."[46] Only an unmanly coward would refuse to protect his mother, wife, sister, or daughter from the degradation of bearing mercenaries' bastard children.

The founders contrasted redcoat corruption to American militiamen's "manly resistance" and "manly spirit." They idealized militiamen as family farmers who mustered for service as dutiful citizen soldiers. One officer explained, "There is a difference between troops that fight only for the mastery and 6d. Sterling a day, and those that fight for their religion, their laws, their liberties, their wives and children and everything else that is dear to them." For the next century, Americans would attribute to regular soldiers all variants of vice and criminality but project onto militiamen all the virtues of republicanism. Simultaneously, however, Americans knew that militia virtues were often more symbolic than real, and they worried that sober family men who entered the militia would revert to bachelor-like licentiousness. Laurel Thatcher Ulrich comments that New England ministers and wives complained that freeholders in the militia were corrupted in camp by drink, profanity, and blasphemy. Don Higginbotham reports that Virginia parents demanded local militia officers be held accountable for overseeing their sons' "moral conduct," primarily by keeping them away from "gaming, profaneness, and debauchery."[47]

General Washington did not idealize militiamen. He complained, "The militia instead of calling forth their utmost efforts to a brave and manly opposition . . . are dismayed, intractable and impatient." Militiamen were unskilled and apt to be "timid and ready to fly from their own shadows." They were "accustomed to unbounded freedom and no control" and often refused to submit to "the restraint which is indispensably necessary to the good order and government of an army, without which licentiousness and . . . disorder triumphantly reign." Washington's alternative to the licentious militia was a continental standing army. This proposal encountered considerable criticism because, as Russell Weigley suggests, "The dangers of a standing army as a threat to liberty were close to everyone's thoughts." For example, "Caractacus" argued that yeomen and artisans serving in a standing army would lose "the gentleness and sobriety of citizens," while Samuel Adams and Benjamin Rush asserted that regular officers and soldiers would develop a sense of separateness and superiority tending toward tyranny.[48]

Americans accepted the standing army during the war, but they maintained suspicions of it that were periodically reconfirmed. When voluntary enlistments flagged and desertions flourished, the Continental army turned to bounties, bribes, and coercion to fill troop quotas. After 1778, Robert Gross notes, towns that once warned out transients began to welcome them if "they stayed only long enough to have a drink, take their bounty, and go off to fight." Even slaves were allowed to become "men" just long enough to enlist. Meanwhile, many freeholders took advantage of laws that allowed for marriage exemptions, hiring substitutes, or paying monetary fines. The result was that America's regular army was filled with indentured servants, vagrants, felons, and slaves—the same riffraff that wore red coats. Furthermore, critics charged the American military with aristocratic corruption. One fruit of that corruption, Franklin argued, was the Society of the Cincinnati, which was composed of former officers who had "been too much struck with the ribbons and crosses they have seen . . . hanging to the buttonholes of foreign officers." William Manning condemned the Cincinnati as a conspiratorial, aristocratic elite leading "a standing army of slaves to execute their arbitrary measures."[49]

Antifederalists zeroed in on the U.S. Constitution's unification of purse and sword as a foundation for tyranny. The "Federal Farmer" warned that the new government would create a standing army that would serve as "a very agreeable place of employment for the young gentlemen" who would delight in gutting the treasury and serving tyranny. "John DeWitt" argued that the new regime would provide emoluments to young aristocrats practiced in arms and ardent for a government "of force" that would absorb every other authority on the continent. A ratified Constitution would be "a hasty stride to universal empire in this Western world, flattering, very flattering to young ambitious minds, but fatal to the liberties of the people." An anonymous Philadelphia man went further: he was certain that American aristocrats already had usurped liberty and were now trying to formalize their power by means of a Constitution that was part of "a deep-laid scheme to enslave us . . . probably invented by the Society of the Cincinnati."[50]

Antifederalists also worried that a peacetime standing army would have decent citizens living amid armed thugs. "John Humble" called the standing army a home for "the purgings of the jails of Great Britain, Ireland, and Germany." Benjamin Workman argued that the army would recruit "the purgings of European prisons" as well as "low ruffians bred among ourselves who do not love to work." John Dawson stated that the soldiers' "only occupation would be idleness [and] the introduction of vice and dissipation," while an "Impartial Examiner" added that the officers would force soldiers into "unconditional submission to the commands of superiors," reduce them to "slavery," and make them "fit instruments of tyranny and oppression." Eventually, these "dregs of the people" would return to society to "become extremely burdensome."[51] Federalists did not wholly disagree. Alexander Hamilton advocated a standing army but showed little trust in it. When he suggested that freeholders did not want to be "dragged from their occupations and families" to perform the "disagreeable duty" of manning western garrisons, he reinforced the belief that only marginal men would voluntarily enlist. When he argued that Americans need not fear the officer corps because the military would "be in the hands of the representatives of the people," he lent credence to Whig suspicions that officers were corrupt men who needed external governance.[52]

The founders saw bachelorhood, libertinism, rape, sodomy, itinerancy, pauperism, frontier violence, slave unrest, and military disorder as the crest of a wave of male degeneracy that was swelled by men's daily dealings in blasphemy, alcoholism, gambling, prostitution, adultery, fighting, dueling, thievery, and murder. So many men seemed to be "intemperate zealots"; so many men participated in "the most shameful depredations"; so many men demanded liberty and asserted democracy only to join mobs that committed "indecent outrages"; so many men followed "factious demagogues" who beckoned tyranny. The founders employed the grammar of manhood to stigmatize, ridicule, degrade, humiliate, and shame disorderly men to consent to and comply with consensual norms of manhood but, cognizant of men's corruptibility, they also relied on state coercion to control, punish, deter, and possibly reform disorderly men.[53]

State Coercion

Death was the prescribed punishment for most serious crimes at the time of the Revolution. However, Enlightenment criminology considered the death penalty a relatively poor deterrent. Cesare Beccaria explained, "It is not the terrible but fleeting sight of a felon's death which is the most powerful brake on crime" but "the long-drawn-out example of a man deprived of freedom." A male deprived of independence, separated from his family, and made dependent on his captors lost not only his liberty but also his manhood. Capital punishment, in contrast, gave him an opportunity to redeem his manhood. That happened at a double hanging where, Benjamin Franklin reported, one convict was "extremely dejected" but the other exhibited "a becoming manly constancy."[54]

The most striking instance of a criminal being executed only to redeem his manhood occurred when British Major John André was hanged for spying during the Revolution. Upon his capture, André sent to General Washington a letter marked "with a frankness becoming a gentleman and man of honor and principle." He asked to "die as a soldier and man of honor [by being shot], not as a criminal [by being hanged]." Washington denied the request but praised André for exhibiting "that fortitude which was to be expected from an accomplished man and gallant officer." When a teary-eyed servant brought him a dress uniform for the scaffold, André ordered, "Leave me until you show yourself more manly." When he was hanged, "the tear of compassion was drawn from every pitying eye that beheld this accomplished youth a victim to the usages of war." Alexander Hamilton was one of many notable Americans who memorialized André for having been "a man of honor" whose final request was that "I die like a brave man."[55]

Nearly two decades later, Benjamin Rush was still rankled by André's celebrity: "The spy was lost in the hero; and indignation everywhere gave way to admiration and praise." Men who saw courage before the gallows as a shortcut to manly dignity had an incentive to commit capital crimes. Furthermore, the "admiration which fortitude under suffering excites has in some instances excited envy [and] induced deluded people to feign or confess crimes which they had never committed on purpose to secure to themselves a conspicuous death." Rush asserted that a proper punishment protected society from the criminal and dissuaded others from emulating his actions. Following Beccaria, he argued, "The death of a malefactor is not so efficacious a method of deterring from wickedness as the example of continually remaining . . . a man who is deprived of his liberty."[56]

A man deprived of liberty suffered a living death of emasculation, family separation, and social isolation. Reformers opposed public punishments (such as cleaning streets and repairing roads) that afforded criminals an opportunity to see family members or engage "crowds of idle boys" in "indecent and improper conversation." Criminality was infectious; it needed to be quarantined. Rush supported sending convicts to isolated prisons. He proposed, "Let a large house . . . be erected in a remote part of the state. Let the avenue to this house be rendered difficult and gloomy by mountains or morasses. Let its doors be of iron; and let the grating, occasioned by opening and shutting them, be increased by an echo from a neighboring mountain, that shall extend and continue a sound that shall deeply pierce the soul." Within these soul-piercing prisons, older convicts were to be isolated from younger ones, and the most vicious were to be locked in isolation cells. Rush reasoned that "attachment to kindred and society is one of the strongest feelings in the human heart" and, therefore, isolation from family and friends "is one of the severest punishments that can be inflicted upon a man."[57]

Most founders agreed that isolation was painful. James Otis, Jr., called "solitude" an "unnatural" state in which men "perish." John Dickinson thought "that to be solitary is to be wretched." Thomas Jefferson stated that isolation from loved ones "is worse than death inasmuch as [death] ends our sufferings whereas [isolation] begins them" and transforms a man into a "gloomy monk sequestered from the world." Samuel Quarrier put it best. Petitioning to be released from a debtors jail, he wrote President Jefferson, "This ignominious imprisonment unmans the heart."[58]

The belief that isolation "unmans" the heart made imprisonment both painful and promising. Isolated men suffered a humiliating loss of manhood. Officials locked them up and treated them as children. Their sole hope for reclaiming self-respect and social status was to cooperate with reformers who urged them to use solitude to repent, suppress passion, and learn useful trades. Rush rhapsodized at the prospect of a reformed convict returning to society: "I already hear the inhabitants of our villages and townships . . . running to meet him on the day of his deliverance. His friends and family bathe his cheeks with tears of joy; and the universal shout of the neighborhood is, 'This our brother was lost and is found—was dead, and is alive.'"[59] One can imagine a similar reaction by family and friends when an apparent lifelong bachelor announced plans to marry a virtuous woman.

The founders also considered punishing disorderly men by banishing them to distant places. Debating a new state constitution in 1783, a South Carolina writer noted that the main problem with banishing a criminal was that other states or nations might retaliate and "cast forth their outlaws upon us." This was what happened when libertines were banished from polite society in one village only to appear at social gatherings in another locale, or when itinerants were sent packing from one town to the next, or when disorderly slaves were sold from one plantation to another. Still, banishment had big benefits. It removed the immediate danger. It was an effective deterrent because it threatened to isolate men from their land, family, and community. Finally, it afforded a chance for rehabilitation because, if a man's character "is not absolutely forfeited, he is laid under a necessity of behaving with more prudence in another society, lest he should again be subjected to the inconvenience of a removal or to a less mild punishment." Alexander Hamilton generally agreed, arguing in 1794 that Whiskey rebels should "be compelled by their outlawry to abandon their property, houses, and the United States."[60]

The founders' most extensive experiment in banishing disorderly males was the practice of sending regular troops to the frontier. From the beginning of nationhood, American legislators limited the number of regular soldiers in the standing army, governed them with severe rules, and sent them far from civilized society. Americans exhibited a lasting hostility to "military institutions and the military function" by refusing to support a large peacetime establishment. They distrusted rank-and-file soldiers and subjected them to drastic discipline, including flogging, branding, hanging, and the firing squad. Most important, they isolated soldiers from respectable society by marching them to the frontier, where their lust and licentiousness were sublimated into building roads and forts and keeping peace between settlers and Indians. Hopefully, some soldiers would take advantage of their situation to mature into manhood, acquire frontier land, start their own families, and assume the rights and responsibilities of citizenship.[61]

Marginal Men

George Washington wrote a nephew, "You have now arrived to that age when you must quit the trifling amusements of a boy and assume the more dignified manners of a man." The Bachelor and other disorderly men did not quit the trifling amusements of a boy. They were marginal men who indulged passion, impulse, and avarice to foment disorder in the ranks of men as well as to seduce innocent women, patronize prostitutes, rape lower-class and slave women, commit incest, marry for lust or money, and cheat on wives. Jeremiah Atwater declared, "Man is always prone to what will center in himself only; hating restraint of any sort and considering it, of itself, as an evil; aspiring at domination over others; fond of possessing power, and prone to abuse it. Human nature appears in its true colors, without artificial disguise, in children. It is, in general, very hard to make children submit to what is proper. They are self-willed and extremely apt to rebel. What children are in a family, mankind are as subject to the restraints of law and order."[62] One reason the founders disputed emerging ideals of self-made manhood was that they believed men's self-centered childishness and rebellious selfishness had to be restrained if they were to assume the more dignified manners of manhood and submit voluntarily to the restraints of law and order.

The founders used the grammar of manhood to encourage the Bachelor and other disorderly men to exercise liberty with self-restraint and assume adult responsibilities consistent with civic order. They stigmatized marginal men as effeminate, slavish, and especially childish creatures who did not merit the rights of men or the respect of society. This informal pressure was generally sufficient to encourage most young white males to conform to consensual norms of manhood. Youth with libertine tendencies could achieve self-mastery and independence by disciplining their sexuality; single men could measure up to manhood by marrying, siring legitimate children, and governing their dependents; itinerants, vagrants, paupers, backwoodsmen, and soldiers could reform themselves by acquiring land and settling into stable families and communities. The founders believed that men who conformed to hegemonic masculinity in order to avoid humiliation and earn esteem were likely to comply with legitimate political authority.

The founders' grammar of manhood did not and could not motivate all males to conform to hegemonic norms. On the one hand, some white males continued to engage in lustful deceit, commit rape and sodomy, brutalize slaves, provoke conflict with Indian peoples, and commit other crimes and outrages that fostered conflicts in society. On the other hand, white prejudice precluded black and Indian men from manhood, and formal laws excluded them from citizenship. The founders spoke as if all of these marginal men suffered a case of male immaturity; they were grown children in need of guidance and governance. This was the discursive context in which the founders invoked hegemonic norms of manhood to legitimize discretionary use of state coercion, in order to control and discipline men's childish conduct and to promote their reformation and maturation. Magistrates could refuse to act when the victim was a greedy old bachelor, or they could enforce breach-of-promise laws to punish libertine treachery. Ultimately, they could imprison disorderly men who exhibited what "Amicus Republicae" called a "licentious disposition" that invited "tumults and insurrections."[63]

The grammar of manhood contained an idiom of childishness that many founders used to criticize, stigmatize, and penalize what Washington described as "unmanly behavior" in "refractory individuals." For example, George Rogers Clark tried to win over Britain's allies by persuading them that the English "are no men . . . and are become like children," while Alexander Hamilton emphasized General Charles Lee's misconduct at the Battle of Monmouth by labeling his acts "truly childish." Leaders debating the Constitution employed the same idiom. David Ramsay dismissed state constitutions as "hastily instituted by young politicians," and Edmund Randolph thought them "too youthful to have acquired stability." Simeon Baldwin wanted to lop off "the libertinism of juvenile independence" manifested in the Articles of Confederation. Federalists then appropriated maturity for the new government. Tench Coxe applauded the requirement that the president be "matured by years of experience." Also, he was pleased that "no ambitious, undeserving, or unexperienced youth" could acquire a seat in the House until "thirty years have ripened his abilities." For "Civic Rusticus," that rule ensured the election of men "past 'the heyday of the blood,' weaned from the intoxicating dissipation of youth and the hot allurements of pleasure." Similarly, Noah Webster portrayed the Senate as a place for men "venerable for age and respectability" and free from "the bias of passions that govern the young." Antifederalists responded in kind, claiming that their opponents were guilty of launching "projects of young ambition." Ratification debaters regularly accused each other of throwing "fits of passion" that were "perfectly boyish," making "childish arguments," behaving like "disgraced school boys," "children in the marketplace," and "children making bubbles," or simply "act[ing] like children."[64]

The idiom of childishness identified a subterranean level of manhood. The founders portrayed the Bachelor and other disorderly men as immature, childish minors who disregarded or denied consensual norms of manhood.

They were males who did not aspire to or achieve manly independence, family continuity, and patriarchal governance. Instead, they were itinerants in time and space, who fit in nowhere and deserved to be distrusted everywhere. They were destroyers, not procreators. They congregated in the democratic mobs that elevated passion over virtue and they filled the ranks of libertine suitors who manipulated, deceived, and abused women rather than loved, governed, and protected them. They were the Other—what young males had to outgrow to gain respectability as family men and to attain civic standing as citizens.

4

The Family Man and Citizenship

In a 1612 essay titled "Of Marriage and Single Life," Francis Bacon argued that families were an "impediment" to men's greatness. Wives and children distracted men from public affairs and made them reticent to take risks essential to performing great deeds. That was why "the best works . . . have proceeded from the unmarried or childless men which, both in affection and means, have married and endowed the public." However, family men were notable for one crucial virtue. They were husbands and fathers who exhibited "the greatest care of future times, unto which they know they must transmit their greatest pledges."[1] The American founders urged some men to greatness. However, given fears of democratic disorder, they used the grammar of manhood to encourage most men to devote themselves to family life. They agreed with Bacon that marriage catalyzed caution and motivated young males to mature into sober, orderly adults responsible for protecting and provisioning dependents. A common cure for male license was a marriage license.

The founders generally agreed that the Bachelor's tendency toward licentiousness intensified America's democratic distemper and invited men to abuse women. They also agreed that the single young man should be encouraged to resist the Bachelor within by settling a piece of land and marrying a respectable woman to share affection, carry his seed, nurture his infants, and contribute to his estate. He thereby assumed responsibility for family protection, productivity, and posterity; exchanged self-interest for family interest; and sacrificed personal pleasure to provide property and patrimony for his heirs, educate them in "the moral character of the *man*," and prepare them to perpetuate the family dynasty.[2] The founders drew on the grammar of manhood to endorse enthusiastically the Family Man who honored his debt to ancestors, fixed a respectable place for himself in the community, and developed a dynastic stake in the future.

The Family Man's presumptive caution, maturity, responsibility, sobriety, and orderly conduct legitimized his power over women and earned him republican citizenship. A worthy man committed himself to protect rather than persecute women. A proper husband and father wielded patriarchal authority in private and public life to govern female dependents for their own good and to defend his family and community from dangers that included women's disorderly conduct and men's licentious behavior. Patriarchal protection was preferable to persecution, though it still amounted to a protection racket. Furthermore, the Family Man's concern for the future suggested that he could exercise liberty with restraint and participate in politics with moderation. He was not apt to indulge passion or act on impulse lest he imperil his dependents and family dynasty. Many founders felt that the Family Man's sense of self-restraint and caring for posterity qualified him as a trustworthy man and deserving citizen.

Better Than Bachelorhood

Young American males pondering marriage could anticipate four benefits from it. The first was love and happiness. A seventeen-year-old Alexander Hamilton rhapsodized, "Believe me, love is doubly sweet in wedlock's holy bands." He later described marriage as "a state which with a kind of magnetic force attracts every breast to it in which sensibility has a place," though "the dull admonitions of prudence" might tempt young men to resist it. Ideally, the tension was resolved in favor of sensibility over prudence by a virtuous woman. Hamilton explained that his betrothed, Elizabeth Schuyler, was such a woman: "The most determined adversaries of Hymen can find in her no pretext for their hostility, and there are several of my friends, philosophers who railed at love as a weakness, men of the world who laughed at it as a fantasy, whom she has presumptuously and daringly compelled to acknowledge its power and surrender at discretion."[3] Hamilton echoed the emerging belief that men could achieve true happiness only in companionate marriages.

What was the relationship between men's happiness and marriage? Contemporary writers believed that the fiery passions that drove many men into marriage ideally gave way to feelings of benevolence and friendship within marriage. Judith Sargent Murray prescribed that a young man "tranquilize his deportment" and show "a dignified and manly manifestation of tenderness" as he anticipated his nuptials, and then exhibit manly moderation and mildness when he became a husband. His betrothed and then wife was to use all means at her disposal to inspire in him rectitude. Alice Izard asserted that a good wife "guides where she does not govern" and leads her husband "to worthy pursuits." Furthermore, a married man could expect to achieve a sense of meaning and immortality by siring legitimate heirs. One American magazine quoted John Milton: "In the existence of a married man, there is no termination." An anonymous poet added that wives suffered a "loss of freedom" but were compensated by husbands' love and by being "renew'd immortal in a filial race." The model republican family was constituted by a husband and wife who fostered benevolence and friendship, made a joint commitment to righteousness and virtue, and experienced a reassuring sense of intergenerational continuity that contributed to their enduring happiness.[4]

Second, marriage was an opportunity for a young male to prove his manhood by governing a woman. The challenge was to ply a narrow pathway between the Bachelor's slavery to passion and a husband's potential subordination to his wife. Initially, a young husband was expected to demonstrate manly self-discipline by giving up promiscuity, itinerancy, drinking, gambling, and other selfish vices associated with his bachelor years. Next, he was to exhibit manly merit by achieving family mastery. George Washington hinted at the difficulty when congratulating Marquis de Chastellux on his marriage: "I can hardly refrain from smiling to find that you are caught at last [by] that terrible contagion, domestic felicity." Washington's mirth mirrored a general sense that new husbands were easily enslaved by love and subordinated by domineering wives. What was a young husband to do? Benjamin Franklin announced, "Any man that is really a man is master of his own family." Manly mastery meant wielding authority without tyranny. A "man that really is a man" restrained his wife's lust lest her adulterous behavior undermine his family dynasty; controlled her profligacy lest it destroy his estate; and monitored her intemperance and negligence lest she had "no longer that prudent care for their family to manage well the business of their station nor that regard for reputation which good women ought to have." Law and custom supported a husband's dominion over disorderly wives, but it was a man's own ability to govern effectively without becoming a "he-tyrant"—to rule firmly but lovingly—that enabled him to sustain conjugal affection and win other men's respect.[5]

One guidebook identified "a wise husband" as one who "by knowing how to be a master" did not let his wife "feel the weight of it" because his "authority is tempered by his kindness" along with his tenderness and esteem. Several writers suggested that a truly masterful husband could cement his authority by choosing an educated woman for a wife or by allowing his wife to be educated. Judith Sargent Murray explained that men benefited from marrying educated women who possessed "invigorated" judgments that prevented "an unhappy Hymen." Mary Fish Noyes drew up a "Portrait of a Good Husband" that praised the spouse who gratified his wife's "reasonable inclinations," especially her desire to read books "for [her] perusal and improvement." An anonymous poetess instructed men, "Be generous then, and us to knowledge lead / And happiness to you will sure succeed / Then sacred Hymen shall in triumph reign / And all be proud to wear the pleasing chain."[6] The traditional patriarch ruled by virtue of near absolute authority, but modern norms of republican manhood indicated that male dominion could be fortified if men practiced a hegemonic masculinity that mostly relied on kindness, consideration, and respect to win a wife's consent to her own subordination.

Third, marriage was the primary means by which young men matured into adult responsibilities. Benjamin Franklin announced that marriage was "the cause of all good order in the world and what alone preserves it from the utmost confusion." A young man "could never thrive" until married. Then he became "more firmly settled." He minded his "business better and more steadily" and was "sooner trusted . . . than if he is single." His sense of responsibility and his industry were augmented by a "good and faithful helpmate" who kept his house, assisted in his business, bore his children, and helped transmit his estate to them. Franklin told this story about a printer's patrimony: "On his decease, the business was continued by the widow who [was] born and bred in Holland, where . . . the knowledge of accompts makes part of the female education." Concerned about family welfare, many American men agreed that women should be educated to contribute to family enterprises, protect family estates from "crafty men" who preyed on widows, and maintain family businesses "til a son is grown up, fit to undertake and go on with it, to the lasting advantage and enriching of the family."[7] Marriage challenged men to assume adult responsibility for managing a family economy and dependents, and planning for future contingencies, including death and dynastic longevity.

The fourth anticipated benefit was that marriage gave men a familial stake in the community. A married man had a family to provision and protect and, therefore, a family interest to join with neighbors in mutual-aid projects that promoted family prosperity and in military ventures against enemies who threatened family welfare. Silas Downer urged communal protest in 1768 by appealing to family interest when warning that British efforts to quarter soldiers in colonists' homes would result in redcoats taking "absolute command of our families." Thomas Jefferson hoped to strengthen patriot solidarity in 1774 by invoking family interest to criticize British attempts to have colonists stand trial in England: "Who are to feed the wife and children whom he leaves behind and who have had no other subsistence but his daily labor?" American leaders idealized citizen-soldiers as husbands and fathers who fought "for their wives, their children, their liberty, and their all" in order to motivate men to participate in community-based militia units. They also demonized the English aristocracy by exploiting fears that the enemy was targeting patriots' families as well as their liberties. George Washington reacted to a 1775 rumor that Virginia's governor was going to arrest his wife, Martha, by declaring, "I can hardly think that Lord Dunmore can act so low and unmanly a part as to think of seizing Mrs. Washington by way of revenge upon me."[8] The founders condemned the Bachelor's selfishness, but they condoned the Family Man's self-interested effort to feed, shelter, and defend his family as a significant source of patriotic cohesion and community good.

Young men who understood that family loyalty, governance, and responsibility were the basis for happiness, manhood, adulthood, and community membership did not necessarily achieve these goals. Many youth failed to restrain lust long enough to choose a proper spouse. "In the composition of human nature," Washington warned, "there is a good deal of inflammable matter [and] when the torch is put to it, that which is within may burst into blaze." Even self-disciplined males were easily dazzled by the brilliance of female "beauty" and blinded to the "virtue" that "fades not in seventy years." The founders counseled young men to choose virtue over beauty but John Adams complicated the choice by observing that a beautiful wife could be a family asset. Franklin's description of Moravian marriage customs intimated that most matches were serendipitous:

> As these elders of both sexes were well acquainted with tempers and dispositions of their respective pupils, they could best judge what matches were suitable, and their judgments were generally acquiesced in. But if, for example, it should happen that two or three young women were found to be equally proper for the young man, the lot was then recurred to. I objected, "If the matches are not made by mutual choice of the partners, some of them may chance to be very unhappy." "And so they may," answered my informer, "if you let the parties choose for themselves"—which, indeed, I could not deny.[9]

Questions about the essential ingredients for happy marriages plus awareness of young people's growing freedom to choose their own mates prompted Thomas Jefferson to suggest that marriage and procreation had become matters of "fortuitous concourse."

Nevertheless, most founders were convinced that fortuitous marriages were better than bachelorhood. Joel Barlow wanted to reduce the legal age of majority to induce young men into "early marriages [to] encourage purity of morals." Samuel Williams applauded "the wishes of parents to see their children settled" into early marriages and set in "the way of virtue, reputation, and felicity." Simultaneously, law and custom opposed the practice of ending bad marriages. Divorces were difficult and rare. Noah Webster's reaction to revolutionary France's liberal divorce laws explains why. He condemned "the decree of the Convention authorizing divorces upon the application of either party, alleging only unsuitableness of temper," as a manifestation of "the little regard in which the morals of the nation are held" and as an invitation "to infidelity and domestic broils."[10] Marriage had to be sanctified if it was to settle down young men, coax them into responsibility, and stabilize society.

William Byrd recalled, "The Spartans had so much regard for marriage that they enacted a law by which they condemned all old bachelors above the age of 24 to be whipped publicly." The founders' Spartanlike commitment to marriage was based on their hopes for human happiness and their fears of the Bachelor's "licentiousness" assuming "the sacred name of liberty." Stephanie Coontz detects an early American consensus that "individual rights did have limits and that the family was the natural place to establish them." Public notification of an impending marriage was an affirmation that a young man had volunteered to exchange licentious individualism for the Family Man's devotion to durable happiness, family responsibility, and the community good. The betrothed male promised to act like a mature adult and thereby earned what "An Impartial Citizen" called "a man's reputation" to enjoy and pass on as part of his legacy to posterity.[11]

Provisioning Posterity

The Family Man's highest duty was to procreate and provision posterity. John Demos observes, "All adult men [were] expected to become fathers." Marriage was the only legitimate outlet for sex, and sex resulted in procreation. Most men aspired to legitimate fatherhood. Mary Beth Norton notes, "Childlessness indicated a husband's failings as a man," whereas fatherhood attested to his manhood. Jay Fliegelman adds that fathers hoped to be "immortalized" in their children. The quest for symbolic immortality prompted fathers to provide for children's current and future needs by accumulating and disbursing property and patrimony to enable sons to perpetuate the family line. Providing for posterity in an era of uncertain economic change was particularly tough. George Mason thought that even wealthy fathers could no longer be confident that their sons would be able to sustain family prosperity: "However affluent their circumstances or elevated their situations might be, the course of a few years not only might but certainly would distribute their posterity throughout the lower classes."[12]

The Family Man's economic strategy was to accumulate a sufficient if not substantial estate. He labored, invested, and sacrificed to amass real and personal property that he could distribute and bequeath to his children. To this end, he might speculate in frontier property. Mason explained to George Jr. that he spent one thousand pounds to acquire western lands because "they will in twenty years be worth forty or fifty thousand pounds to my family." The larger a man's estate, the better the chance that his heirs would be able to preserve it, cushion the impact of adverse economic forces, and take advantage of new opportunities. Artisan fathers practiced a variation on this theme. Scholars suggest that artisans aspired to a "comfortable existence" by devoting themselves to building craft skills and small shops. They identified their skills with "manly competence" and used control of apprenticeships to convert their skills into "a form of property" that they passed on to sons. Overall, the Family Man's economic interest was more a matter of paternal aggrandizement than possessive individualism although, in the late eighteenth century, family loyalties increasingly commingled with an emerging capitalist mentality.[13]

How should the Family Man distribute his estate to his children? Many founders opposed primogeniture on principled grounds. It was unjust for fathers to favor oldest sons. Thomas Paine wrote, "By the aristocratical law of primogeniture, in a family of six children, five are exposed. Aristocracy never has more than one child. The rest are begotten to be devoured." Privileged older sons "begin life by trampling on all their younger brothers and sisters" while younger sons, "by aristocracy, are bastards and orphans." Thomas Jefferson added that primogeniture fostered a "brutality" borne of vast economic inequalities and class conflict. For him, "legislators cannot invent too many devices for subdividing property" and distributing it among "all the children or to all the brothers and sisters or other relations in equal degree."[14] Primogeniture robbed posterity of liberty and equality.

Most founders considered relatively equal distributions of family property useful for perpetuating family dynasties. They agreed that fathers wanted to accumulate sufficient patrimony to make their children "forever independent." Still, they criticized older sons who received huge inheritances only to become spoiled youth who indulged vice and squandered family fortunes. The founders reserved their highest accolades for young men who received modest family shares and then demonstrated personal merit by cultivating manly virtues and talents advantageous to economic productivity. Writers used Benjamin Franklin (the youngest son of a youngest son for five generations) as an "illustrious example" of the "self-made man" who transformed a meager family legacy into a substantial estate. Nathanael Emmons instructed young Americans to emulate Franklin and "show yourselves men." David Ramsay honored the "self-made, industrious men" who "laid a foundation for establishing personal independence," and who also were "successfully employed in establishing that of their country."[15] Significantly, this nascent image of self-made manhood was situated in a familial context. It depicted young men who inherited family wealth and merited additional prosperity; and it recognized accumulated wealth as a means to establish, support, steward, promote, and perpetuate family estates.

Ironically, the founders' support for equitable family distributions made great fortunes seem safe for the Republic. Charles Cotesworth Pinckney argued that egalitarian inheritance laws would encourage a natural, periodic redistribution of wealth. Once instituted, "we may suppose that in the future an equal division of property among the children will in general take place in all the states." This supposition had two implications. One was that men who owned huge estates probably deserved them because they likely accumulated most of their assets by dint of their own effort and merit. The other implication was that men who had immense holdings posed no great danger to the community because they did not transmit intact riches from generation to generation. Their wealth was safe because it would be subdivided among numerous heirs.[16] This reasoning helped legitimize an economic aristocracy of virtuous, talented, manly heirs able to metamorphose modest patrimonies into magnificent family fortunes.

Where did fathers find manly heirs? Jefferson wanted the pool to be as large as possible. He supported an equal distribution of family wealth to create "an opening for the aristocracy of virtue and talent" among traditionally dispossessed younger sons. He also argued that "females shall have equal [inheritance] rights with males." That way, fathers could seek an opening for virtue and talent among their sons-in-law—who had legal control of their wives' wealth. Benjamin Franklin argued that a dynastic diversification strategy made sense during times of uncertainty. A man should "raise a large family" with many sons and launch each boy into manhood with a modest stake. That way, regardless of "contrary winds, hidden shoals, storms, and enemies," there was a good chance that at least one son would "return with success" enough to perpetuate the family dynasty.[17]

Many fathers had no property or patrimony to pass on to sons, and many young men came of age and married having received no family wealth. Few

American writers saw poverty as an impenetrable barrier to family prosperity and social stability. William Bradford argued that, in Europe, the impoverished "wretch" had little chance to transform his labor into a family estate. With no alternatives, he often engaged in disorderly and criminal conduct to support his family and better his children's prospects. But poverty was different in America, where "every man is or may be a proprietor" and his "labor is bountifully rewarded." Even America's poorest fathers and sons could invest individual effort in economic opportunity to build family estates and even accumulate substantial patrimony for the next generation. John Adams suggested that the realistic prospect of family aggrandizement in America helped defuse discontent among "the idle, the vicious, the intemperate." Robert Coram added that universal public education would further enlarge men's economic prospects and secure even greater social harmony.[18]

The Family Man's efforts to provision his family and seek prosperity for posterity encouraged him to cultivate "free and manly habits" conducive to family accumulation. His industry and thrift enabled him to feel "the dignity of human nature" and share in the productivity and mobility that contributed to social order. Whether he inherited great wealth or no wealth, he "showed himself a man" by engaging in paternal aggrandizement to support his family and perpetuate his family line. The cautious Family Man was no Baconian hero striving after greatness but, Noah Webster proclaimed, he deserved to be ranked among "the laborious and saving" who were "generally the best citizens."[19]

Educating Posterity

The young Benjamin Franklin left home and journeyed hundreds of miles to establish his own business and family. The lines of kinship in his family were distended and frayed, but they did not snap. The aged Franklin approvingly recalled his father: "His great excellence was a sound understanding and a solid judgment in prudential matters. . . . He turned our attention to what was good, just, and prudent in the conduct of life." Franklin saw a good father as an exemplar and teacher of "prudence" and "temperance" along with virtues such as order, frugality, industry, sincerity, justice, moderation, cleanliness, tranquillity, chastity, and humility.[20] He taught his sons to excel in manly virtues that were essential to perpetuating the family dynasty.

Republican ideals enjoined a father to govern his sons in the same way that a husband governed his wife. Melvin Yazawa explains that he had to strike "a balance between love and authority" to build a relationship of "affection and duty, affection energizing duty, duty controlling affection." Thomas Jefferson applauded "affectionate deportment between father and son" as a foundation for teaching "correct conduct." A wise father appealed to his sons' innate sensibilities ("pride of character, laudable ambitions, and moral dispositions") as "correctives" to youthful "indiscretions." When these correctives failed, the father withdrew affection and used shame to discipline children. Mild measures had "a happier effect on future character than the degrading motive of fear." Nevertheless, most founders did not restrict paternal rule to mildness. They saw "discretion" as "the soul of 'fatherly' administration." John Dickinson advocated the "mild features of patriarchal government" but admitted the occasional utility of coercion. "Plough Jogger" argued that a "father . . . may prefer mildness in his family," but "necessity obliges him sometimes to use rigorous measures." Peter Thacher concluded that the best guide to paternal governance was actual results: did sons learn "judgment and discipline . . . to check their effervescences" even after they left their father's home?[21]

Paternal lessons in judgment and discipline were to eliminate the Bachelor's vices from boys' behavioral repertoire. John Adams taught his sons to reject libertine "vanities, levities, and fopperies" and instead to practice "great, manly, and warlike virtues." He relied on Abigail's assistance and instructed her, "Train them to virtue. Habituate them to industry, activity, and spirit. Make them consider every vice as shameful and unmanly." The Adams boys were to become "great and manly." Fathers who taught manly shame and pride expected several payoffs. Jefferson believed they would experience "the most sublime comforts in every moment of life and in the moment of death" because fathers' immortality hinged on sons' manly excellence. At times, Sally Mason reports, the deepest family feelings shifted from affection "between husband and wife" to bonding "between son and father." Americans expected this male bonding to produce an intergenerational friendship. According to Jay Fliegelman, the father would be "revered long into his child's adulthood" and his adult son would be "loved long after he has left home."[22] The ideal father-son friendship transcended intergenerational time and continental space.

The founding generation enjoined fathers to make necessary sacrifices for their sons' good breeding and their families' future prospects. Nathanael Emmons called on fathers to elevate their moral words and deeds in order to serve as proper models for boys: "Let the dignity of man appear in all your conduct, and especially in your conduct towards your children. Let them see the dignity of human nature exemplified. . . . Take heed that none of your words, none of your actions, none of your pursuits be unworthy of men."

Likewise, Emmons expected sons to give up licentiousness to earn their fathers' respect. He instructed young men: "Flee youthful lusts which war against both the body and the mind. Shun that all-devouring monster, intemperance, by which so many strong minds have been cast down and destroyed. Avoid bad company and unmanly diversions which are an inlet to every vice. Hold steady contempt for beaus and fops, those butterflies which live upon the filth and dregs of the earth."[23] Both fathers and sons were to cast aside their egos in order to measure up to mutual expectations and manly aspirations.

Nature and nurture fortified the father-son bond. Jefferson wrote, "Experience proves that the moral and physical qualities of man, whether good or evil, are transmissible from father to son." A good father might sire base sons but he was more apt to produce virtuous ones. Adams agreed that "Wise men beget fools, and honest men knaves; but these instances . . . are not general. If there is often a likeness in figure and feature, there is generally more in mind and heart." Most founders thought that fathers transmitted virtues and talents to sons. Thus, when a father achieved an esteemed reputation, people presumed that his sons would earn and merit the same respect. The result was that an eminent man's son was likely to find that other men were predisposed "to honor the memory of his father, to congratulate him as the successor to his estate, and frequently to compliment him with elections to the offices he held." What Adams called "the family spirit" denoted a thick father-son bond that supported the transfer of manly virtue, reputation, standing, and even political power from one generation to the next.[24]

The founders reinforced intergenerational bonding when honoring fathers by favoring their sons. Learning Congress had authorized Jefferson and himself to appoint American consuls in Europe, Adams recommended Winslow Warren in familial terms:

> Otis his grandfather, the famous James his uncle, his other uncles, and his father have been to my knowledge . . . among the firmest and steadiest supporters of the American cause. I declare, I don't believe there is one family upon earth to which the United States are so much indebted for their preservation from thralldom. There was scarcely any family in New England [that] had such prospects of opulence and power under the royal government. They have sacrificed all of them. It is true, and I know you act upon the maxim that the public good alone is the criterion, but it is equally true that the public good requires that such conspicuous and exemplary services and sacrifices should not be neglected, and therefore considerations of this sort ever did and ever will and ever ought in some degree to influence mankind.

Jefferson mostly agreed that deserving men's sons should be rewarded. He responded, "I think with you too that it is for the public interest to encourage sacrifices and services by rewarding them, and they should weigh to a certain point in the decision between candidates."[25]

This intergenerational reward system was manifested in the practice of providing notable men's sons with letters of introduction. George Mason sent Patrick Henry his son's "thanks for the testimonial you were so kind to give him under the Seal of the Commonwealth. It has been of great service in recommending him to the notice of many gentlemen of rank and fortune." These letters usually highlighted both family standing and individual merit. Jefferson introduced Mr. Lyons to Adams as a "son of one of our judges" and "a sensible worthy young physician." He recommended Mr. Rutledge by writing, "Your knowledge of his father will introduce him to your notice. He merits it moreover on his own account."[26] A good father exemplified manly virtues, transmitted a respected family name, and provided appropriate connections; ultimately, however, each young man would be judged "on his own account."

Among the most important lessons a father taught his sons was how to be judged positively. That required lessons in "civility." Franklin explained that good breeding involved "searching for and seizing every opportunity to serve and oblige." He "made it a rule to forbear all direct contradiction to the sentiments of others and all positive assertion of my own." That made him a more pleasant companion, procured him a ready listening audience, and increased the likelihood that he would prevail in disagreements. Conversely, "He that is displeased with your words or actions commonly joins against you. . . . You have enemies enough by the common course of human nature." Franklin's Junto was organized around civility. It consisted of young men who sought to establish reputations for "character and credit" and increase their "influence in public affairs."[27] Jefferson applauded Franklin's advice and added that civility, politeness, mild flattery, and the sacrifice of small pleasures gratified and conciliated other men. He emphasized "good humor as one of the preservatives of our peace and tranquillity" and stated that ingratiating oneself with companions was a cheap price for "the good will of another." A young man who cultivated "unaffected modesty and suavity of manners" would be "endeared" to polite society. Jefferson opposed sending youths to Europe, for fear of sexual corruption, but he did "wish my countrymen to adopt just so much of European politeness as to be ready to make all those little sacrifices of self which really render European manners amiable and relieve society from the disagreeable scenes to which rudeness often subjects it."[28] Where impassioned men claimed individual liberty, manly civility contributed to social harmony.

George Washington epitomized manly civility. At age nine, he copied 110 "Rules of Civility and Decent Behavior in Company and Conversation" to help balance "that little spark of celestial fire called conscience" with respect for other people in society. He noted that civility enabled a young male to develop a reputation for being "manful, not sinful," and he tried to build and maintain such a manly reputation throughout his life. As a soldier, he hoped to walk "in such a line as will give the most general satisfaction." In his farewell orders to the Continental army, he challenged demobilizing soldiers to do the same:

> All the troops . . . should carry into civil society the most conciliating dispositions; and . . . they should prove themselves not less virtuous and useful as citizens than they have been persevering and victorious as soldiers. . . . The private virtues of economy, prudence, and industry will not be less amiable in civil life than the more splendid qualities of valor, perseverance, and enterprise were in the field. Everyone may rest assured that much, very much of the future happiness of the officers and men will depend upon the wise and manly conduct which shall be adopted by them when they are mingled with the great body of the community.[29]

Twenty years later, Mercy Otis Warren remembered Washington for having exhibited "a certain dignity united with the appearance of good humor."[30]

A responsible father who combined love and discipline, transmitted and taught manly virtues, secured a respected family name and useful social connections, and fostered in his sons a habit of civility afforded them maximal opportunity to become trustworthy and trusted members of society. Still, the Family Man's efforts to provide patrimony, encourage filial merit, and secure social respect for his heirs were all for naught unless he also protected his family, encouraged his sons to participate in family defense, and freed them to merit manhood and grow independent branches of the family tree.

Protecting Posterity

Responsible fathers protected their posterity. In 1776, Thomas Paine pushed patriotism against overwhelming odds by reminding colonists that their cause was not "the concern of a day, a year, or an age" but that "posterity are virtually involved in the contest." A decade later, an "Officer of the Late Continental Army" rallied voters against the U.S. Constitution by warning fathers to act "like men, like freemen and Americans, to transmit unimpaired to your latest posterity those rights, those liberties, which have ever been so dear." The Family Man who protected his posterity exhibited manhood, earned personal honor, and deserved social esteem. He alone could "take his child by the hand and bless it without feeling the conscious shame of neglecting a parent's duty" because he alone secured his "good name" and left a memorable legacy that "blunts the sharpness of death."[31]

Most founders saw paternal self-sacrifice to protect posterity as natural. Simeon Howard observed that fathers were bound to their children "by the common tie of nature," and any man who "has the bowels of a father" felt duty-bound to defend his children against dangers such as "the iron scepter of tyranny." Paternal vigilance was reinforced by intimations of immortality. "The Preceptor" argued that a man's willingness to put himself at peril for his children's liberty "will make him venerable and beloved while he lives, be lamented and honored if he falls in so glorious a cause, and transmit his name and immortal renown to his latest posterity." Americans agreed that the one force in life more powerful than men's Hobbesian drive for self-preservation was their desire to preserve their posterity. This agreement was manifested in George Mason's conviction that a father "will be quickly converted into a soldier when he knows and feels that he is to fight not in defense of the rights of a particular family or prince but his own."[32]

Nevertheless, fathers had to put their posterity at risk to teach their sons to defend their family dynasties. They required young men to test their manhood by joining with them to bear arms in militia units established to defend liberty and locality. Robert Gross describes the militia muster as a sort of "family reunion." John Adams affirmed a willingness to put his posterity at risk when he wrote in 1777, "I wish my lads were old enough. I would send every one of them into the army in some capacity or other. Military abilities and experience are a great advantage to character." Military service challenged youth to show they were not Thomas Paine's "summer soldiers and sunshine patriots" but citizen-soldiers who merited "the love and thanks of man and woman." The challenge could be daunting. Paine explained, "Some men have naturally a military turn, and can brave hardships and the risk of life with a cheerful face; others have not. . . . I believe most men have more courage than they know of and that a little at first is enough to begin with." Jefferson prescribed that young men who found courage, braved hardship, risked death, and survived earned "a quiet and undisturbed repose in the bosom of their families."[33]

Of course, young men who went to war exposed themselves to disability and death, and potentially imperiled their families' dynastic futures. If they served with honor and died, they would be celebrated with "recollections of manly sorrow," but their deaths would eliminate future branches of their family trees. That was why George Washington was ambivalent about sending into battle a step-grandson who was "the only male of his great great grandfather's family" and thus the sole hope for dynastic survival. Anticipating war with France in 1798, Washington recommended that the boy become a Cornet of Horse. "If real danger threatened the country," he wrote, "no young man ought to be an idle spectator in its defense." But he hoped real danger would be averted. That way, the boy would "be entitled to the merit of proffered service without encountering the dangers of war" and likely live long enough to perpetuate his bloodline.[34]

An important challenge of fatherhood was passing liberty to adult sons by allowing them to make their own decisions about family procreation, provision, and protection. Many fathers had an economic stake in keeping older sons dependent on them because filial labor contributed to family farms. Some fathers simply did not want to give up authority. A father might bless a son's marriage and give him use of land for his family but retain legal title as a means to maintain paternal control. Or a father could use the prospect of inheritance and the psychological lever of intergenerational friendship to pressure adult sons to conform to paternal expectations. Sooner or later, however, fathers were expected to perform what Paine called "an act of manhood" by renouncing paternal authority and freeing adult sons to achieve independence, family status, and governance of their own dependents. Renunciation was risky. Once freed, as Jefferson recognized, a man's sons could "disavow" him, forsake family obligations, and put personal pleasure above family security and longevity.[35] In general, the founding generation was ambivalent about whether fathers should encourage liberty among their children or instead seek to protect posterity from its self-destructive tendencies.

The founders midwifed an "improvement ethic" conducive to the liberty of new generations. Bernard Bailyn argues that this ethic "reflected the beginnings of a permanent motion within American society by which the continuity of the generations was to be repeatedly broken." Father-son bonds were weakened as more fathers lacked the resources and knowledge needed to guide and assist youth, and as more sons left home in search of independence and prosperity. Some founders did not see this trend as troublesome. Often, sons separated from and even rebelled against their fathers to become just like them, that is, to become independent landowners and farmers. Also, youthful independence was a recognized source of innovation. Jefferson argued that the doctrine that "we must tread with artful reverence in the footsteps of our fathers" was a barrier to "the progress of the human mind." Paine detested the "vanity" of men who sought to govern from "beyond the grave" and applauded the prospect that "children grow into men" who were free to follow the light of their own reason.[36]

The founders themselves participated in efforts to improve on the world of their fathers and procreate a better world for their sons. They set precedents by denying filial loyalty to Great Britain and by analogizing an independent America to a "young heir arrived at a mature age who, being freed from the restraints of tutors and governors, takes the management of his own estate into his own hands and makes such laws for the regulation of his domestic affairs as he judges will be most conducive to establish peace, order, and happiness in his family." Federalists rejected the authority of yesterday's state constitutions and the Articles of Confederation to support the U.S. Constitution. Their attitude was captured in James Madison's observation that Americans showed "a decent regard to the opinions of former times" but avoided "a blind veneration for antiquity, for custom, and for names." That enabled them to exhibit a "manly spirit" and produce the "numerous innovations displayed on the American theater."[37]

Simultaneously, most founders were troubled by the notion that fathers were fated for obsolescence. Madison praised *his* generation's innovations because they promised to suppress the "mutability" of state laws and support a Constitution designed to "decide forever the fate of republican government" and "last for the ages." He advocated a Bill of Rights that strengthened "the frame" of the Constitution and rendered men's liberties "perpetual." Later, he called on Washington's administration to honor past treaties with the France (though the French government had been revolutionized), claiming that Americans were obliged to keep past promises lest every change or reform constitute a "destruction of the social pact, an annihilation of property, and a complete establishment of the state of nature."[38] Like Plato, Madison tended to praise one-time innovations intended to create a stable and relatively unchangeable legacy.

Most founders shared this tendency. They saw the Revolution and Constitution as one-time affairs that produced enduring institutions. Antifederalists such as "John DeWitt" argued against the Constitution because ratification would not be "temporary but in its nature perpetual," creating "a government . . . for ages." Patrick Henry warned, "If a wrong step be now made, the republic may be lost forever." Federalists such as Alexander Hamilton, arguing for the Constitution, agreed that a misstep now meant that republican government "would be . . . disgraced and lost to mankind forever." The founders consistently spoke as if every decision would fix the course of posterity, in John Adams's estimation, for "thousands of years." Much of this was political rhetoric, but it was rhetoric that reflected an anxiety, identified by Michael Lienesch, that future generations would seek to "play the roles of revolutionaries and constitutionalists themselves, emulating the example of the framers by destroying their government and preempting their place as founders."[39] The founders did not intend to be preempted by their children.

Lienesch suggests that the founders "marched into the future fearfully, and always with an eye to the past." They articulated an improvement ethic but also recalled that men's passionate, impulsive, and greedy nature gave rise to public disorders that destroyed past achievements and prevented future advances. They wondered if their sons and grandsons, who had never suffered British tyranny or fought for independence, would appreciate manly freedom and patriotic sacrifice, or instead lapse into selfish, childish behavior that undermined the Republic. Federalists complained loudest about men's tendency to abuse liberty and practice licentiousness, but even Jefferson and his followers, their faith in human progress notwithstanding, worried about men's excesses. Jefferson approved of "the spirit" of Shays's Rebellion but thought the rebellion itself a mistake. He opposed the Alien and Sedition Acts, in part, to counteract policies that were "driving these states into revolution." He supported protests prior to the French Revolution in the hope that they would spawn modest reforms that averted bloodshed. Often, Jefferson promoted the rhetoric of liberty but was cautious about its practice among masses of disorderly men.[40]

A few founders were explicit about wanting their generation to bind future ones. John Adams saw written documents as an important means to foster order in the ranks of men: "The social compact and the laws must be reduced to writing. Obedience to them becomes a national habit and they cannot be changed but by revolutions which are costly things. Men will be too economical of their blood and property to have recourse to them very frequently." Adams wanted American men's liberty to be tempered by a habitual obedience reinforced by marriage and fatherhood, which provided men a family interest in safeguarding their "blood and property" rather than risking them in protest and rebellion.[41] For Adams, the cautious Family Man who protected his family and estate and habitually obeyed the law was the backbone of republican order.

Thomas Paine's description of a republic as a timeless polity was a creative effort to resolve intergenerational tensions. A republic, he wrote, was "never young, never old . . . subject neither to nonage, nor dotage . . . never in the cradle, nor on crutches." It possessed "a perpetual stamina" that presented itself "on the open theater of the world in a fair and manly manner." A republic did not suffer childish delusions of inevitable progress or senile fears of inevitable decline. Rather, it relied on an understanding that manhood was a source of continuity across time and space. The responsible Family Man procreated, provisioned, and protected his sons and left behind a manly legacy likely to be remembered by his sons even as they sought to demonstrate their own merit through experimentation and innovation. This promise of filial remembrance was fulfilled in exemplary fashion at the death of Henry Laurens by his son John, who "reared an altar on which he burnt the body of the patriarch and carefully gathered the ashes from the hearth, deposited them in a silver urn, and placed them in his bed-chamber with reverence and veneration . . . at once a mark of the respect due to the memory of both the patriot and the parent."[42]

The Parent and the Patriot

Significant similarities united the parent and the patriot. Both roles required men to discipline their passions and forgo the Bachelor's egomaniacal search for gratification. Both roles demanded that men engage in responsible, industrious, orderly conduct that benefited other people. Both roles enjoined men to govern women, ideally, with women's consent. Both roles called for men to procreate posterity and devote themselves to the good of posterity. Finally, both roles challenged men to measure up to consensual norms of manhood in order to earn self-respect and social respectability. Most founders were convinced that the self-disciplined, responsible, respectable Family Man was qualified for citizenship and deserved to share in the rights and responsibilities of citizenship.

Americans inherited the English belief that only substantial freeholders were sufficiently independent and committed to the public good to be trusted with citizenship, but two aspects of the American experience urged flexibility. First, America's rhetoric of liberty and equality suggested that all men were potentially worthy of citizenship. This created a presumption for inclusiveness. Second, America's abundance of land seemed to afford every young man an opportunity to acquire property, marry, and raise children. Theoretically, every male could become a modest freeholder and Family Man. While the founders continued to put the substantial freeholder at the center of citizenship, they began to expand citizenship by situating the Family Man near the center of public life.

Benjamin Franklin observed, "A man remarkably wavering and inconstant . . . can never be a truly useful member of the commonwealth." Unlike the Bachelor, the Family Man was "in the way of becoming a useful citizen." Poor young men could "begin first as servants or journeymen, and if they are sober, industrious, and frugal, they soon become masters, establish themselves in business, marry, raise families, and become respectable citizens." Economic opportunity was a basis for marriage; marriage was a foundation for fatherhood; and fatherhood promoted the stability essential to citizenship. Samuel West suggested that "the tender affection that we have for our wives and children [and] the regard we ought to have for unborn posterity" counteracted men's selfishness and encouraged the manly self-denial, family responsibility, and modicum of civic virtue essential to citizenship. Ultimately, the Family Man's independence, family loyalty, and commitment to the future encouraged him to exhibit "a gigantic manliness" by provisioning and protecting a family within "a well-constituted republic."[43]

The close association of the Family Man and citizenship was a recurring theme in the founders' speeches and writings. In 1776, for example, Thomas Jefferson wrote to Edmund Pendleton, "I cannot doubt any attachment to his country in any man who has his family and peculium in it. . . . I [am] for extending the right of suffrage (or in other words the rights of a citizen) to all who [have] a permanent intention of living in the country. Take what circumstances you please as evidence of this, either the having resided a certain time, or having a family, or having property, any or all of them." Contemporaries were generally willing to entertain formally and affirm informally the proposition that a man who headed a family had an enduring attachment to the public good. That was George Mason's reasoning when he proposed enfranchising the Family Man at the Constitutional Convention:

> A freehold is the qualification in England and hence it is imagined to be the only proper one. The true idea [is] that every man having evidence of attachment to and permanent common interest with the society ought to share in all its rights and privileges. Was this qualification restrained to freeholders? Does no other kind of property but land evidence a common interest in the proprietor? Does nothing besides property make a permanent attachment? Ought . . . the parent of a number of children whose fortunes are to be pursued in his own country to be viewed as suspicious characters and unworthy to be trusted with the common rights of their fellow citizens?[44]

Franklin added that "the sons of a substantial farmer," though not yet independent freeholders or family heads, anticipated becoming family men and, therefore, "would not be pleased at being disfranchised." Madison hinted at a greater degree of inclusiveness when observing that America had "the precious advantage" of having a male majority of "freeholders, or their heirs, or aspirants to freeholds."[45] Men who owned family estates, those likely to inherit them, and even those who aspired to acquire them might be trusted to combine independence and public loyalty to merit citizenship.

Ruth Bloch comments that "American men were advised that good republican citizenship . . . would follow ineluctably from true love and marriage." They were also led to believe that good citizenship was foreclosed to bachelors, whose vices enslaved them and estranged them from the public good. Thus, when Benjamin Rush made a plea for tax-supported public education in the early republic, he assumed that the Family Man was sufficiently civic-minded to understand the need to subsidize schools that taught young men "virtue and knowledge in the state." However, he felt compelled to make a special, utilitarian case that appealed to the Bachelor's self-interest. He argued that public education would reduce crime and disorder and, therefore, "the bachelor will in time save his tax for this purpose by being able to sleep with fewer bolts and locks on his doors."[46]

The connection between the Family Man and citizenship was loudly proclaimed by federalists in the debates over the U.S. Constitution. They argued that the Family Man's self-restraint and family interests guaranteed that he would act the part of a responsible citizen who made reasonable choices. Fisher Ames detested democracy's "loud clamors of passion, artifice, and faction," but he supported biennial elections to the House of Representatives "as security that the sober, second thought of the people shall be law." His faith in voter sobriety and thoughtfulness was based on his confidence in "the calm review of public transactions which is made *by the citizens who have families and children, the pledges of their fidelity.*"[47] Often, federalists promoted a family-oriented image of voter sovereignty that qualified liberty with family sobriety.

Federalists also employed the image of the Family Man to suggest that the new government was committed to the public good. John Jay tried to cast away fears that the president and Senate would ratify treaties contrary to the public good by noting that "they and their family estates will . . . be equally bound and affected with the rest of the community." James Iredell did not worry about a government that united the purse and sword because it was improbable "that our own representatives, chosen for a limited time, can be capable of destroying themselves, their families, and fortunes, even if they have no regard to their public duty." Alexander Hamilton saw no need to be alarmed by federal control of state militia because "our sons, our brothers, our neighbors, our fellow citizens" manned the militia. Finally, Zachariah Johnston did not see the Constitution as oppressive because federal representatives "will probably have families [and] they cannot forget them." A representative would not arbitrarily burden citizens because he "will be averse to lay taxes on his own posterity."[48] Federalists proclaimed that national officials would be trustworthy because they too would be fathers responsible for their families' welfare.

Federalists also construed family status as a bond of trust between citizens and leaders. Hamilton suggested that the Family Man would trust a leader who, like himself, was the father of "children to whom the ties of nature and habit have attached me." After all, a father in a position of leadership would not choose "the precarious enjoyment of rank and power" by participating in "a system which would reduce his . . . posterity to slavery and ruin." Rather, he would approach the future cautiously, with his children serving as "the dearest pledges of [his] patriotism." Furthermore, the average Family Man was apt to consent to political authority when it was bathed in the benign language of fatherhood. That was James Wilson's assumption when he argued that just as a responsible father gave priority to the welfare of his children, so too would the new president "watch over the whole with paternal care and affection."[49] Federalists used paternal imagery to make the Constitution and new government feel familiar and friendly.

David Ramsay summarized the federalist identification of the Family Man with citizenship when he called on the American people to "honor the men who with their own hands maintain their family and raise up children who are inured to toil and capable of defending their country." These honorable men were sufficiently steady and trustworthy to wield the rights and responsibilities of citizenship; and they were sufficiently respected and trusted by other men to be considered for positions of political leadership and authority. The federalist faith in the Family Man who voted in elections and consented to be governed by other family men prompted Timothy Pickering to express a father's ultimate plea for ratification: "If I were now on my dying bed and my sons were of mature age," he wrote, "my last words to them would be adopt this constitution."[50]

This connection between the Family Man and citizenship effectively foreclosed the possibility of identifying the Family Woman with citizenship. In large part, the founders believed the Family Man was sufficiently trustworthy to participate in politics because he was responsible for governing, as well as provisioning and protecting, a spouse and children. A dutiful husband settled down into patriarchal responsibility. He learned to differentiate authority and tyranny by governing his wife. He exercised family mastery to control disorderly female tendencies. He claimed an exclusive sex right to his wife's body to guarantee his paternity and secure his dynastic stake in the future. The result, according to Linda Kerber, was that "formulations of citizenship and civic relations in a republic were tightly linked to men and manhood." A whole new language had to be devised even to contemplate women's citizenship. That language focused on the role of the republican wife and mother who served as a moral monitor and civic educator for her family. Whether this role afforded women significant influence in an informal "fourth branch of government," as Kerber suggests, or kept them "locked in step behind the legal status of men," as Joan Hoff argues, it certainly reflected the founders' consensus that the Family Woman was excluded from public deliberations and suffrage, as well as jury service and the militia muster.[51]

The founders' faith in the Family Man as a citizen was substantial—but still limited. He manned the front lines of authority. He headed a family, provisioned and protected it, ruled dependents, and taught lessons in benevolence, productivity, civility, and deference to authority. Ideally, he lightened the burden of women's subordination and prepared young males to practice good citizenship. His family was a crucial building block for a stable republic. However, the founders did not forget that the Family Man was still a male creature who often failed to restrain passion, fulfill responsibility, or reconcile family interests with the public good. Like western Massachusetts farmers or Philadelphia artisans, he sometimes claimed that his family's welfare justified disobedience to established political authority. The founders presumed that the Family Man would be a trustworthy citizen, but they also sought security against his lapses from good citizenship.

The Limits of Family-Based Citizenship

Most founders agreed that family ties were a powerful source of unity and stability among men. Antifederalist "Cato" explained, "The strongest principle of union resides within our domestic walls. The ties of the parent exceed that of any other. As we depart from home, the next general principle of union is among citizens of the same state, where acquaintance, habits, and fortunes nourish affection and attachment." Federalist Alexander Hamilton concurred "that a man is more attached to his family than to his neighborhood, to his neighborhood than to the community at large."[52] The Family Man's affections, loyalties, and interests radiated out from his family to neighbors, community, state, and nation. Family ties bound men to the larger public; but they also promoted parochial loyalties that potentially conflicted with the public good.

In the 1760s and 1770s, radical artisans argued for the right of family men to vote and hold office. They also invoked their status as independent householders to legitimize their participation in political rallies, clubs, campaigns, petition drives, and elections. Gary Nash argues that American civic leaders were horrified by this "crumbling of deference." A more modest outlook on the Family Man was better attuned to the founders' desire for orderly politics. Joseph Lathrop stated, "He that practices every virtue in private life and trains up a family in virtuous principles and manners is no useless or unimportant member of society."[53] Lathrop implied that the Family Man achieved a sort of plateau. He was not a disorderly bachelor; thus, he could be a citizen. Nonetheless, his virtue was not necessarily sufficient to qualify him for political action and leadership. Why not?

The founders had limited trust in the Family Man for several reasons. First, a thin line separated the Family Man from the Bachelor. The Family Man vowed to control his appetites and fulfill his responsibilities, but his practice often fell short. Benjamin Franklin made a good living writing about the foibles and failings of weak and bumbling husbands and fathers. Many were guilty of licentiousness; many did not settle down into family life; many proved themselves social misfits. Joel Barlow went so far as to suggest that fathers were sometimes "too ignorant and often too inattentive or avaricious to be trusted with the sole direction of their children." Recalling common Puritan practice, he suggested that the state should supervise the Family Man's governance of his dependents.[54]

Second, even the most benign Family Man had the potential to act against the public good. Benjamin Rush advocated a system of public education that taught each young man "to love his family but . . . at the same time that he must forsake his family and even forget them when the welfare of his country requires it." The sheer strength of the Family Man's attachment to his closest relations diminished the likelihood that he would forsake or forget his family for the public good or allow his sons to do so. George Washington's constant complaint against militiamen was that they quickly demobilized or deserted to return to their families rather than contributing to the public good by fighting for the duration of the war. In 1783, Washington attributed the threat of a military insurrection to the fact that unpaid officers were forced "to participate their estates" to support themselves while in the service. They had "contracted heavy debts" and "spent their patrimonies."[55] Even honorable gentlemen would act in rebellious ways when they felt their families, estates, and posterity were threatened by undue sacrifices for the nation.

Third, the founders felt the Family Man's interests could be a source of political corruption. Antifederalists such as Melancton Smith worried that "pride of family" was so infectious and commanded so much influence among all classes of Americans that voters would elect to public office only men from noteworthy families. The likely result, according to "Brutus," was that "large family connections" and mutually profitable combinations among "the well-born and highest orders" would create a political monopoly among aristocrats who were ignorant of the sentiments and interests of "the middling class." Federalists such as John Adams agreed that family pride played an inevitable role in American politics. His fear was that men's family loyalties stopped short of the public good. The majority of men "confine their benevolence to their families," and "very few indeed extend it impartially to the whole community." The consequence was that Americans suffered from a parochialism powerful enough "to blind our eyes, darken our understandings, and pervert our wills."[56] For Adams and others, men who could not overcome family partiality lacked the virtue and talent necessary to be ranked among the Better Sort of men who were qualified to lead society and fill public offices.

Finally, many founders feared that the Family Man, who devoted his life to building and perpetuating a family dynasty, harbored an unspoken admiration for Europe's powerful aristocratic families, which had sustained themselves over many generations. The Society of the Cincinnati, an exclusive organization of Revolutionary War officers that perpetuated itself by making membership an inheritance of eldest sons, attracted many critics who considered its existence evidence that American officers and gentlemen were infatuated with aristocratic corruption. John Adams went so far as to suggest that Europe's aristocratic families attracted the secret devotion of virtually all Americans. He wrote to Jefferson, "If the duke of Angoleme, or Burgundy, or especially the Dauphin should demand one of your beautiful and most amiable daughters in marriage, all America from Georgia to New Hampshire would find their vanity and pride so agreeably flattered by it that all their sage maxims would give way; and even our sober New England republicans would keep a day of Thanksgiving for it, in their hearts."[57] Alas, the Family Man often preferred family pride and prejudice to the public good.

The founders' limited faith in the Family Man prompted them to construct for him a truncated conception of citizenship. On the one hand, the Family Man was sufficiently procreative to start a family, provision dependents, and prolong his family dynasty. He was relatively sober, safe, and predictable, and could claim liberty and equality without automatically lapsing into anarchic libertinism or democratic leveling. He could be trusted to become what Michael Lienesch describes as a "private citizen"—someone who cultivates a farm, pursues family interests, contributes to his community, and occasionally votes for public officials.[58] On the other hand, the Family Man's procreativity was parochial. His family interests did not necessarily encourage him to exhibit the elevated manly virtue and talent needed to cultivate social harmony or generate the public good. Nor did he demonstrate the political potential to resolve major crises, found new nations, or build a better future for humankind. Guilty of familial parochialism and innocent of Baconian greatness, the average family man was a private citizen in need of public leadership.

Indeed, the founders could not imagine a simple republic of men based solely on the exclusion of the Bachelor and the inclusion of the Family Man. Democratic disorders persisted. Internal exigencies were a daily occurrence. External dangers were omnipresent. A crucial question was whether the average family man would continuously conform to norms of common decency and contribute to the public good. Most founders believed that the Family Man needed strong leadership. They sought men of great virtue and talent, even a few heroic men, to calm democratic disorders, make and administer law, resolve crises, defeat enemies, and lead the citizenry down the path of providence.

Even before the Revolution, a "gentleman" could not automatically claim standing as a natural leader of men. After the Revolution, the rhetoric of liberty and equality reinforced patriots' refusal to recognize any man's natural superiority or authority. Consider this exchange between two "servants" in Royall Tyler's play, *The Contrast*:

> JESSAMY. I say, Sir, I understand that Colonel Manly has the honor of having you for a servant.
>
> JONATHAN. Servant! Sir, do you take me for a neger? I am Colonel Manly's waiter.
>
> JESSAMY. A true Yankee distinction, egad, without a difference. Why, Sir, do you not perform all the offices of a servant? Do you not even blacken his boots?
>
> JONATHAN. Yes, I do grease them a bit sometimes; but I am a true blue son of liberty, for all that. Father said I should come as Colonel Manly's waiter to see the world, and all that; but no man shall master me. My father has as good a farm as the Colonel.[59]

If all white male property owners and their heirs were true blue sons of liberty, not servants or slaves, why would they recognize or comply with men claiming leadership authority? Tyler's play suggested two answers. First, compliance was a matter of contract. Jonathan waited on Colonel Manly who, in return, provided his waiter an opportunity to see the world. This was a relatively weak basis for consent because it was contingent on both parties' satisfactory performance. Second, compliance was a function of respect. Jonathan deferred to Colonel *Manly* because he recognized, admired, and deferred to the Colonel's exceptional manly virtues and talents. Arguably, this was a stronger, more enduring basis for consent because it was built on consensual norms of manhood and reputed character rather than on utility and performance.

The founders' political discourse often focused on rationality and contract as a basis for legitimate leadership, but it also centered on evolving norms of manly respectability and deference. In the aristocratic past, commoners were expected to value and obey gentlemen's authority. In the revolutionary present, gentlemen's status was suspect and democratic equality defied deference. The founders became obsessed with reestablishing order in the ranks of men. They needed to identify "an alternative form of male cohesion" in order to sort out and stabilize what Nancy Cott calls "shifting hierarchies" among men.[60] They turned to the grammar of manhood to foster male cohesion. They applied it to put the Family Man at the center of citizenship and then to encourage the sober citizenry to comply with the leadership of the Better Sort of man.

5

The Better Sort and Leadership

The Family Man fit into the fraternity of men. The marriage contract was a fraternal contract that transformed a single man into a husband who claimed an exclusive sex right over his wife, agreed to other men's monopoly over their wives, and thereby established a "cooperative agreement" among the "brotherhood of free appropriators" of women's bodies. Men's joint "jurisdiction over women" helped to knit together male society. Additionally, the Family Man was a protector who enlisted in the Revolution to defend and bequeath liberty. He achieved solidarity with the "manly citizenry" that stood in opposition to the "effeminate imperial power" of the "mother country." Finally, the Family Man was a citizen who projected corruption onto womanhood and allied civic virtue to the male birthing of society and procreation of new republics, thereby actualizing Jefferson's fantasy about men reproducing without women.[1] In sum, early American fraternity presumed patriarchal domination and political exclusion of women.

However, that fraternity was threatened by intramale conflict. The Bachelor and other disorderly men threatened to destroy fraternal unity by acting on "unmanly ambition" to upset individual lives, destroy families, and ruin social harmony. Ann Fairfax Withington reports that scores of popular plays dramatized a world of "rakes, thieves, sharpers, libidinous old men, . . . dupes, and 'chattering crop-eared coxcombs'" who generated constant chaos in the ranks of men. Judith Sargent Murray especially worried that the Family Man's passion and parochialism, in tandem with his claims to freedom and equality, fueled a factionalism capable of sinking a sword of discord into "the vitals of that infant constitution" only to cut loose "hell-born anarchy." The founders sought to subdue democratic disorder and reinforce fraternal unity by employing the grammar of manhood to encourage the Family Man to identify especially trustworthy men and submit voluntarily to their leadership. A mid-eighteenth-century visitor to Portsmouth, New Hampshire, identified the leadership pool when he remarked, "The better sort of people here live very well and genteel."[2]

Beyond Basic Membership

Benjamin Franklin had "great hopes" that his nephew Benny would mature into "a worthy man." George Rogers Clark aspired to a higher status. He wanted to earn the respect of all virtuous and wise men and made it his "fixed principle" not to accept any honor but "to merit it first." Similarly, jurist James Kent advised ambitious young lawyers to exhibit "a manly determination" to merit their membership in the legal fraternity. The founders put great stock in a father's obligation to provide patrimony for his sons, but they especially honored the young man who demonstrated personal merit and achieved the distinction of being "observed, considered, esteemed, praised, beloved, and admired by his fellows."[3] Ultimately, an individual's character, accomplishments, and social recognition were what elevated him into the ranks of the Better Sort.

The Family Man earned elevated standing first by honoring family responsibilities and then by shedding some selfishness and parochialism to identify with an extended family of men. Prior to the Revolution, the Better Sort of man demonstrated fidelity to fellow colonists and British brethren by engaging in "manly and spirited but yet respectful and loyal petitioning" to redress colonial grievances. He affirmed manly freedom for Americans and maintained "brotherly love" for the English. In 1776, the Better Sort exhibited fraternal solidarity with revolutionaries. John Witherspoon applauded patriots' commitment to domestic "order and public peace" amid the chaos of the war, while Samuel McClintock congratulated patriots for being "a band of brethren" that averted internal "anarchy and confusion" to unify against the enemy. After the Revolution, writers honored American men's sense of fellow feeling and respect for authority. David Ramsay praised patriots for forging "a social band" while submitting to a Congress whose "recommendations were more generally and more effectually carried into execution than the laws of the best regulated societies." Mercy Otis Warren called the Revolution "a singular phenomenon in the story of human conduct" because laws and governments were annihilated but "recommendations of committees and conventions [were] equally influential and binding with the severest code of law."[4] American men demonstrated during the war that they could transcend individualism and localism to procreate an extended fraternal order and an independent nation.

One basis for that extended fraternal order was American men's opposition to unmanly British vices. Philip Greven suggests that American protesters and rebels sought "to be manly rather than effeminate" by supporting republican independence and frugality against English luxury and effeminacy. Withington recalls that the First Continental Congress drew up a code of moral conduct that banned English-identified vices such as cockfighting, horse racing, the theater, and lavish funerals. The code articulated a unifying vision "that made colonists aware of themselves as a people" who were "worthy of liberty." It cut across class and sectional differences by proscribing regional extravagances, such as northern theatricals and southern horse races. It urged colonists to build a sense of manly pride and community in opposition to various vices associated with libertines, gamblers, transients, backwoodsmen, immigrants, blacks, and Indians as well as Englishmen. Patriots united in opposition to a deceitful mother country and to marginal men infected by licentiousness.[5]

Communities enforced the congressional code mostly by employing social pressure, humiliation, and ostracism. Local committees and leaders demanded that offenders recant and rejoin the community. They stigmatized men who tried to conceal their vices by accusing them of "unmanly equivocation," subjecting them to ridicule, and urging them to confess and conform. They forced perpetrators who seemed beyond persuasion to endure rituals of public humiliation that included being tarred and feathered, drummed out of town, or "associated with blacks." A profligate patriot or duplicitous Tory might be degraded and marginalized by being handcuffed to a black man for a period of time or by being publicly whipped by a black man before being banished from the vicinity. Rituals of public humiliation and social ostracism helped unify fraternal insiders as well as identify deviants and "render them impotent."[6]

What motivated American men's loyalty to extended fraternal families? Most founders believed that men naturally desired society. Assertions that "man is a gregarious animal" were accompanied by avowals that man's "happiness" is rooted in society, his misery in "solitary existence." Simultaneously, most founders felt that men's natural sociability was weak. Thomas Paine contrasted men's desire for society to their selfish "wickedness," which demanded government restraints. Alexander Hamilton was absolutely awed by men's wickedness. While others applauded wartime solidarity, Hamilton warned that men's "passion . . . for opposition to tyranny and oppression very naturally leads them to a contempt and disregard for all authority."[7] Approaching victory, many founders were greatly concerned about whether American men could parlay wartime solidarity into peacetime sociability.

Contemporaries generally agreed that wartime experiences fostered fraternal feelings likely to outlast the war. David Ramsay noted that the Revolution extended men's bonds from their families and localities to all of the former colonies. An isolated farmer might not have seen the relationship between his family interests and British taxation or even national independence, but he certainly identified with American men across the continent who, in one way or another, suffered redcoat "depredation." That prompted him to "extinguish selfish passions," sacrifice parochialism "on the altar of patriotism," and forge "a common bond of union cementing us together." Furthermore, patriotic soldiers who died in the struggle left a legacy of enduring memories for their children, which would continue to provide "the firm cement of an extensive union" for generations to come. Military historian Don Higginbotham concludes that American men's Revolutionary War experiences were "the bricks and mortar of nationality."[8]

The war certainly stretched American men's sense of time, space, and politics. James Madison observed a new cosmopolitanism among easterners who became familiar with the frontier during the war and later acquired western lands "for their children." They formed "a new class of advocates" for western brethren and children, for example, on issues related to the free navigation of the Mississippi River. Ramsay located another source of cosmopolitanism in the continental relationships that soldiers fashioned during their marches and encampments. Sometimes these relationships blossomed into "intermarriages between men and women of different states," projecting family feeling across generations and geography to provide "an additional cement to the union." Continuing friendships and extended family feelings eventually became a centerpiece in the federalist case for a strong national government. John Jay argued that Americans "fighting side by side throughout a long and bloody war" became "a band of brethren [who] united to each other by the strongest ties should never be split into a number of unsocial, jealous, and alien sovereignties." Madison summoned "the mingled blood" of America's warriors to "consecrate" the proposed new union.[9]

The founders prolonged wartime solidarity by honoring and rewarding veterans. For example, Thomas Jefferson provided James Monroe a letter of introduction which emphasized that Monroe "served some time as an officer in the American army and as such distinguished himself in the affair of Princetown as well as on other occasions. . . . Should any circumstances render your patronage and protection as necessary as they would be always agreeable to him, you may be assured they are bestowed on one fully worthy of them." An honorable veteran was presumed to be deserving of men's trust and good offices. Conversely, a nonveteran might encounter men's presumptive distrust. Pelatiah Webster attacked Pennsylvania antifederalists by claiming that very few of them had fought in the war. They should not have opposed the Constitution but, instead, they should have given thanks for the "lenity" of the deserving citizens who "permitted" them "to live among us with impunity."[10] Implicitly, only members of the Revolution's martial fraternity could speak with authoritative public voices.

Despite their belief in men's natural sociability and their efforts to perpetuate wartime unity, most founders feared that postwar solidarity would not be "so great as will be necessary for the general good." Jefferson observed that few friendships borne of war stood the test of time. Men quickly "forget themselves but in the sole faculty of making money." As early as 1778, Phillips Payson reported a trend among men toward self-aggrandizement and warned that the man who finds virtue solely in "what he hoards up in his barn or ties up in his purse" would be unable to practice good citizenship after the war. In 1783, George Mason announced that American ethics already had degenerated into a "depravity of manners and morals" that destroyed "all confidence between man and man." He wondered whether victory "shall prove a blessing or a curse."[11]

Many of America's foremost political and military figures were disenchanted by men's postwar behavior. Selfishness and parochialism appeared to have replaced civic virtue and cosmopolitanism. George Washington wrote, "We have probably had too good an opinion of human nature in forming our confederation." Some founders accepted the inevitability of possessive individualism and hoped to sublimate it into an emerging semblance of self-made manhood. But most founders continued to urge men to transform their wartime virtue into a peacetime civility consistent with the ideals of republican manhood. Washington instructed his demobilizing troops to cultivate "conciliating dispositions" and discipline themselves to engage in "wise and manly conduct." Later, Secretary of the Treasury Alexander Hamilton issued an exemplary directive to revenue-cutter captains who had been detailed to curtail smuggling: "[They] will always keep in mind that their countrymen are freemen and as such are impatient of everything that bears the least mark of a domineering spirit. . . . They will endeavor to overcome difficulties . . . by a cool and temperate perseverance in their duty, by address and moderation rather than by vehemence or violence."[12] If martial courage and fortitude bound soldier to soldier in wartime, then perhaps self-restraint and sociability could bind citizen to citizen in peacetime. The founders called on Americans to cultivate civility.

It was one thing to promote civility among American men but quite another to expect most men to practice it. Many founders agreed with Noah

Webster's assessment that the male majority suffered from "rough passions" that distracted them from "the civilities of refined life." Even well-bred Americans often failed to discipline their passions to conciliate other men. Jefferson observed in 1797, "I have formerly seen warm debates and high political passions. But gentlemen of different politics would then speak to each other and separate the business of the Senate from that of society. It is not so now. Men who have been intimate all of their lives cross the street to avoid meeting and turn their heads another way lest they should be obliged to touch their hats. This may do for young men with whom passion is enjoyment but it is afflicting to peaceable minds." The Better Sort of man was not an impassioned youth who fostered factional conflict. Rather, James Madison suggested, he was one of the trustworthy few who was able to maintain manly integrity and "make friends" of opponents.[13]

The Trustworthy Few

The trustworthy few reconciled aristocratic manhood and republicanism. They distinguished themselves by restraining their animal instincts and exemplifying the morals and manners of "civilized" beings. The *United States Magazine* reported in 1778, "A man without taste and the acquirements of genius [is an] orangutan with the human shape and soul of a beast." By contrast, a man with taste emulated worthy gentlemen, understood social subtleties, and studied courtesy books to master the innumerable details of appropriate dress, speech, and conduct. His success depended as much on his effort and merit as on his birth and breeding. The *Polite Philosopher* explained, "It is want of attention, not capacity, which leaves us so many brutes." Theoretically, all men could cultivate gentility and move up in society. As Richard Bushman puts it, middle- and low-status men could "strive for elevation rather than resent subordination."[14]

Bushman asserts that men striving for elevation and those who achieved it were "the cement and soul" of society. Forrest McDonald argues that the founders considered social climbing a virtue when it involved soliciting "the esteem of wise and good men." In turn, high-status men were obligated to be benefactors to low-status men. "The Preceptor" explained that gentility required "the true gentleman, rather than shunning or scoffing at inferiors, show affability and condescension to all who were below him." Gentility also enjoined gentlemen to "defend and patronize their dependents and inferiors" in order to ensure that America's "diversity of ranks and conditions" blended into fraternal harmony. John Perkins thought fulfilling this obligation was challenging because "the rustic" often despised "the gentle manner and obliging behavior of the well-bred and polite" and considered gentility incompatible with "manly fortitude and resolution." Perkins expected the Better Sort to resolve the tension between aristocratic manners and republican simplicity by reforming the rustic, encouraging him to redefine manhood as refinement, and teaching him proper behavior. Similarly, John Adams called on gentlemen to spread among commoners a gospel of "good humor, sociability, good manners, and good morals . . . some politeness but more civility."[15]

Refined morals and manners were especially important markers of male worth in a mobile society where a steady stream of strangers poured into established communities and carved out new ones. The founders wanted men to settle down and raise families but knew that many youth had to traverse time and space to demonstrate merit and earn an independent, respectable place for themselves and their families in the city or on the frontier. Who among them could be trusted? Strangers were judged by their dress, speech, and conduct. Those considered crude, lustful, and impulsive attracted other men's distrust whereas those exhibiting manly refinement gained eligibility for admission into polite society. Bushman points out that, in an era of change, the ability to exhibit good morals and manners "enabled wanderers to claim a place, forge an identity, and establish a recognized hierarchy."[16] Refinement helped order the ranks of strangers.

A refined order was a hierarchical order with the Bachelor on the bottom, the Family Man in the middle, and the Better Sort at the top. Most founders believed that few men sufficiently mastered the challenges of refinement to deserve top ranking. Mastery was difficult. It went beyond exhibiting proper morals and manners; it also meant maintaining manly independence and integrity in difficult circumstances. A man was truly respectable only if he exhibited "a free and manly spirit." He had "to think with boldness and energy, to form his principles upon fair enquiry, and to resign neither his conscience nor his person to the capricious will of men." Few men demonstrated this independence and integrity, along with sincerity and honesty, when pressed to conform to conventional ideas and prevailing opinions. Moreover, mastery entailed balancing manly integrity with civility in order to reconcile independent thought with social order. George Washington advised that "manly candor" should be accompanied by a "manly tone of intercourse" and a disposition to deal "freely" with another man by treating him "like a friend." Alexander Hamilton proposed a union of openness and modesty, recommending that President John Adams exhibit "*manly* but *calm* and *sedate* firmness . . .

without strut." Edmund Randolph exemplified the ideal of aristocratic manhood in a republic: he harbored "no indifference to public opinion, but resolved not to court it by an unmanly sacrifice of my own judgment." John Stevens praised Randolph for his "manliness"—for his "candor" and "delicacy" in paying homage to public opinion even when opposing it.[17]

The Better Sort possessed "the most attractive merit and the most diffusive and established characters." They made independent decisions but acted "in conjunction with others" to promote a "moral culture of the heart" that fostered "all endearing ties of gratitude and love which unite man to man in the discharge of reciprocal duties." They were an elite skilled at mediating individual liberty and fraternal order. This made them particularly qualified to be leaders and lawmakers. Unfortunately, many founders feared, the male majority often confused the trustworthy few with deceivers and manipulators who feigned manly integrity and civility to acquire base popularity, "an adulteress of the first order." Speakers alerted Americans to pretenders. Samuel Wales differentiated worthy leaders who earned "true popularity" by gaining the "esteem of the virtuous and wise" from dangerous demagogues engaged in a "mad pursuit of low popularity" by "flattery." Noah Webster distinguished the respectable man of "real worth" from the "popularity-seeker, or mere man of the people" who "banishes candor and substitutes prejudice."[18] The founders were quite concerned that the man of real worth, rather than the deceiver, establish an elevated reputation to secure hegemony by inspiring common men to invest their trust, consent, and quiescence in his leadership and authority.

A Man's Reputation

Virtually all founders agreed with James Madison that "distinctions [among men] are various and unavoidable." Many concurred with Judith Sargent Murray that liberty "dreadeth that tumultuous and up-rooting hurricane which, inmingling the various classes of mankind, destroyeth the beautiful gradation and series of harmony." Some concluded with Peres Fobes that distinctions among men produced natural inequalities that invited domination and subordination: "We behold in the countenance of some persons a kind of dignity which at once beams reverence and designates for dominion; in others, we observe such a vacancy and prostration of dignity as equally marks them for subjection." Perhaps the norm among the founders was Noah Webster's notion that the Better Sort of man had "just claims" to elevated social status and "influence and authority."[19] Republicanism did not destroy hierarchy. Rather, it called on the Better Sort to build manly reputations in order to attract sufficient public trust to be entrusted with political authority.

From the onset of colonization, Americans considered "a good name" of the utmost importance. Mary Beth Norton states that a man had to establish and maintain his "credit" and "reputation of being worthy of belief or trust" to participate in the oral agreements that shaped social interactions and to maintain his status in a society where legal supports for the male pecking order were mostly absent. The significance of reputation persisted into the founding era when, for example, Martin Howard proclaimed "the high value of a good name and how dear it is to men of sentiment and honor." A good name fortified a man's self-esteem, enhanced his opportunities, increased his admirers, and enabled him to circulate among the Better Sort, be favored by them, and become one of them. Thomas Jefferson was "never happier than when . . . performing good offices for good people, and the most friendly office one can perform is to make worthy characters acquainted with one another." Worthy men needed good friends to disseminate their good names as well as to defend their good names against "the assassin who stabs reputation."[20]

Some founders ranked reputation above law. For example, George Mason wrote George Washington about a young relative who killed his opponent in an unlawful duel. The young man "may not be strictly justifiable in a legal sense [but] I am entirely of the opinion that he has done no more than any man of sensibility and honor would have thought himself obliged to do under the same circumstances of provocation . . . an attempt to blast the reputation of a young lady of family and character allied to him by the nearest ties of blood." The youth had to protect his reputation and family honor by shedding blood. Alexander Hamilton (later to die in a duel with Aaron Burr) emphasized the importance of duelists' proper conduct. A second to John Laurens in a duel with Charles Lee, Hamilton reported, "It is a piece of justice to the two gentlemen to declare that, after they met, their conduct was strongly marked with all the politeness, generosity, coolness, and firmness that ought to characterize a transaction of this nature."[21] Both duelists demonstrated their manhood and reinforced their good names.

Many founders were obsessed with what other notable men said and wrote about them. Early in the Revolution, Washington worried that his reputation would "fall" if he continued his military command with too few soldiers only to be charged with incompetence, or if he resigned his command only to be attacked for disloyalty. He fretted about the "impossibility of serving with reputation" and instructed his cousin Lund to issue a "declaration made in credit to the justice of my character." The founders generally considered men's devotion to reputation less a matter of self-indulgence and more a positive stimulus to virtue. Theophilus Parsons explained that a major reason public officials could be trusted and empowered with authority was that their concern for their "own reputation would guard them against undue influence." They were unlikely to engage in deceit, dishonesty, or corruption because they knew that "the censure of the people will hang on their necks with the weight of a millstone."[22]

Concern for reputation also was central to discussions about free expression. Benjamin Franklin wrote a satire favoring "liberty of the press" and "liberty of the cudgel"—the right of men to thrash anyone who unjustly attacked their reputations. Franklin defended a free press but added, "If [it] means the liberty of affronting, calumniating, and defaming another, I, for my part, own myself willing to part with my share of it . . . and shall cheerfully consent to exchange my liberty of abusing others for the privilege of not being abused myself." Supporters of a free press expected journalists to qualify liberty with civility. They agreed with Washington that defamation was "incompatible with truth and manliness" as well as with Tunis Wortman that defamation constituted "unmanly . . . calumny." However, supporters of the Sedition Act did not trust journalists' truthfulness or manhood. They demanded legal restraints on the press, especially to protect political leaders' reputations. Such restraints, they announced, were alarming only "to slanderers, to libelers, to robbers of reputation."[23]

Some founders considered a man's reputation so important that it "ought to be guarded as of the next consequence to his life." One reason was personal. Franklin wrote, "It is so natural to wish to be well spoken of, whether alive or dead." This desire to be warmly remembered was a part of men's quest for symbolic immortality. Franklin used this insight to try to lure Washington to France: "You would, on this side of the sea, enjoy the great reputation you have acquired, pure and free from those little shades that the jealousy and envy of a man's countrymen and contemporaries are ever endeavoring to cast over living merit. Here you would know and enjoy what posterity will say of Washington." Judith Sargent Murray's "Gleaner" made reputation central to the very meaning of men's lives and deaths when declaring his most cherished goals: "I would be distinguished and respected by my contemporaries; I would be continued on grateful remembrance when I make my exit; and I would descend with celebrity to posterity."[24]

A second reason was that many founders felt men's concern for reputation helped moderate their conduct and keep it within the boundaries of propriety. Colonial protesters who participated in mock funerals and executions experienced considerable social pressure to maintain decorum and order if they were to protect their good names. Many neutrals and Tories who remained in their communities during the Revolution learned to speak and act with restraint, so that they might maintain sufficient respectability to insulate themselves from public anger, humiliation, and worse. Patriots who aspired to upward mobility and leadership positions sought to establish good civic reputations to gain the respect and deference of friends, neighbors, and supporters who otherwise treasured their manly independence and maintained skepticism toward leadership and authority.[25]

Another reason the founders dwelled on reputation was that they saw it as a bond between citizens and leaders. Charles Pinckney argued that most men would trust leaders who "connect the tie of property with that of reputation." Noah Webster thought that citizens would put their confidence in officials whose jealousy of their reputations was a "guarantee" that they would faithfully discharge public duties. Pelatiah Webster stated that lawmakers made themselves "fit to be trusted and worthy of public confidence" when concern for "personal reputations with all the eyes of the world on them" induced them to exhibit "noble, upright, and worthy behavior." The founders were convinced that most men did not excel at manly sensibilities, candor, and civility; however, they believed that most men admired the few who did excel at manhood and most men would voluntarily submit to manly leaders who earned reputations for gentility, integrity, civility, and civic virtue. Annis Boudinot Stockton captured this belief when she announced that "the free born" would resign their "native rights" only to "*Men.*"[26]

The Natural Aristocracy

The men who filled the ranks of the Better Sort constituted what the founders often considered "the natural aristocracy." Elizur Goodrich called the natural aristocracy an "institution of heaven," designed by God to ensure that leaders with a "sincere regard to the public good" gained men's "cordial affection, veneration, esteem, and gratitude." Most founders doubted neither the existence of a natural aristocracy nor its significance for the stability of the Republic. But many founders questioned whether the *language* of natural aristocracy was appropriate in a republic. Did it provide a terminology that helped the majority of men to identify the trustworthy few and entrust authority to them? Or was it so closely associated with English corruption and tyranny that, as Gordon Wood argues, the "destruction of aristocracy, including Jefferson's 'natural aristocracy,' was the real American Revolution"?[27]

Alexander Hamilton stated, "There are strong minds in every walk of life that will rise superior to the disadvantages of situation and will command the tribute due to their merit, not only from the classes to which they particularly belong, but from the society in general." At the New York ratifying convention, he labeled these men "aristocrats." Their leadership inspired "the confidence of the people" from all classes. Two days later, Robert Livingston referred to "the natural aristocracy" as a repository of men's virtue, wisdom, eminence, and learning. He asked, "Does a man possess the confidence of his fellow citizens for having done them important services? He is an aristocrat. Has he great integrity? Such a man will be greatly trusted. He is an aristocrat." Livingston tied the natural aristocracy to democracy by expressing a hope that Americans were all "men of merit" and "all aristocrats."[28] For their part, antifederalists affirmed the conceptual substance of the natural aristocracy. Melancton Smith stated that "the author of nature has bestowed on some greater capacities than on others—birth, education, talents, and wealth, creating distinctions among men as visible and of as much influence as titles, stars, and garters." He agreed that such men constituted a "natural aristocracy" that deserved recognition, which they would likely receive because "pride of family, of wealth, of talents . . . command influence and respect among the common people." The "Federal Farmer" wrote that a "few men of wealth and talent" constituted a natural aristocracy, and "Brutus" asserted the likelihood that "the natural aristocracy of the country will be elected."[29]

Two divisive issues centered on the language of aristocracy and the trustworthiness of natural aristocrats. First, federalists had mixed feelings about using the language of natural aristocracy to identify and legitimize manly leaders. Many federalists avoided the language of aristocracy for fear that it would alienate potential supporters. Like James Wilson, they preferred to characterize the new president as "the Man of the People" rather than a natural aristocrat. However, some federalists used, refined, and defended the language of aristocracy, for example, when confronted by opponents' charges that supporters of ratification were "monarchy men, military men, aristocrats, and drones." They drew distinctions between Europe's "hereditary aristocrats," the critics' "phantom aristocrats," and America's "natural aristocrats" who contributed to the public good.[30] Often, however, their distinctions were not particularly persuasive to American men steeped in the rhetoric of liberty and equality against aristocracy.

Second, federalists and antifederalists debated whether natural aristocrats were worthy of most men's trust. Federalists argued that natural aristocrats were trustworthy leaders and lawmakers. They were family men loath to engage in actions that might harm their posterity and gentlemen whose jealousy of their reputations allied them to the public good. Antifederalists contended that natural aristocrats, like all men, were flawed beings. Samuel Bryan claimed that they had a "love of domination" in proportion to their "talents, abilities, and superior acquirements." Even those with "the greatest purity of intention" were apt to become "instruments of despotism in the hands of the artful and designing." Unfortunately, the public was often blind to their failings and yielded "an implicit assent to the opinions of those characters whose abilities are held in the highest esteem." Some antifederalists suggested that the "illustrious" were no "more free from error" than common men but were more insensitive to people of modest means. Other antifederalists repeated the warning that the public was sometimes so "dazzled by the splendor of names as to run blindfolded into what may be our destruction."[31]

Most federalists and antifederalists did agree that Benjamin Franklin, George Washington, and other framers of the Constitution were natural aristocrats. Federalists argued that these "distinguished worthies" favored ratification and the common man who respected them ought to favor ratification too, as well as "manfully oppose" those whose "wicked intent" was to destroy these great men's labors. Noah Webster emphasized that "some of the greatest men in America with the venerable FRANKLIN and the illustrious WASHINGTON at their head" had written the Constitution. They deserved public support. James Madison recognized that the framers' reputations were crucial to ratification: "Had the Constitution been framed by an obscure individual instead of the body possessing public respect and confidence, there can be no doubt that . . . it would have commanded little attention from most of those who now admire its wisdom."[32]

Antifederalists did not attack Franklin and Washington for being aristocrats. At times, they even congratulated the American public on its propensity to honor these great men by associating their good names with worthy deeds. The main opposition tactic was to stress individual men's responsibility to make independent judgments about the Constitution while pointing out the framers' flaws. Thomas Wait explained that, initially, "I loved George Washington—I venerated Benjamin Franklin—and therefore concluded that I must love and venerate all the works of their hands." Soon, Wait realized that blind veneration was a "violence of passion" more appropriate to "European slaves" than to "the freemen of America." He consulted manly "candor," engaged in "cool and impartial examination," and chose to oppose the Constitution. But why did America's great men support the Constitution? Bryan reminded readers that "the illustrious and highly revered Washington" was "fallible on a subject that must be in great measure novel to him." Moreover, his "unsuspicious zeal" for America along with the "honest mistaken zeal of a patriot" made him vulnerable to the "flagitious machinations of an ambitious junto."[33]

The conviction that the ranks of men were capped by a cadre of natural aristocrats who were more or less trustworthy as leaders of men was ubiquitous throughout the founding era. As late as 1794, Noah Webster openly applauded the existence of the natural aristocracy and added that even "the most noisy democrat" demonstrated a belief in "natural aristocracy" when he sought a "respectable family" to take his son as an apprentice, inquired into the "family connections and fortune" of a son's or daughter's proposed spouse, or rallied around the banner of "certain influential men in the democratic clubs." In time, however, most founders discovered that the language of natural aristocracy was so laden with emotional baggage that it could not be used without controversy. John Adams learned by experience. Despite innumerable efforts to distinguish hereditary from natural aristocracy, he was constantly on the defensive. In 1790, he felt compelled to explain that his assertion of the inevitability of "noble families" referred to "the natural and actual aristocracy" of talent and virtue. In 1791, he tried to counteract accusations that he supported aristocracy by writing Jefferson, "If you suppose that I have ever had a design or desire of attempting to introduce a government of king, lords, and commons, or in other words an hereditary executive or an hereditary senate, either into the government of the United States or that of any individual state in this country, you are wholly mistaken." Adams was still on the defensive in 1800, when critics continued to insist that his "principles would wrest the government from the hands of the people" and substitute "hereditary power and hereditary privileges."[34]

Attacks on men who spoke the language of natural aristocracy or who openly intimated its existence became quite vicious. William Manning's 1799 *Key of Liberty* was a vitriolic tract against the conspiracies of "the Few." Manning paid homage to great men whose wisdom, virtue, and service earned them public respect and trust. The problem with the natural aristocracy was the "solemn truth that the higher a person is raised in stations of honor, power, and trust, the greater are his temptations to do wrong." Eminent men's selfishness and pride "create a sense of superiority" and then a "hankering and striving after monarchy or aristocracy where the people have nothing to do in government but to support the Few in luxury and idleness." This hankering was heightened when "leading men" felt they could "never receive compensation and honors enough from the people for their services" and urged the people "to reverence and respect" them rather than "to see for themselves."[35]

Manning asserted the temporality of all natural aristocracies and emphasized their antagonism to men's liberty.

Unlike Manning, nearly all founders believed that the Better Sort—by whatever label—should be recognized, trusted, and empowered to compensate for common men's passions, selfishness, and parochialism by leading them toward fraternal unity and exercising lawmaking authority over them. Legitimizing the leadership of the Better Sort was an ongoing challenge because any justifying language that hinted at the social or political superiority of a few men was sure to generate controversy. Thomas Jefferson believed in a natural aristocracy founded on a few men's great virtue and talent, and he even considered it "the most precious gift of nature" for "the instruction, the trusts, and government of society." Nonetheless, he understood that all talk about aristocracy, natural or not, was repugnant to men steeped in the rhetoric of "the equal rights of men." Accordingly, he advised George Washington to refuse membership in the Society of the Cincinnati, which critics condemned as an aristocratic organization.[36]

Alexander Hamilton came to recognize that the distance between men and their leaders in a republic could not be too great or too narrow. Men had to feel close enough to their leaders to be familiar with them, develop trust in them, and eventually render habitual respect and obedience to them. And leaders had to reinforce public familiarity and trust by claiming to be like other men. Simultaneously, leaders had to appear sufficiently elevated and esteemed to merit men's respect and obedience. Advising Washington on precedent-setting etiquette for the first presidency, Hamilton stated, "Men's minds are prepared for a pretty high tone in the demeanor of the Executive, but I doubt whether for so high a tone as in the abstract might be desirable. The notions of equality are yet in my opinion too general and too strong to admit of such a distance."[37] The language of natural aristocracy proved to be too high-toned and put too much distance between the Better Sort and the common man. Alternatively, the founders experimented with a rhetoric of fame and infamy that emphasized the close proximity of citizens and leaders even as it justified men's deference to hegemonic elites.

The Rhetoric of Fame and Infamy

The founders put "equality" at the heart of their revolutionary creed: "God made all mankind originally equal"; adult sons were "equal in rank to their parents"; men in society deserved "equal esteem or equal respect"; and "government was a political institution between men naturally equal." They also suggested that American men were destined for equality. As individuals, they faced God's "two great levelers, death and endless retribution"; as a nation, they adopted "a gospel of equality and fraternity" and encouraged "universal redemption of the human race." At the same time, the founders were convinced that men were born unequal and died unequal. John Adams argued that men were born with varied abilities and a "passion for distinction" that motivated them to achieve superiority over others and to acquire a celebrity that continued beyond the grave, where it "Adorns our hearse, and flatters our tombs."[38] How did the founders reconcile natural equality with the actual inequality represented by the Better Sort of man?

The founders relied on the grammar of manhood to discuss equality and inequality in the ranks of men. They conceptualized male equality as a function of patriarchal domination of women, joint opposition to unmanly vices associated with effeminacy and marginality, and support for fraternal sociability and wartime solidarity. They talked about inequality as a matter of men's varying efforts and abilities to achieve high standards of manly refinement, candor, civility, and reputability. In late-eighteenth-century America, being a Family Man in a patriarchal society conferred dignity and justified citizenship; being a Family Man who exhibited great manly merit conferred social status and legitimized leadership. The passion for distinction and ambition was the driving force of manly merit and the quest for fame was its highest expression.

John Adams applauded the passion for distinction when it urged men to emulate noble ancestors and worthy contemporaries, but he feared it when it fostered jealousy, envy, and also "destructive factions, wasting seditions, and bloody civil war." Mercy Otis Warren called men's desire for distinction "a noble principle" with "benevolent effects"—except when it produced "mortifying instances of profligacy, tyranny, and the wanton exercise of arbitrary sway." John Stevens considered men's "ambition" a "noble passion" and "laudable desire" but worried that it sometimes stirred men's "insatiate lust of domination and despotic sway." If many writers appreciated ambition as a source of a "manly and martial spirit" and "heroism," others were quick to warn that ambition for "pomp, power, and greatness" often corrupted men, even "our better sort."[39]

Judith Sargent Murray's mixed belief that manly ambition was both "a noble principle" that was "productive of the most valuable consequences" and a "time server ready to answer the purpose of every base employer" reflected contested ideals of manhood. Ambitious young men were free to measure up to republican manhood by establishing and governing families, perpetuating family dynasties, and positioning themselves to be fondly remembered by their children and neighbors. But they were also invited to measure up to aristocratic manhood by fitting into fraternal society, earning an esteemed reputation in it, and positioning themselves to be fondly remembered by men of virtue and wisdom, if not by all posterity. Unfortunately, the disorderly bachelor and the deceiving demagogue were likely to be equally ambitious in the cause of personal pleasure and power against fraternal unity and the public good. Both were self-made men but, by the founders' standards, neither was a true "man."[40]

The highest object of ambition was "fame." For most founders, Douglass Adair explains, a man ambitious for fame wanted "to make history" by acquiring "the largest possible human audience" and imprinting "his name and his actions" in the minds of worthy men everywhere so that he was "never to be forgotten." He sought "immortality" by way of "public service." David Ramsay considered fame the ultimate reward for men "who stepped forward in the cause of liberty." George Washington admitted that he was driven by ambition, reputation, and especially fame. He explained that "the height of my ambition" was "to merit the approbation of good and virtuous men." Fame would be "full compensation for all my toils and suffering." According to Garry Wills, what most distinguished Washington from other leaders was his "willingness to be rewarded *only* in fame." Washington's quest for fame made him like other men, but his willingness to be rewarded only in fame made the "immortal Washington" into what William Emerson called "a man among men." If ordinary citizens identified with Washington "the man," they adored Washington "the man among men." Wills concludes that his fame became "a social glue . . . for the republic."[41]

Occasionally, Washington's colleagues sought to influence him by positioning themselves as defenders of his fame. For instance, James Madison opposed Washington's 1793 Proclamation of Neutrality. Madison did not directly criticize Washington or the Proclamation but argued instead that it was "mortifying" to the President and his friends that the Proclamation undermined his "fame" because it appeared to be "an assumption of prerogative" that was not found in the Constitution but "copied from a monarchical model." Americans often took it upon themselves to uphold Washington's fame. In a sermon celebrating the Revolution, for example, George Duffield called on congregants to "let the illustrious Washington . . . live perpetual in the minds and the praises of all." He enjoined his listeners to "aid feeble fame with her hundred wings and tongues to proclaim his worth; and . . . convey down through every age the unsullied remembrance of the patriot, the hero, and citizen combined, and deliver his name and his praise to the unbounded ocean of immortal esteem."[42]

The rhetoric of fame was also applied to more ordinary officials. Daniel Shute proclaimed that men's reward for the "faithful and intrepid execution of the duties of their offices" was the chance to "transmit their names with honor to posterity who, in futurity, will participate in the blessing." Phillips Payson noted that men's faith in public officials was justified by magistrates' ambition "of transmitting their names to posterity with characters of immortal honor." During the constitutional ratification debates, Madison resurrected the argument that citizens could safely entrust authority to elected officials who sought fame through public service. Other federalists relied on the desire for fame to build a case for a powerful presidency. Gouverneur Morris opposed a single-term presidency because it would "destroy the great incitement to merit public esteem by taking away the hope of being rewarded with reappointment," perhaps "shut the civil road to glory," and compel ambitious men to seek fame "by the sword" rather than by public service. Hamilton, agreeing that "love of fame" was "the ruling passion of the noblest minds," argued that presidents should have unlimited terms of office to enable them to seek and achieve fame. Peres Fobes added that officials were most trustworthy when they were "fired with a noble emulation of transmitting their names to posterity in laurels of honor."[43]

The rhetoric of fame reserved its highest honors for leaders and lawmakers, but it also offered degrees of immortality to more ordinary men. Duffield's celebratory sermon first praised Washington and then his fallen officers by instructing, "Number them not of the dead. They are enrolled in the list of glory and fame, and shall live immortal, beyond the death of the grave." Next, Duffield widened the scope of remembrance by stating, "From the commander in chief down to the faithful centinel, let the officer and soldier who have bravely offered their lives and nobly dared death and danger in the bloody field . . . be remembered with kindness." Sometimes, even men who fought for liberty but failed could expect their share of fame. An admirer told the Pennsylvania minority that lost its struggle against ratification, "We rejoice that your names will shine illustriously in the pages of history and will be read with honor and grateful remembrance in the annals of fame."[44] Fame trickled down from the Better Sort of men to more ordinary men and thereby narrowed the distance between them.

The rhetoric of fame also helped close the gap between lofty political rhetoric and everyday personal experience because its glowing terms were familiar and friendly to common men. Few individuals achieved fame by being great leaders and public officials, but every family man sought "fame" by wishing to be remembered by his descendants. Orators played on this point. In a July 4 speech, Simeon Baldwin recalled "the sons of freedom" who with "manly firmness" withstood British tyranny and transmitted "their names, their virtues, and their noble deeds to posterity, by whom they will be revered as the most distinguished benefactors of mankind and eminent examples for future generations." Baldwin then linked these great warriors to America's family men, who did their noble share to provide for "the protection of their estates, families, persons, fame, and lives."[45] The rhetoric of fame justified inequality in the ranks of men, but it also reinforced Americans' sense of shared manhood.

The familiarity of fame freed it from the baggage weighing down the language of natural aristocracy. Most men of distinguished birth or great wealth did not achieve fame, but some men of humble origins (such as Benjamin Franklin) were numbered among the famous. John Stevens expressed the equal opportunity idiom of fame as follows:

> No government that has ever yet existed in the world affords so ample a field to individuals of all ranks for the display of political talents and abilities. Here are no patricians who engross the offices of state. No man who has real merit, let his situation be what it will, need despair. He first distinguishes himself amongst his neighbors and township and country meeting; he is next sent to the state legislature. In this theater his abilities, whatever they are, are exhibited in their true colors, and displayed to the views of every man in the state; from hence his ascent to a seat in Congress. . . . Such a regular uninterrupted gradation from the chief men in a village to the chair of the President of the United States, which this government affords to all her citizens without distinction, is a perfection in republican government heretofore unknown and unprecedented.[46]

Ambitious men who sought distinction had to undergo a trial by political ordeal to achieve fame. Like the Jeffersonian educational system intended to "rake . . . from the rubbish" those who proved themselves "the best geniuses," republican politics provided tiered tests of manhood to separate the less deserving many from the meritorious few who were sufficiently trustworthy to lead men and wield political authority.[47]

Of course, the founders were greatly concerned that men's quest for fame could be perverted by "the bold effrontery of those interested and avaricious adventurers for place who, intoxicated with the ideas of distinction and preferment, have prostrated every worthy principle beneath the shrine of ambition." Mercy Otis Warren believed such men were more than malevolent; they were also foolhardy because they exposed themselves to the eternal pain of "infamy." The grammar of manhood suggested that a worthy person preferred a manly death to infamy. David Ramsay recounted a battle in which George Washington exposed himself to the enemy "as if in an expectation that by an honorable death he might escape the infamy he dreaded from the dastardly conduct of troops on whom he could place no dependence." It was terrible to die forgotten; but it was worse to be eternally remembered as a scoundrel like Benedict Arnold, who would be forever associated with "the blackest crimes" of "treason" and "patricide."[48]

The founders thought that men's dread of infamy provided a modest guarantee of their integrity and leadership. A pretender to popularity would think twice about deceiving other men because his self-aggrandizement might be exposed and open him to humiliating charges of infamy. A respectable official would be a cautious decision maker lest he make serious mistakes that invited infamy. That was Benjamin Franklin's warning to Lord Howe shortly after the British went to war with its colonies: "I consider this war . . . as both unjust and unwise; and I am persuaded cool dispassionate posterity will condemn to infamy those who advised it; and that even success will not save from some degree of dishonor those who voluntarily engaged to conduct it." Finally, a truly worthy leader would endure significant self-sacrifice rather than risk infamy for himself and his loved ones. When General Horatio Gates lost a key battle, he immediately tendered a "manly resignation" to avert infamy. And when Henry Laurens, imprisoned by the British for his role in the Revolution, was offered a pardon in return for a public apology, he declared, "I will never subscribe to my own infamy and to the dishonor of my children."[49]

The founders conceptualized "the love of fame" as a manly motivation and compelling justification for free and equal men to aspire to membership among the Better Sort and to recognize, respect, and obey the leadership of the Better Sort. Fame was the carrot. The many men who sought it and the few who partook of it were enticed by posterity's grateful remembrance. Thus, Gouverneur Morris eulogized Alexander Hamilton by instructing mourners, "I charge you to protect his fame—it is all he has left." Infamy was the stick. It poked and prodded ambitious men to avoid disgrace and humiliation by disciplining their passions, exercising liberty with restraint, and sustaining order in the ranks of men. Men who misdirected their ambitions potentially mutilated themselves with "a deep and . . . lasting mark of infamy."[50]

Fraternity and Fratricide

Many men tested their masculinity, cultivated refinement, established reputations, and sought fame by participating in fraternities that joined norms of self-improvement and social civility to more-or-less intricate ranking systems. For example, "Shopkeepers, traders, and merchants bonded into clubs and societies" that fostered "mutual consideration," "mutual benevolence," and "friendly feeling." Membership was often a tryout for social fit and mobility. Apprentice printers and artisans complied with craft norms as a means to survive and advance. Apprentice status provided the contrast needed to bolster masters' social standing "by highlighting the value of craft skills, the significance of training, and the achievement of manly respectability through work." In the legal fraternity that emerged in the late eighteenth century, aspiring and new lawyers were expected to excel at "responsible manhood" to establish their place in the profession. The "manly advocate" could anticipate moving up in the ranks.[51]

John Adams was a master psychologist of fraternal life. He argued that men first sought to fit into social groups and then to rise above their peers: "Every man desires not only the consideration of others but he frequently compares himself with others . . . and in proportion as he exults when he perceives that he has more of it than they, he feels a keener affliction when he sees that one or more of them are more respected than himself." Adams's mix of fraternal membership and hierarchical status aptly described Freemasonry. Benjamin Franklin wrote of his fellow Masons, "They speak a universal language and act as a passport to the attention and support of the initiated in all parts of the world. . . . They have made men of the most hostile feelings and most distant religions and most diversified conditions rush to the aid of each other and feel social joy and satisfaction that they have been able to afford relief to a brother Mason." Freemasonry coupled international fraternal equality to a complex ranking system that challenged members to demonstrate manhood and earn elevated status by performing prescribed deeds and secret rituals. All Masons were brethren but some, like George Washington, demonstrated exceptional merit and earned elevated status.[52]

Freemasonry opened its meritocracy to most white men. Mary Ann Clawson suggests that it helped to "deny the significance of class difference" by creating a "kin-like bond" among members and leaders. Masonic lodges were quite popular among veteran soldiers and officers, providing them an opportunity to perpetuate martial fraternities and hierarchies in peacetime. DeWitt Clinton claimed that Freemasonry procreated an "artificial consanguinity" that operated with "as much force and effect as the natural relationship of blood." The ideal Mason was an extended family man who would sacrifice individual interest and even family aggrandizement to promote fraternal good. His willingness to cooperate with a fellow Mason rather than compete against him in the marketplace helped "moderate the excesses of the emerging capitalist system." Gordon Wood concludes, "Freemasonry . . . repudiated the monarchical hierarchy of family and favoritism and created a new hierarchical order that rested on 'real worth and personal merit' along with 'brotherly affection and sincerity.'"[53]

Two of the most controversial fraternities of the founding era were the Society of the Cincinnati founded in the 1780s and the Democratic Societies that proliferated in the 1790s. The Cincinnati was an exclusive "society of friends." Membership was limited to former officers and inheritable by their oldest sons. Its ideology was that postrevolutionary America was threatened by disorder in the ranks of men and Cincinnati members were responsible for fostering "liberty without anarchy." General Henry Knox believed the Cincinnati was "the only bar to lawless ambition and dreadful anarchy." Members played key roles in quelling Shays's Rebellion, promoting the U.S. Constitution, and sustaining the memory of "immortals." One manifestation of their immortalizing mission was the practice of naming their sons after war heroes, as in George Washington Cobb, Horatio Gates Cook, William Augustus Steuben North, Henry Knox Hall, Rufus Putnam Stone, and Alexander Hamilton Gibbs.[54]

Critics condemned the Cincinnati as an aristocratic, factional organization. Benjamin Franklin and Mercy Otis Warren argued that members were infected by an envy for monarchy and aristocracy during their association with Washington's European officer corps. Jefferson described members as "monocrats" and suggested that the Society was "carving out for itself hereditary distinctions, hovering over our Constitution eternally, meeting together in all parts of the Union, periodically with closed doors, accumulating capital in their separate treasury, corresponding secretly and regularly . . . to suppress the friends of general freedom." If Jefferson saw the Cincinnati as an elitist secret society, William Manning portrayed the Cincinnati as a self-conscious power elite conspiring to rule the "swinish multitude."[55] Critics focused on its exclusiveness, hereditary membership policy, questionable intentions, and destructive effects.

By contrast, Jefferson praised the Democratic Societies as champions of men's rights and "the republican principles of our Constitution." These fraternities opposed "the chains of customs and outworn creeds" to support policies aimed at greater equality, penal reform, public education, women's rights, and antislavery and democratic politics. Henry May suggests that the Democratic Societies generally "stopped short of advocating any sweeping changes in existing institutions in the American republic." Their primary purpose was to encourage "the vigilance of the people" in order to preserve and protect liberty. Manning proposed a continental version of the Democratic Societies in his plan to create a national "Society of the Many" that would apply the Cincinnati's organizational acumen for democratic ends. He wrote, "If the Many were one-quarter part so well organized as the order of Cincinnati . . . , they would always carry their points in elections—being in numbers so vastly superior." Once organized and empowered, the common people would have little cause to promote social and political disorder.[56]

David Osgood and others saw the Democratic Societies as groups of men whose passions were inflamed "to a degree of fury" by "demagogues well skilled in the business of faction." Noah Webster excoriated these "self-created" societies for lawless violence and belittled their members for sacrificing "independence of mind" to become "dupes of other men." Alexander Hamilton called the Democratic Societies the "Grecian horse to a republic"; they praised liberty but practiced licentiousness. Washington thought they were "instituted by artful and designing" schemers "to impede the measures of government" and "destroy the confidence which is necessary for the people to place . . . in their public servants."[57] The critics emphasized members' unmanly slavishness, leaders' licentious demagoguery, and the groups' divisive impact on society.

If fraternalism promised male solidarity and order, actual fraternities as well as emerging political parties seemed to produce factional conflicts and fratricidal tendencies. That was why President Washington argued that Americans should submerge their petty differences and identify with the one national brotherhood borne of constitutional government. He used the same reasoning to convince Secretaries Hamilton and Jefferson to set aside their differences for the greater good of the administration, government, and nation. A few years later, President Jefferson was the one seeking to counteract men's fraternal prejudices, party factionalism, and fratricidal tendencies by reminding American men that they were all "brethren of the same principles."[58]

One National Brotherhood

On one plane of analysis, most founders could imagine that the stigmatized but redeemable Bachelor, the meritorious but parochial Family Man, and the reputable but ambitious Better Sort of man provided a manly foundation for a unified, orderly, stable republic. Brutish men would be restrained and reformed. Responsible fathers would provision and protect families, govern women, and perform the basic functions of citizenship. Many men would aspire to leadership, but only the trustworthy few would be empowered to serve as leaders and lawmakers. Consensual norms of manhood would bind American citizens and their leaders into one national brotherhood.

James Madison suggested that the gap between ordinary men and their leaders might be narrowed in time. The Family Man was likely to become less parochial and more cosmopolitan when participating in elections. His views would be refined and enlarged "by passing them through the medium of a chosen body of citizens whose wisdom may best discern the true interest of their country and whose patriotism and love of justice will be least likely to sacrifice it to temporary or partial considerations." A more sophisticated citizenry would be less apt to be deceived by demagogues and more likely to elect to public office men of real worth. Gradually, voters would develop a "manly confidence" in public officials who were from the people but "particularly distinguished" among them as contributors to the "dearest interests of the country." Relatedly, Edmund Randolph suggested that consent of the governed registered through a national electoral process would encourage a sense of "fellow-feeling" between the farmers who comprised the bulk of the citizenry and the lawmakers chosen "by and from the people" to represent them.[59]

Madison argued that men's sense of fellow feeling would be reinforced by constitutional guarantees that leaders could "make no law which will not have its full operation on themselves and their friends as well as on the great mass of society." He called this one of "the strongest bonds by which human policy can connect the rulers and people together." Alexander Hamilton heartily agreed. The principle that legislators and citizens were obliged to obey the same laws sounded "true and . . . strong chords of sympathy between the representative and the constituent." In addition, Hamilton believed that national fraternal bonds would be fortified by ties of "common interest" that urged manufacturers and mechanics to view the merchant as "their natural patron and friend," landholders to recognize a shared "natural interest" against excessive taxation, and members of the learned professions to gain the confidence of all classes. Ultimately, common interest would be "the surest bond of sympathy" between voters and an elected government staffed by "landholders, merchants, and men of the learned professions."[60]

On another plane of analysis, however, most founders doubted that fraternal unity between citizens and leaders was sufficient to ensure enduring order in the ranks of men and lasting stability for the Republic. A strong bond between the Family Man and the Better Sort may have provided a sufficient foundation for republican government in ordinary times. But most founders were convinced that they lived in extraordinary times. They daily encountered uncertainties, exigencies, emergencies, and crises that aroused citizens' furious passions; and they beheld unprecedented opportunities to guide, shape, and improve a future that demanded more wisdom and virtue than even reputable leaders and lawmakers could muster. Needed in extraordinary times were a few heroic men who could neutralize the people's unruly passions and inspire public support for innovative measures that promised a better future for America and all posterity.

Writing as "Solon, Junior," David Howell suggested that the destiny of the Republic ultimately depended on the actions of a few extraordinary men. How did America win the Revolution? Howell answered, "During the war and while that was the rage of the day, was not an act passed putting every freeman in the state under martial law to be inflicted by a general over whom even the Legislature had no control? Yet the people bore it—and those who complained of it being unconstitutional were answered that the safety of the people is the highest law." Great generals who stood above positive law led the Revolution and most patriots followed them. Now, what were the prospects for the new U.S. Constitution? Howell argued, "Whatever the new federal Constitution is in itself, its administration is all that can ever affect the people."[61] Howell's insight and the founders' sacred truth was that the future of the Republic depended not simply on citizen consent to worthy lawmakers and laws but also on citizen compliance with the great authority and extralegal prerogative of a few heroic men.

6

The Heroic Man and National Destiny

The founders agreed that "law ought to be king." The problem was that law was a blunt instrument for resisting men's democratic passions, reforming their morals and manners, and maintaining order among them as well as for resolving national crises and realizing historic opportunities. Law was slow, cumbersome, and rigid, but the times that tried men's souls demanded quick thinking and creative action. Law reflected "an excess of popularity" rather than excellence in manly virtue and vision. Law mirrored the prejudices of "pygmies" who lacked the "candor and unbiased minds as becomes men," not the integrity and charisma of "giants" who sought political "manhood" by "rigorous measures," regarded "the public good more than their own humor," and established hegemony to procreate a republic of men. Unfortunately, giants were rare. George Washington repeatedly asked, "Where are our men of abilities?"[1]

The founders saw everyday politics as a matter of restraining and reforming the Bachelor, trusting the Family Man with citizenship, and entrusting leadership and lawmaking to the Better Sort; but they also felt the Republic needed truly exceptional men to lead the nation to its destiny. They sought to identify and empower the Heroic Man and thereby reinforced the contested ideal of the traditional patriarch. The Heroic Man was a national father figure who required manly independence and patriarchal discretion to defy law and resist public opinion without forsaking popular consent. Women too could be heroic, but only in a secondary sense. Judith Sargent Murray thought women's "heroism cannot be surpassed" and Thomas Paine wanted "some Jersey maid" to emulate Joan of Arc to "spirit up her countrymen"; but Murray's women mostly succored male warriors and Paine's maid shamed recalcitrant men into combat. These heroines were what Teresa Brennan and Carole Pateman refer to as "auxiliaries to the commonwealth." Ultimately, the founders' faith in the Heroic Man completed their grammar of manhood by promoting a patriarchal discourse that lifted up a few great men over the democratic masses and played down women's political potential as citizens and leaders.[2]

A Few Great Men

The founders consistently described their immediate circumstances in the idiom of crisis, contingency, emergency, exigency, expediency, fortune, and necessity. The urgency of their terminology informed their belief that the extraordinary threats, challenges, and opportunities of their times beckoned a few great men to step forward; assume positions of leadership, authority, and power; and preside over the course of national affairs. The ubiquitous rhetoric of liberty and equality continued to cast suspicion on concentrated power but, most founders believed, the initiative and influence of some heroic men were essential for achieving America's destiny as a model republic and world-class nation.

American intellectuals drew ideals of political heroism from thinkers ranging from Plato to Plutarch but especially from Lord Bolingbroke's *The Idea of a Patriot King*. A Patriot King was a majestic leader who governed "like the common father" whose "true image of a free people" was "a patriarchal family." He had a "love of liberty," and he defended and extended liberty to his national family. He displayed affection toward citizens and exhibited clemency by reforming rather than exacting retribution from his "rebellious children." Importantly, he epitomized manhood. He acted with "decency and grace," refused flattery and resisted factionalism, practiced manly virtues, and avoided vices "unworthy of men," such as the libertinism and adultery associated with Alexander the Great, Julius Caesar, and Augustus Caesar. His manly efforts earned him a "true popularity" that enabled him to rule on the basis of widespread consent, ensuring that he would be "reverenced and obeyed" in life and accorded "fame after death."[3]

Prior to the Revolution, Americans called on George III to play the part of a Patriot King who protected colonial liberty against corrupt officials. Initially, colonial writers approved of royal and parliamentary prerogative, even as they protested particular laws and policies. "On some emergencies," wrote Daniel Dulany, "the King . . . hath an absolute power to provide for the safety of the state . . . like a Roman dictator." Thomas Fitch added that "reasons of state" and "necessity" legitimized Parliament's authority to be "supreme director over all His Majesty's dominions." Americans mostly assumed the legitimacy of political prerogative but pleaded with both king and Parliament to exercise it on their behalf. When Parliament continued to enact controversial measures, colonists looked to the king to rein in Parliament. Even after blood was shed at Lexington and Concord, members of the Continental Congress professed to be King George's "loyal and dutiful subjects . . . still ready with our lives and fortunes to defend his person, crown, and dignity" when he asserted his prerogative against "his evil ministry."[4]

Simultaneously, Americans questioned whether English rulers exercised their powers properly and effectively. Did they make laws and exercise discretion to achieve the good of the empire or the good of England at the expense of the colonies? Were they proximate enough to the colonies to understand and resolve local crises? Americans protested abuses of prerogative and invoked local crises to justify colonial authority. Richard Bland and Oxenbridge Thatcher claimed that "sudden emergencies" in the colonies justified the transfer of British authority to American officials who were more intimately acquainted with the colonial landscape and better positioned to act with dispatch. When Parliament rejected these claims, Americans called on "necessity" to legitimize illegal protests. Mercy Otis Warren spoke of "laws of self-preservation" to justify a Boston Tea Party that otherwise was an unwarranted "attack upon private property," and David Ramsay called on "the great law of self-preservation" to support "the destruction of the tea." The founders regularly invoked exigency to legitimize patriot prerogative to break existing laws in the cause of defending liberty.[5]

By 1776, Americans denounced kingship, royal prerogative, and executive authority as tyrannical but, as Ralph Ketcham observes, "The cloud that descended over executive power . . . did not entirely obscure the practices and tradition of active leadership that had been both dominant and admired in the more than 150 years since the founding of the first colonies." George Washington promoted active leadership. He argued that military and civilian leaders had a duty to exercise "extensive powers" in difficult times. Accordingly, he reminded Joseph Reed that Pennsylvania had vested him with martial-law authority "to take such measures as the exigency may demand." He enjoined Reed "to exert the powers entrusted to you with a boldness and vigor suited to the emergency" and assured him that "the popular mind" was prepared to comply by making "sacrifices both of ease and property."[6] In a republic, powerful leadership was justifiable and desirable on the basis of exigency and anticipated public support.

Claims of exigency often elicited public support. A declared crisis aroused public anxiety and encouraged men to seek strong leaders to resolve the crisis and reduce their anxiety. The public's demand for great leadership invited ambitious men to prove themselves heroes by displaying the virtuous manhood needed to master fortune and make history. Katherine Auspitz reminds us that the Latin root of *virtue* is *vir*, which connotes "manliness or prowess." The Heroic Man exhibited manly prowess. He disciplined his passions and interests "to take events into his own hands and shape them according to his own will." Often, he sacrificed personal pleasure, family prosperity, and social respectability to protect liberty and secure order against "the flux, wildness, and frenzy of fortune." Alexander Hamilton exhibited manly prowess by refusing to make "an unmanly surrender" to love. He left his new wife at home so he could follow the path of public service. Nathanael Greene's military victory at Eutaw Springs also exemplified manly prowess. Washington wrote to him, "Fortune must have been coy indeed had she not yielded at last to so persevering a pursuer as you have been. I hope now that she is yours she will change her appellation of fickle to that of constant." The Heroic Man's prowess required his separation from women and his conquest of the disorderly female forces affiliated with fortune.[7]

Earning public respect was one thing; ensuring public obedience was another. The founders distrusted powerful men. They led a rebellion against a king, kingship, and consolidated authority; they framed state constitutions that limited executive authority and a U.S. Constitution that fragmented political power. They cultivated what Joyce Appleby calls "a culture of constitutionalism" that endorsed the "voluntary sphere of action" but limited the public sphere.[8] Still, the founders often repressed their impulse to limit political authority. They suspended skepticism of powerful leaders whenever a crisis called forth the Heroic Man to save the nation and secure its destiny. Most notably, their distrust melted away each time that Washington agreed to assume the helm of public affairs. He was widely perceived as a man among men, a hero who avoided corruption and performed great service because, like Moses, he was inspired by God and chosen by acclaim. Washington surveyed "the road which providence has pointed us to so plainly" and led voluntary legions of American men into the republican future.[9]

The Heroic Man had a complex relationship to law. John Adams saw him as a patriot who sought to establish "a government of laws and not of men" but also as a leader who knew that the way to secure a government of laws was "to depute power from the many to a few of the most wise and good." The road to impersonal politics was paved by a few heroic personalities. Thomas Jefferson agreed. A great leader supported the rule of law but recognized that exigencies and opportunities might demand extralegal initiatives: "A strict observance of the laws is doubtless one of the high duties . . . but it is not the highest." The Heroic Man had to ignore law and risk infamy "on great occasions when the safety of the nation or some of its very highest interests are at stake." Jefferson took that risk to acquire the Louisiana Territory. He acted "beyond the Constitution" out of a sense of paternal duty. It was "the case of a guardian investing the money of his ward in purchasing an important adjacent territory and saying to him when of age, I did this for your good; I pretend no right to bind you; you may disavow me and I must get out of the scrape as I can; I thought it my duty to risk myself for you." Jefferson hoped to open up farmland for family men and to secure the Mississippi Valley with "our own brethren and children" rather than "strangers of another family." He was convinced that his actions would "confirm and not weaken the Constitution" by promoting the public good and winning men's eventual consent.[10]

Most founders felt that the elevation of great leaders above legitimate laws during moments of crisis and opportunity promised multiple payoffs. First, the Heroic Man exhibited what R. W. Connell calls "the public face of hegemonic masculinity." He modeled independent manhood.[11] His public exhibition of manly prowess heightened other men's awareness of their own masculine shortcomings and encouraged them to strive for male maturity. His manly language and masterful deeds provided criteria by which most men could measure, judge, and rate one another. His public persona as a self-disciplined man who transcended personal prejudices, parochial loyalties, and factional politics fostered a sense of fraternal solidarity and national pride that bound men together. One truly exceptional man could be crucial for curbing male licentiousness, ordering the ranks of men, and encouraging fraternal harmony.

Second, the founders' faith in the Heroic Man who wielded extensive powers during difficult times reinforced traditional patriarchalism. Continuing a line of thought running from Plato through Bacon and Machiavelli to the present, the founders perpetuated the idea that a great leader separated himself from women and conquered antagonistic female forces. He kept women at a distance to avoid distraction, temptation, and seduction from public duty. That explained why General Howe was no great leader. Thomas Paine scorned Howe for capturing Philadelphia only to hide "among women and children" in the city rather than pursue a dispirited American army across the countryside. A manly leader left women behind; then he took the initiative to conquer effeminate vices and fickle fortune. For instance, President Washington made "manly" overtures to strengthen U.S. relations with Great Britain by issuing an extralegal Proclamation of Neutrality and by pursuing treaty options with the Crown when America's alliance with France was unsettled by the

French Revolution. Alexander Hamilton denounced Washington's critics for harboring a "womanish attachment to France."[12] The Heroic Man was a patriarch who exercised authority in opposition to women and womanhood.

Third, a few exceptional men acting in concert could procreate a new nation for posterity. The framers of the Constitution saw themselves as fertile men (demigods) who resolved a national crisis by bringing forth a new republic. They did not dwell on mundane matters of due process and lawful conduct. Edmund Randolph explained, "There are certainly seasons of a peculiar nature where ordinary cautions must be dispensed with, and this is certainly one of them." Washington agreed. Anticipating the Constitutional Convention, he admitted that it "may not be legal" and even suggested that Congress give it legal coloring "without proceeding to a definition of the powers." After the convention, Washington predicted that the "transient circumstances and fugitive performances which attended this crisis" would be forgotten, while the noble principles that informed the Constitution would merit "the notice of posterity."[13] In the interim, federalists had to legitimize the planning process and plans for a new national republic.

Federalists used the language of crisis to justify their role as heroic leaders who ended one government and originated another. John Jay explained:

> They who have turned their attention to the affairs of men must have perceived that there are tides in them, tides very irregular in their duration and seldom found to run twice exactly in the same manner or measure. To discern and to profit by these tides in national affairs is the business of those who preside over them, and they that have had much experience on this head inform us that there frequently are occasions when days, nay, even when hours, are precious. . . . As in the field, so in the cabinet, there are moments to be seized as they pass, and they who preside in either should be left in capacity to improve them.[14]

Jay argued that great leaders with significant powers and public support were needed to seize the moment to avert catastrophes and realize possibilities. Madison and Hamilton applied Jay's reasoning to the convention and the Constitution.

Madison indicated that a national crisis forced convention delegates to disregard their charge to revise the Articles of Confederation and obligated them to reinvent national government. "If they had exceeded their powers," he wrote, "they were not only warranted but required by the circumstances in which they were placed to exercise the liberty which they assumed." Moreover, even "if they had violated both their powers and obligations in proposing a Constitution," their decision was legitimate because it was "calculated to accomplish the views and happiness of the people of America." Madison did not intend to suggest that all leadership initiatives focused on public happiness were justified. Rather, he suggested that extralegal initiatives were warranted when great men confronted "the absolute necessity" of defending "the great principle of self-preservation" by making "great changes of established governments." In 1776, America had been blessed with heroic leaders who instituted momentous changes "by some informal and unauthorized propositions," with "no ill-timed scruples, no zeal for adhering to ordinary forms." Again in 1787, Madison argued, America was blessed with heroic men who formulated innovative changes in national government.[15]

Hamilton agreed that convention delegates were obliged to exercise prerogative "to provide for the exigencies of the Union" and secure "the happiness of the country." His enduring concern was to ensure that the leaders of the new government would be sufficiently powerful to provide for all exigencies because "too little power is as dangerous as too much, that it leads to anarchy, and from anarchy to despotism." Hamilton searched the Constitution's words (e.g., "necessary and proper") and concepts (e.g., "implied powers") to support an interpretation that provided national leaders with enough authority to address "necessities of society," which took precedence over "rules and maxims." Necessities included "existing exigencies" and "probable exigencies of the ages." Hamilton proposed that Americans empower their leaders "to provide for future contingencies as they may happen" rather than "fettering the government with restrictions that cannot be observed." And because future contingencies were "illimitable," leaders' capacity to address them had to be illimitable too.[16]

Madison was more ambivalent about concentrated power but, like Hamilton, he did not want to fetter government officials with "constitutional barriers to the impulse of self-preservation." He believed that great public leaders ought to have ample authority to "maintain a disciplined army" against potential enemies and to resist men's "temporary errors and delusions" in order to blend "stability with liberty" and ensure domestic harmony and national security. Hamilton hoped that leaders' ample authority would grow through informal means. The Heroic Man could accrue considerable influence by voicing words and performing deeds that captured "the esteem and good-will" of citizens. A leader with a memorable track record positioned himself to "hazard with safety" unpopular actions "in proportion to the proofs he had given of his wisdom and integrity, and . . . the respect and attachment of his fellow-citizens." He could accumulate surplus legitimacy and oppose public opinion without provoking mass disobedience.[17]

Antifederalists warned Americans against so-called heroic leaders. They alerted the public to the "danger to be apprehended from vesting discretionary powers in the hands of man" and encouraged citizens "to regulate the discretion of rulers." However, as Michael Lienesch suggests, antifederalists also "admitted the power of fortune in public affairs" and recognized the advantages of prerogative for the public good. Patrick Henry was quite willing to prescribe a strong dose of extralegal justice for one Josiah Philips,

> a fugitive murderer and an outlaw—a man who commanded an infamous banditti. . . . He committed the most cruel and shocking barbarities. He was an enemy to the human name. Those who declare war against the human race may be struck out of existence as soon as they are apprehended. He was not executed according to those beautiful legal ceremonies which are pointed out by the laws in criminal cases. The enormity of his crimes did not entitle him to it. I am truly a friend to legal forms and methods; but, Sir, the occasion warranted the measure. A pirate, an outlaw, or a common enemy to all mankind may be put to death. It is justified by the laws of nature and nations.[18]

For Henry, as for Hamilton, the Heroic Man respected law but recognized occasions when it was necessary to demonstrate manly "ability and faithfulness" by subordinating law to the more "weighty concerns of the state."[19]

Patriarchal Hegemony

Several scholars identify an "erosion of patriarchal authority," an "antipatriarchal revolt," and a "revolution against patriarchal authority" in late-eighteenth-century America. Fathers lost authority over sons; gentlemen were scorned by commoners; and hereditary kingship was replaced by contractual politics. "Almost at a stroke," writes Gordon Wood, "the Revolution destroyed all the earlier talk of paternal . . . government." Wood's judgment is premature. Just as the contested image of the traditional patriarch continued into the founding era, the image of the Heroic Man as a "common father" of a "patriarchal family" persisted in Jefferson's justification of the Louisiana Purchase as a paternal duty and, more generally, in the founders' belief that great leaders established hegemony by reconciling patriarchal authority and republican consent.[20]

The founding era was filled with the language of political fatherhood. In 1774, Gad Hitchcock addressed public officials as "honored fathers" and "civic fathers." In 1778, Phillips Payson referred to American leaders as "civil fathers." In 1780, Samuel Cooper described the framers of the Articles of Confederation as "fathers of their country" filled with "parental tenderness." In 1784, Samuel McClintock honored New Hampshire's framers as "fathers of their country," "fathers and guardians of their people," and "fathers, guides, and guardians." In 1788, Samuel Langdon called public leaders "fathers of a large family." In 1791, Israel Evans told the nation's political "fathers" that citizens would "be their political children as long as they are good parents." In 1792, Timothy Stone enjoined officials to be "civil fathers" who treated citizens with the "tender care of natural parents." In 1794, Judith Sargent Murray asserted that men wanted "the protecting hand of a guardian power" and gave their guardian "the august title—The Father of his Country." In 1795, Peres Fobes noted that "a ruler is the father of his country" and that slandering him was "parricide." In 1804, Samuel Kendal called on Massachusetts's "venerable fathers" to care for the people.[21] Patriarchal expressions of political leadership were commonplace for decades after the Revolution.

Federalists often used patriarchal language to reduce men's fears that ratification of the U.S. Constitution would invite despotic leadership. Early in the debates, for example, James Wilson trumpeted the prospect that the new president would be not a tyrant but a father figure to "watch over the whole with paternal care and affection." Madison, Hamilton, and other federalists felt fortunate that the nation's greatest father figure, George Washington, was likely to become the Republic's first president. Ministers, writers, and citizens considered Washington "the father of the country." Zephaniah Swift Moore called him "our political father," and Alexander Addison addressed him as "the great father of his country." Annis Boudinot Stockton even described him in regal terms. Americans ratified a new Constitution "When lo! HIMSELF, the CHIEF rever'd, / In native elegance appear'd, / And all things smil'd around / Adorn'd with every pleasant art, / Enthron'd the Sov'reign of each heart, / I saw the HERO crown'd." Noah Webster praised President Washington's patriarchal ability to inspire filial loyalty:

> The long and eminent services of our worthy President have filled all hearts with gratitude and respect; and by means of this gratitude and respect and the confidence they have inspired in his talents and integrity, he has a greater influence in America than any nobleman, perhaps than any prince in Europe. This respect has hitherto restrained the violence of parties. . . . This is the effect of his personal influence and not a respect for the laws or Constitution of the United States. *Americans rally round the man*, rather than round the executive authority of the union.[22]

Six years later, Henry Holcombe eulogized Washington as a manly leader who "ruled his appetites and passions in scenes of the greatest trial and temptation" to serve as "the father, friend, benefactor, and bulwark of his country."[23] Washington epitomized the Heroic Man—a national father figure whose manly prowess and procreative abilities animated citizens' confidence, consent, and compliance.

Washington was unique. Many founders worried that other potentially great leaders had difficulty establishing hegemony. After all, public censure was "the unfailing lot of an elevated station" and public envy was "the tax of eminence." The Heroic Man who earned high public standing was vulnerable to charges of aristocracy. His motives and values were subject to public skepticism and trivializing opposition. His words and deeds were apt to be misinterpreted and used against him. Misunderstanding between heroic leaders and common citizens was predictable because great and ordinary men were divided by vast differences. A towering intellect such as James Madison relied on insights beyond the comprehension of the average man who, for example, could not understand how "inconstancy" could be a virtue for Madison (who opposed and then proposed a Bill of Rights) but a vice for others. Great leaders were not bound by the foolish consistency that hobgobbled little minds. However, they were obliged to legitimize their authority by soliciting the consent of uncomprehending citizens.[24]

A key function of the grammar of manhood was to employ patriarchal language to transform threatening images of tyrannical leaders into friendly portraits of familiar father figures. Most Americans presumed that a father was devoted to his family. He was responsible, settled, and trustworthy. The founders used patriarchal language to convey a parallel presumption that a "civic father" was devoted to his political family and was equally likely to be responsible, settled, and trustworthy. American writers regularly used family fatherhood as a foundation for discussing public leadership. For example, Samuel Langdon drew lessons from patriarchal family life as a basis for instructing New Hampshire's "much honored fathers" in public affairs: "Without constant care of your families, you will have bad servants, and your estates will be wasted. So [you] must pay constant attention to the great family . . . to be a free and happy people."[25] Patriarchal language signified that leaders were caring men who merited public obedience.

Patriarchal language also suggested that obedience to heroic leaders was consistent with manhood and citizenship. American men were accustomed to paternal authority. They honored ancestral fathers and expected sons to honor them. As such, political leaders who successfully presented themselves as civic fathers could elicit considerable citizen deference. Although images of civic father figures put common citizens in the symbolic role of children, Reid Mitchell points out that "at least they do not make them sound like slaves or an inferior class or the dregs of society." Generally, American men still associated paternal rule with "benign authority." An adult son could honor his biological father with obedience without sacrificing his sense of independence; similarly, a citizen could honor a political father by obeying him without feeling he had sacrificed manly liberty. Meanwhile, patriarchal language made dissent more daunting. It was one thing to oppose a tyrant but quite another to turn against a loving father. As Mitchell puts it, "The parental metaphor made rebellion a primal sin."[26]

Patriarchal language had the additional advantage of stability. When George III failed to act as a Patriot King, colonists finally denounced him as a bad ruler and condemned kingship as a tyrannical institution. The terms of republican discourse changed suddenly, and only highly educated men could fully appreciate the dramatic reconceptualization of citizenship and leadership. By contrast, the terms of patriarchal discourse barely changed. Mary Beth Norton argues that they survived as elements of "a metaphorical language" that identified the norms of fatherhood as legitimate criteria for leadership. For example, "Philanthrop" explained that fears of corruption by "the head of the family" did not eliminate the institution of marriage; by analogy, fears of corruption by leaders "selected to preside at the helm of [public] affairs" should not eliminate leadership authority. A few bad fathers did not destroy fatherhood; a few bad leaders should not end assertive leadership. Extending this logic, John Smalley criticized corrupt patriarchs but supported strong patriarchal leaders. He denounced "libertine" males who acted in office like immature "children" by failing to hold the reins of government "with sufficient force" or "discretion." He advocated replacing them with powerful father figures who would use sufficient force to secure public order.[27]

Most founders positively celebrated the conjuncture of fatherhood and politics when they applauded ancestral fathers for pioneering the continent, celebrated colonial fathers for spearheading protests against Great Britain, commemorated revolutionary fathers for achieving independence, and honored civic fathers for procreating new states and a new nation. At times, their profuse praise for their political fathers was a prelude to expressing present fears that the age of patriarchal heroes was past and, henceforth, Americans were doomed to suffer mediocre leadership. "Where are our fathers?" cried Stanley Griswold. "Where are our former men of dignity . . . who in their day appeared like men?" Could America "bring forward another band of sages" when, alas, American males seemed to be "more disposed to act like children than men"?[28]

Many founders dwelled on the "abundance of rubbish" that constituted contemporary manhood and political officialdom; but most agreed with Abigail Adams that there was still some "sterling metal in the political crucible." John Tucker applauded manly individuals who with "great resolution and firmness" distinguished themselves by their ability "to maintain a calmness of mind and to guide with a steady hand in tempestuous seasons." Gad Hitchcock praised men who demonstrated the ability "to lead and advise [the public] in the more boisterous and alarming as well as in calm and temperate seasons." John Jay thought that the Heroic Man usually emerged from among those "highly distinguished by their patriotism, virtue, and wisdom in times which tried the minds and hearts of men." And James Madison certainly expected that, under the Constitution, "the purest and noblest characters" would arise to confront the nation's crises and restore peace, dignity, and prosperity to America.[29] Adversity not only demanded great leaders and justified powerful ones; it also called forth, tested, and identified the Heroic Man who measured up to the highest standards of manhood.

The standards were diffuse but known. They included preeminence in "ability and virtue" along with disciplined passion, family responsibility, and social civility. John Adams emphasized "exemplary morals, great patience, calmness, coolness, and attention," while Elizur Goodrich highlighted "knowledge, wisdom, and prudence, courage and unshaken resolution, righteousness and justice tempered with lenity, mercy, and compassion, and a steady firmness . . . and a sacred regard to the moral and religious interests of the community." Whatever the particular mix of virtues, the founders felt that great leaders made themselves known by their powerful and positive impact on ordinary men. Zephaniah Swift Moore suggested that great leaders were men of "character and example" who had considerable "influence in forming the public mind." Zabdiel Adams asserted that great leaders exhibited "exemplary conduct" and "contagious" manners, providing a "shining example" to improve men's conduct and support public order.[30]

Ultimately, the Heroic Man distinguished himself from the Family Man and the Better Sort by transcending intergenerational time and parochial space. He honored the ancestral past but acted in the present to fulfill his calling to produce a memorable legacy for the future. He was exquisitely selfless and supremely public-spirited. He also claimed an extraordinary degree of manly liberty to follow conscience and maintain "integrity" by demonstrating "fortitude" and "resolution" against "unprincipled" foes who slandered him with "unmanly but unavailing calumny." He asserted his right to vindicate "the dignity of men" by acting with a higher regard for the public good than for his own family and friends. He could act against both malicious enemies and misguided friends because he sought neither leadership status nor public acclaim. Like Washington, he preferred home life; like Franklin, he accepted the burdens of leadership solely to enlarge his capacity for "doing good"; and like history's most memorable heroes, he risked fortune, fame, and immortality to procreate a better future for humankind.[31]

Madison wrote, "The aim of every political constitution is, or ought to be, first to obtain for rulers men who possess the most wisdom to discern, and the most virtue to pursue, the common good of society; and in the next place, to take the most effectual precautions for keeping them virtuous whilst they continue to hold their public trust." Many founders were far more interested in legitimizing and empowering manly leaders than in instituting precautionary measures. They were convinced that the Heroic Man was best qualified to pursue the public good while attracting the trust and consent of sober citizens. Most certainly, he should be applauded rather than rotated out of office. John Adams opposed mandatory rotation schemes because "the ablest men in the nation are rooted out" and people were "deprived . . . of the service of their best men and . . . obliged to confer their suffrages on the next best until the rotation brings them to the worst." Robert Livingston called mandatory rotation "an absurd species of ostracism—a mode of proscribing eminent merit and banishing from stations of trust those who have filled them with the greatest faithfulness."[32] The Heroic Man was a huge asset. A republic treasured his presence rather than squandered his talents.

Most founders also opposed mandatory instruction schemes that invited the mediocre masses to bind talented, virtuous leaders. Noah Webster despised such schemes for fostering a "spirit of exalting the *people* over the . . . magistrate" and miscasting leaders in the role of "*servants of the people.*" Instruction schemes tended "to degrade all authority, to bring the laws and the officers of government into contempt, and to encourage discontent, faction, and insurrection." They "unmanned" leaders by denying them conscience, integrity, and choice. Washington asserted that a public official who ignored his own convictions to follow public instructions was more slave than man: "What figure . . . must a delegate make who comes there with his hands tied and his judgment forestalled?"[33] Joel Barlow urged leaders to ignore flawed instructions: "When the delegate receives instructions which prove to be contrary to the opinion which he afterwards forms, he ought to presume that his constituents . . . are not well informed on the subject and his duty is to vote according to his conscience." Roger Sherman added that a leader was "bound by every principle of justice" to elevate conscience over instructions.[34] The founders subscribed to an informal creed which asserted that the Heroic Man had a paternal duty to reject errant public opinion for the public's own good.

Could a leader reject public opinion and still attract the consent of the governed? A great leader could. When Madison asserted that a leader was not "bound to sacrifice his own opinion," he implied that the Heroic Man was revered less for his brilliant reasoning and astute decision making than for his exceptional manhood. He epitomized the consensual norm of manly independence by exhibiting self-discipline, courage, fortitude, candor, and integrity in the midst of adversity. Most citizens would honor such noble displays of manhood with deference, even if they disputed resulting decisions. Jeremiah Wadsworth reported instances when leaders "disregarded their instructions and have been re-elected." Conversely, a leader who chained himself to public opinion was apt to be scorned as unmanly, even though his decisions reflected public opinion. Here, Wadsworth cited instances when "representatives following instructions contrary to their private sentiments . . . have ever been despised for it."[35] In part, the Heroic Man's hegemony was based on his ability to exemplify ideals of manly independence and insulate himself against charges of effeminacy, slavishness, and childishness.

Manhood above Public Opinion and Law

Most founders agreed that the Heroic Man needed extraordinary freedom to guide America to its destiny. He had to be able to forgo popularity and ignore legality, for example, when confronting the crisis that called forth the Constitutional Convention in 1787, addressing the problems that prompted the Proclamation of Neutrality in 1793, or investing in the opportunities afforded by the Louisiana Purchase in 1803. The Bachelor was contemptuous of people's values and subordinated to legal restraints; the Family Man and Better Sort hoped to reconcile popular consent and political authority; the Heroic Man stood above public opinion and law to procreate a new order for the ages.

The founding generation distinguished popularity from consent. No worthy man or leader solicited a crude popularity borne of vanity, flattery, and show. Such popularity was foolish, fickle, and fleeting. It was identified with demagoguery and effeminacy. However, every worthy leader sought the consent of the sober Family Man and the reputable Better Sort along with the grateful remembrance of future generations. This enduring consent represented the stable trust and respect of solid citizens and the promise of a positive judgment by posterity. Accordingly, the Heroic Man persevered in "the plain path of duty" and remained "unmoved by noisy opposition, undaunted by popular clamor, undismayed by imminent danger." He refused to sacrifice duty to crude popularity, even though his refusal was likely to generate public envy, enmity, and spite. John Adams felt that he had to fortify himself "with a shield of innocence and honor" to govern against public acrimony. Thomas Jefferson thought himself "a constant but for every shaft of calumny which malice and falsehood could form."[36] Predictably, the Heroic Man suffered the wrath of lesser men.

A leader's heroism partly depended on how he addressed adverse public opinion. First, he should recognize the inevitable conflict between manhood and popularity. Samuel Wales observed that a great leader often had to support "a manly opposition . . . to popular prejudice and vulgar error." John Mitchell Mason added that a courageous leader who engaged "in a manly attempt to avert national ruin" sometimes had to expose a "favorite error" of the public only to excite its "resentment." Alas, "none of [the world's] benefactors have escaped its calumnies and persecutions." Second, a great leader approached the conflict between manhood and popularity as a challenge. For Patrick Henry, the challenge was to demonstrate "manly fortitude" and "manly firmness" against "an erring world." Others defined it in terms of exhibiting manly "integrity" and "intrepidity" against "public execration." The Heroic Man bore the weight of public antagonism; a lesser man collapsed under it and was reduced to "a crouching and fawning disposition [that] takes the place of manliness."[37]

James Madison indicated that a tension between manly leadership and public opinion was endemic to republics. Sometimes, "public opinion must be obeyed by the government" and other times it "may be influenced by the government." Who decided whether public opinion or government guidance took precedence? Ideally, a great leader disseminated republican principles so that the citizenry itself knew when to assert sovereignty and when to defer to leadership. Thus, George Washington sought to secure "the enlightened confidence of the people" by teaching citizens "to know and to value their own rights; to discern and provide against invasions of them; to distinguish between oppression and the necessary exercise of lawful authority; between burdens proceeding from a disregard to their convenience and those resulting from the inevitable exigencies of society; to discriminate the spirit of liberty from that of licentiousness—cherishing the first, avoiding the last; and uniting a speedy but temperate vigilance against encroachments with an inviolable respect to the laws."[38] However, most founders did not count on the "enlightened confidence of the people" because they saw men as more impassioned than enlightened. They relied instead on leaders' prerogative to determine when to heed or lead public opinion, when to obey or overstep the boundaries of law.

The founders took their idea of political prerogative from English forebears. In the late medieval period, English jurists recognized the Crown's prerogative to govern in matters of domestic discord and foreign relations. Henry VIII and Elizabeth expanded the scope of royal prerogative, but Stuart abuses of it culminated in a revolution that established restrictions on it. Whigs promoted liberal and republican theories that criticized abuses of royal prerogative but also retained benign versions of leadership prerogative. Locke's liberalism affirmed an executive's prerogative to act "without the prescription of law, and sometimes even against it" for the good of society. Locke memorialized Elizabeth for employing a proper prerogative to unite "her interest and that of her subjects." Bolingbroke's ideal republic was ruled by a Patriot King who exercised prerogative to "renew the spirit of liberty" among citizens. He too praised Elizabeth for having exercised prerogative to unite "the great body of the people."[39]

Most founders had a relatively benign view of prerogative. They applauded or at least accepted royal prerogative up to the moment of revolution. In 1774, Gad Hitchcock distinguished the abuse of prerogative from its proper use by insisting, "Prerogative itself is not the power to do anything it pleases but a power to do some things for the good of the community." The same year, Thomas Jefferson called on George III to assert prerogative to reestablish "fraternal love and harmony through the whole empire."[40] After the Revolution, some founders raised leadership prerogative to the status of a sacred duty. Edmund Randolph explained at the Constitutional Convention, "When the salvation of the republic is at stake, it would be treason to our trust not to propose what we found necessary." The framers were less prone to debate the legitimacy of prerogative than to discuss its proper application. We often remember Hamilton's monarchical bent but we also should recall Madison's support for a republican version of "kingly prerogative":

> A negative in all cases whatsoever on the legislative acts of the states, as heretofore exercised by kingly prerogative, appears to me to be absolutely necessary and to be the least possible encroachment on the state jurisdictions. Without this defensive power, . . . the states will continue to invade the national jurisdiction, to violate treaties and the law of nations and to harass each other with rival and spiteful measures dictated by mistaken views of interest. Another

> happy effect of this prerogative would be its control on the internal vicissitudes of state policy, and the aggressions of interested majorities on the rights of minorities and of individuals.[41]

Convention delegates replaced Madison's "kingly prerogative" with the Supremacy Clause, but they supported a national government that provided presidents, senators, justices, and military officers great discretionary latitude. Their collective memory was filled with the manly deeds of ancestral fathers and revolutionary leaders inspired by "the spirit of the times" to claim extensive authority to make extraordinary history.[42]

The founders did have a problem with articulating and justifying political prerogative. The language of prerogative, like the language of aristocracy, was discredited by its historical association with British tyranny and corruption. In 1787, Madison could speak positively but controversially about "kingly prerogative." A few years later, he found it wiser to associate "prerogative" with "a monarchical model" and then condemn it. Nonetheless, many Americans continued to communicate the conceptual substance of leadership prerogative by employing the grammar of manhood. For example, Mercy Otis Warren praised American diplomats for maintaining an "independent attitude with manly dignity" when, in 1783, they ignored a lawful congressional directive "to be under the councils of France."[43] Most founders agreed that great leaders needed to exercise manly liberty and wield great discretionary power to govern a republic of disorderly men situated in a dangerous world.

Sustaining Hegemony

The founders invoked crises to legitimize the Heroic Man's prerogative to rule. Did a return to "normalcy" signify that great men should retire from public life, rely on the Better Sort to make and administer law, and trust the Family Man to devote himself to provisioning his wife and children? Or was normalcy a temporary interlude when great leaders prepared for the next crisis? The founders aspired to a state of republican normalcy when a government of laws would free most men to devote themselves to their families and farms. But they saw the world as a dangerous place. Men and women were disorderly creatures and their infant republic was surrounded by hostile powers. Anticipating future crises, the founders generally expected the Heroic Man to sustain hegemony and exercise prerogative for the foreseeable future.

Sustaining hegemony, especially in peacetime, was a complex challenge. Judith Shklar observes that republics "rely on mutual trust between governments and citizens to an unusual degree." This interdependence generates intense suspicions because, "Where there is so much reliance on trust, there must also be frequent betrayals." The result is that republics require "a highly personalized politics" in which leaders constantly reassure citizens that trust in them is warranted. Murray Edelman suggests that leaders often ply the art of personalized politics by manipulating cultural symbols, first to arouse and then to assuage people's anxieties. If there is no immediate crisis, leaders can manufacture a symbolic one to legitimize their power and foster mass quiescence.[44] Well aware of the need to sustain public trust amid fears of betrayal, the founders recognized that leaders had to practice symbolic politics to ensure the enduring consent of the governed.

Alexander Hamilton grasped the fundamentals of symbolic politics. He often summoned the specter of past, present, and future crises to arouse public anxiety and then justified powerful political leadership to assuage it. He used the prospect of "national exigencies" to justify presidents' "great latitude of discretion" in choosing appropriate means to achieve the public good. He suggested that leaders had to be as concerned with "appearances as realities." It was crucial that "government appears to be confident of its own powers" because officials who appeared confident inspired "confidence in others" and positioned themselves to make controversial decisions with minimal dissent. Like Wadsworth, Hamilton believed that manly leaders who acted to save the people "from very fatal consequences of their own mistakes" could "procure lasting monuments of gratitude" by exhibiting "courage and magnanimity enough to serve [the people] at the peril of their displeasure." George Washington also understood symbolic politics. During the Revolution, for example, he tried to bolster patriots' confidence in the war effort by spreading exaggerated public praise for his army's performance and prospects, even though he complained privately to friends, relatives, and Congress that his troops were unreliable and ineffective.[45]

Washington's symbolic politics was assisted by Thomas Paine's alchemical transformation of an American military defeat into a symbolic victory. In 1778, General Howe conquered Philadelphia and Washington's army was riddled with dissension. Paine explained to American readers that Howe "mistook a trap for a conquest." His troops were bogged down in Philadelphia where they were "sleeping away the choicest part of the campaign in expensive luxury." Howe was no manly leader. His character was "unmilitary and passive"; his troop movements were motivated by fear and fickleness; and his military prospects were dim. Indeed, America never had "so fair an opportunity of final success as now." Paine proclaimed, "The death wound is already given. The day is ours if we follow it up. The enemy, by his situation, is within our reach, and by his reduced strength is within our power." Victory was simply a matter of Americans demonstrating their confidence by providing solid support for the Continental army.[46] Paine understood that symbolic politics could have tangible consequences.

The founders' symbolic politics was saturated with images of manhood, family, and friendship conducive to leadership prerogative and citizen consent. Reporting on hurricane relief efforts in the West Indies, a young Hamilton lauded the governor for having "shown himself *the Man*" by issuing strict but humane regulations to relieve public distress. The founders often emphasized aspects of manhood that combined strength with caring and justice with mercy above "weakness" and "connivance." Washington conveyed a sense of strength and caring when reporting to Congress his decision to pardon Whiskey rebels: "Though I shall always think it a sacred duty to exercise with firmness and energy the constitutional powers with which I am vested, yet it appears to me no less consistent with the public good than it is with my personal feelings to mingle in the operations of government every degree of moderation and tenderness."[47] Like a father who mixed discipline and love, the Heroic Man infused authority with tenderness to personalize politics and promote citizen confidence in him.

Family symbolism figured prominently in leaders' efforts to solicit and sustain consent. Defending the Alien and Sedition Acts, John Thayer argued that President Adams's motives were honorable by stating: "This great man can have nothing in view but the happiness and prosperity of his fellow citizens, with whose fortunes his own and those of his family are evidently and inseparably connected." A draft of Washington's first Inaugural Address put a different spin on the leader as Family Man. Washington hoped to convince Americans that his presidency posed no threat to liberty by pointing out that he was a stepfather (as opposed to a biological father) with no dynastic prospects: "Divine providence hath not seen fit that my blood should be transmitted or my name perpetuated by the endearing though sometimes seducing channel of immediate offspring. I have no child for whom I could wish to make a provision—no family to build in greatness upon my country's ruins." Tench Coxe saw republican leadership as a variation on stepfatherhood: "As their sons are not to succeed them, they will not be induced to aim at a perpetuity of their powers at the expense of the liberties of the people."[48] The Heroic Man was both a father figure who could be trusted to seek the good of his public family and a stepfather figure who could be trusted because he was not tempted to transform public power into a dynastic legacy. His blood was invested in the Republic.

The founders used images of family and fraternal trust to outline the appropriate relationship between great leaders and common citizens. Noah Webster ridiculed "the man who, as soon as he has married a woman of unsuspected chastity, locks her up in a dungeon," just as he condemned the practice of voters to elect political leaders only immediately to "arm ourselves against them as against tyrants and robbers." Nathanael Emmons argued for a presumption of mutual confidence among all members of America's political family as a basis for criticizing individuals who "trample on human authority" with their "unruly spirit" or "restless, discontented, seditious spirit," foolishly thinking that they played "a noble, manly, patriotic part" when they actually behaved like little boys by "weakening the hands of rulers and destroying the energy of government." Emmons's message was that "nothing but absolute necessity can justify . . . breaking the bands of society." Ultimately, John Adams insisted, the Heroic Man deserved to be respected by "every manly mind." He was resisted only by children.[49]

The Heroic Man fortified public trust by appearing in public as the citizen's friend. Israel Evans observed that "exalted characters in authority feel themselves connected to the whole community by a brotherly, benevolent attachment." Public expressions of fraternal feeling reassured men that their "lives and estates" were "secure." Great leaders neither flaunted high status nor called attention to the social distance that separated them from commoners. Instead, they self-consciously identified with ordinary men and befriended them "to establish esteem and confidence between the people and their rulers." Especially important, great leaders conducted themselves with what Peres Fobes described as "an affable deportment, a complacency of behavior, and such conciliating manners as cannot fail to secure the most commanding influence over the people."[50] Leaders fortified hegemony with civility.

The debate over the Constitution raised the issue of whether the sheer size of the new national government would preclude leaders from cultivating a sense of fellow feeling with most citizens. Antifederalists argued that the great geographical extent of the proposed polity and the huge numbers of men composing each electoral district worked against the likelihood that national leaders would be widely recognized, known, respected, or befriended by citizens. "Brutus" complained, "The people . . . will have very little acquaintance with those who may be chosen to represent them; a greater part of them will probably not know the characters of their own members much less that of a majority of those who will compose the federal assembly; they will consist of men whose names they have never heard and of whose talents and regard for the public good they are total strangers to; and they will have no persons so immediately of their choice so near them, of their neighbors and of their own rank in life that they can feel themselves secure in trusting their interests in their hands." If American men came to view their leaders "as a body distinct from them," the result would be a deficit in public confidence, which guaranteed that factionalism and fratricide would prevail over fraternalism.[51]

Madison agreed that national leaders needed to cultivate "personal influence among the people" to gain men's confidence. He also recognized that most members of the executive and judicial branches would be unknown to citizens. He argued, however, that members of Congress would be in a position to build networks of public friendship. They would be more numerous and accessible than other federal officials; they would "dwell among the people at large" and have "connections of blood, of friendship, and of acquaintance" that extended to "the most influential part of society." The most influential part of society included local notables who would have "ties of personal acquaintance and friendship and of family" to their constituents. Put differently, the Heroic Man would be personally acquainted with the Better Sort, who would intermingle with the Family Man. A great leader could strengthen serial bonds with common men by expressing "a manly confidence in their country" and by lauding the "manly spirit which actuates the people of America."[52] A man, father, and friend to the people honored citizens' manhood.

The founders procreated fraternal twins: (1) an institutional republic of men and laws; and (2) a symbolic politics that legitimized democratic deference to leadership prerogative. During extraordinary times, most founders felt that the Republic's health and survival ultimately depended on the ability of a few men to rule the democratic masses, build public support among them, ensure order in the ranks of men, and meet the historical challenges of the modern era. What best distinguished a great leader was his ability to reconcile leadership prerogative and republican sovereignty. The Heroic Man appeared in public as a confident and caring man, a fatherly and friendly man, who calmed fears of betrayal and earned sufficient citizen trust to govern with widespread compliance and quiescence. Although he sometimes governed regardless of public opinion and law, he had little reason "to recur to force" because he could count on men's "esteem and good will" to sustain the consent of the governed.[53]

A Government of Men

The politics of war and peace was the preeminent domain for manhood and leadership in the service of posterity. The founders told the story of America's struggle for liberty as a battle of virtuous fathers and sons against "cruel and unmanly" enemies opposed to natural rights and national independence. The moral of their story was that the peaceful exercise of liberty required citizens to show manly restraint at home and a "dignified, manly, independent spirit" in their dealings abroad.[54] Because the founders had limited faith in most men's ability to exercise self-restraint and practice civility, they relied on exceptional leaders to identify their own manhood with the nation's fortunes and exercise authority to secure the Republic's survival, safety, and reputation in the world.

The founders enlisted the grammar of manhood to legitimize controversial foreign policy initiatives. For example, President Washington anticipated public outcry if he signed a treaty with Great Britain that contradicted prior agreements with France. He told Secretary Hamilton that he wanted a treaty that could be "assimilated with a firm, manly, and dignified conduct." When the resulting Jay Treaty precipitated predictable opposition, Washington defended his actions as a product of "manly and neutral conduct which . . . would so well become us as an independent nation." He also pointed out the unmanly "misconduct of some of our own intemperate people" who subordinated the public good to French interests.[55] Though they often disputed foreign policy, most founders agreed that national leaders should exercise a manly prerogative to establish, defend, and extend America's independence and respectability in the world.

International respectability was important. During the Revolution, Hamilton argued that unification was desperately needed to enhance America's reputation abroad: "There is something noble and magnificent in the perspective of a great federal republic, closely linked in the pursuit of a common interest, tranquil and prosperous at home, respectable abroad." He was mortified that America was "a number of petty states with the appearance only of union, jarring, jealous, and perverse, without any determined direction, fluctuating and unhappy at home, weak and insignificant by their dissensions in the eyes of other nations." After the Revolution, Paine called on Americans to build "a fair national reputation" to command global "reverence." Jefferson and Jay wanted Americans to gain "respect in Europe" to dispose European powers "to cultivate our friendship [rather] than provoke our resentment."[56] America's reputation abroad would determine its fit, fame, and future in the fraternity of Western nations.

How did a new nation achieve international respectability? The founders tried to create a notable national identity by disseminating the story of their manly struggle for liberty and independence. They related the adventures of freedom-loving fathers, patriotic brothers, and valiant sons of liberty to foster fraternal feelings at home and produce an exalted but fearsome reputation abroad. Their message was twofold. First, Americans' devotion to liberty was so strong that they had defeated the most powerful army and navy in the world. Second, their love of liberty was so enduring that they would mobilize anew to defeat any power that threatened their security. Hamilton liked the message but limited its longevity. American men's memorable deeds and worthy reputation were likely to be compromised by their current excesses. What was happening to French revolutionaries could happen to American citizens:

> A struggle for liberty is in itself respectable and glorious. When conducted with magnanimity, justice, and humanity it ought to command the admiration of every friend to human nature. But if sullied by crimes and extravagances, it loses its respectability. Though success may rescue it from infamy, it cannot in the opinion of the sober part of mankind attach to it much positive merit or praise. But in event of want of success, a general execration must attend to it. It appears thus far but too probable that the pending revolution of France has sustained some serious blemishes. There is too much ground to anticipate that a sentence uncommonly severe will be passed upon it if it fails.[57]

Even with constitutional unification, many founders feared that men's excessive passions and democratic disorders would weaken the United States' global standing.

A government led by great men was needed to protect American liberty by ensuring stability at home and unified purpose abroad. James Madison explained, "An individual who is observed to be inconsistent with his plans, or perhaps carry on his affairs without any plan at all, is marked at once by all prudent people as a speedy victim of his own unsteadiness and folly. His more friendly neighbors may pity him, but all will decline to connect their fortunes with his; and not a few will seize the opportunity of making their fortunes out of his. One nation is to another what one individual is to another." National leaders needed to establish and maintain domestic order as well as develop and pursue national unity of purpose for America to build consistent, cooperative relationships with friendly nations and fend off victimization by hostile ones. Hamilton emphasized that leaders needed considerable political, economic, and military clout to support national unity of purpose when it was necessary, for example, to uphold neutrality or repel aggression to avoid "national humiliation."[58]

Regardless of their expressed fears of powerful leaders, most founders relied on the president to serve as the repository of national unity of purpose in foreign policy. The U.S. Constitution imposed few checks on a president's authority to formulate foreign policy, administer it, and command the military to enforce it. Equally important, Washington's precedent-setting presidency demonstrated that Americans would rally around a great leader while his neutrality proclamation confirmed that citizens would tolerate presidential prerogative in foreign policy. When President Adams conjured up what Madison considered a false crisis that threatened to undermine men's liberty at home and engage them in a foolish war abroad, Madison observed that a president's exercise of prerogative in foreign policy was both inevitable and dangerous. That was why it was crucial that a "cool, considerate, and cautious" individual like Washington rather than a "headlong" person like Adams man the helm of state. In 1800, Madison's preference was Thomas Jefferson, who reaffirmed in word and deed the need for exceptional leaders to map foreign policy and steer the nation through turbulent international waters.[59]

Ultimately, most founders depended on the Heroic Man to frame, govern, and promote a reputable republic. They understood that governance was as much a matter of the "art of definition" as their new science of politics. Madison was attentive to the "pliancy of language." He feared demagogues who manipulated language to mislead men. Thus, he criticized Sedition Act supporters for "sophistry" when making a false distinction "between the liberty and licentiousness of the press" or when attempting the "seduction of expediency" to rob men of liberty. However, Madison also appreciated the utility of language for legitimizing leadership and promoting the public good, and proved quite adept at the art of definition. So too did the "Republican," for example, who reinvented the meaning of "unanimous consent" to announce that the whole Constitutional Convention supported ratification. Yes, three delegates dissented, but they did not count because they acted "from partial considerations that can have no weight with a free and enlightened people." The founders relied on the authority of language to shape public discourse, create a collective identity, promote domestic order and international reputability, and fix their own place in history. Indeed, they defined themselves as living exemplars of the Heroic Man who procreated a republic of men.[60]

Abigail Adams demonstrated remarkable insight when she observed to John that "the art of government" was "a prerogative to which your sex lay an almost exclusive claim." The founders practiced the art of manly politics. They used the grammar of manhood to highlight the procreativity of men and to dim the political potency of women. They also applied the grammar of manhood to justify the rule of a few great men over common men to neutralize democratic passions, foster order in the ranks of men, raise America's standing in the world, and convey to posterity a legacy in which they would be remembered as founding fathers—as fertile men who gave birth, in William Pitt's words, to "a glorious asylum of liberty, of manliness."[61]

7

The Founders' Gendered Legacy

The American founders employed a grammar of manhood that distinguished four ranks of men. The lowest rank was symbolized by the Bachelor, the passionate man who was isolated in time and space, distrusted by other men, and deemed a danger to social order and political stability. He was ridiculed, stigmatized, sanctioned, and sometimes imprisoned. The main rank was represented by the Family Man who disciplined passion to fit into the role of responsible husband, father, and neighbor. He merited sufficient respect to be entrusted with citizenship. A more select rank was constituted by the Better Sort of man who sufficiently mastered the norms of manly integrity and civility to earn personal dignity, social respect, and public influence. He demonstrated virtue and wisdom enough to represent other men and make law for them. The highest rank was reserved for the rare Heroic Man who cultivated civic virtue and procreated a new nation for posterity. He stood above law and public opinion to address the exigencies of fortune but secured hegemony to ensure the consent and quiescence of most men.

Fearful of democratic disorder in the ranks of men, the founders employed the grammar of manhood to encourage men to reform themselves, school their sons to exercise liberty with restraint, and restore and reinforce order in public life. They invoked what James Madison called "the manly spirit" to lift up men in each rank and encourage them to defer to higher-ranking leaders. Some founders considered themselves heroes of the highest caliber, extraordinarily procreative men destined to produce a better world for humankind. Their attitude was both arrogant and insightful. Their arrogance was partly based on patriarchal privilege; they could think and act almost exclusively in terms of men's passions, interests, virtues, aspirations, hierarchies, and authority because they inherited and perpetuated women's exclusion from public life. Their insightfulness was manifested in their impact; their republic of men proved to be durable and influential.

Durable Manhood

For two hundred years, Americans have struggled with varying degrees of success to extend the founders' revolutionary promise of liberty and equality. Major successes include the demise of slavery and the achievement of women's voting rights. However, the relationship between manhood and politics has hardly changed. American males of all races, religions, classes, and regions continue to build hierarchies that stigmatize disorderly men, provide varying degrees of respect and influence to men in the middle, and afford great authority to the few on top. Generation after generation of American boys has adapted to these patriarchal hierarchies, and generation after generation of American men has participated in them.

In his study of American nineteenth-century "boy culture," E. Anthony Rotundo observes that young males who interacted beyond the immediate oversight of their parents regularly established a "series of informal rankings" that challenged each youngster to earn his place in the adolescent "pecking order." The most successful boys displayed "independence" through will, daring, prerogative, and force; they learned "to master the emotions that would otherwise make them vulnerable"; and they employed "ridicule, ostracism, [and] hazing" to establish and enforce their hegemony over others. Most boys earned a modest place by exhibiting exuberance and spontaneity, and also disdain for adult authority. Eventually, these middling boys had to make "the leap from boyhood to manhood" by giving up "heedless play for sober responsibility." Boys lacking proper size, appearance, pluck, or athletic skills sometimes had to fight for their manhood. Those who lost confrontations or ran away from them were likely to be debased as "mama's boys," who had failed to separate from females or overcome effeminacy. They suffered an array of youthful cruelties.[1]

Today's boy culture reproduces a remarkably similar pattern. Barrie Thorne's study of modern gender play suggests that boys' relationships "tend to be overtly hierarchical." Boys "negotiate" and "mark rank" by demonstrating admired qualities and by issuing "insults, direct commands, challenges, and threats" to reinforce rankings. High-status boys command widespread respect and deference; middle-status boys jockey to maintain or raise their position; and low-status boys suffer considerable if not constant humiliation. Thorne captures the extremes in this contrast: "John, who was the tallest boy in the class and one of the best athletes in the school, deftly handled challenges to his authority. Dennis, who was not very good at sports or at academics, was at the other end of the pecking order. John . . . called Dennis 'Dumbo' and insulted him in other ways; in a kind of ritual submission, Dennis more or less accepted the insults." Weaker boys are also humiliated by epithets such as "girls," "sissies," and "fags." High-status boys' hegemony is based on low-status boys' consent to subordination.[2]

Boys become men who participate in and perpetuate adult pecking orders. Joseph Pleck observes that "men create hierarchies and rankings among themselves according to criteria of masculinity" and then "compete with each other . . . for the differential payoffs that patriarchy allows men." R. W. Connell specifies three general rankings among men: "hegemonic masculinity, conservative masculinities (complicit in the collective project but not its shock troops), and subordinated masculinities."[3] Connell's hegemonic masculinity is consistent with what I have represented as the founders' Heroic Man; his conservative masculinities encompass the Better Sort and the Family Man; his subordinated masculinities include the marginal men and minorities epitomized by the Bachelor. In all, the modern rhetoric of liberty, equality, and democracy has not inhibited American men from complying with a seemingly iron law of male oligarchy: a few men rule, the majority of men consent and obey, and marginal men mostly accept subordination.

Why do American men perpetuate these hierarchies? One factor is that high-status males believe they must govern, in order to prevent disorderly men from destroying life, liberty, and happiness. They applaud powerful leaders who exercise prerogative to resolve national crises and realize historical opportunities. They share patriarchal sensibilities that call for manly leaders to protect women from libertines and other dangerous men. William Goode suggests that men's emotional ties to their mothers, sisters, wives, and girlfriends provide them an incentive to protect women from the disorderly men who threaten to harm them. These caring men are "sure of their own goodheartedness and wisdom" but fearful of other men's "exploitative efforts." Accordingly, they believe "that they are to be trusted and so should have great power," but "other men cannot be trusted" and so should be restrained.[4] To the extent that high-status men continue to concur with the founders' belief that most males are disorderly creatures, they locate themselves among the Better Sort who are sufficiently trustworthy to govern the dangerous masses as well as to rule womankind.

A complementary factor is that low-status males have a strong incentive to acquiesce, accommodate, and assent to the male hierarchies that subordinate them. Mark Gerzon asserts that the average American male is fearful that other men will perceive him and treat him "as a boy and not a man." Powerful men have used this understanding to manipulate others. For example, dominant white males reinforced their historical domination of black and Indian males by labeling them "children" and treating them like dependents. Modern leaders still stigmatize enemies by tagging them with male immaturity. President Lyndon Johnson condemned "the talkers and writers and the intellectuals who sat around thinking and criticizing and doubting" as "boys"; but he honored "activists, doers, who conquered business empires, who acted instead of talked" as "men." Why should any male care if powerful men label him a boy? David Leverenz explains that American males harbor "fears of being humiliated . . . by other men." And because humiliation often is a forerunner to severe sanctions, the safest strategy for a low-status male seeking to avoid shame and punishment is to conform to ordinary standards of manhood and achieve at least modest respectability in the male pecking order.[5]

The American consensus on men's main route to modest respectability has not changed in two hundred years. It still involves independence, family commitment, and governing subordinates. Stable norms of manhood declare that males ought to practice intellectual and emotional autonomy as well as secure sufficient wealth or income to settle down, marry, sire children, rule female and male dependents, and perpetuate family dynasties. This declaration is periodically reaffirmed by critics who first complain that bachelorhood is causing family decline and social breakdown and then call on men to recommit themselves to family responsibility and civic order. Late-seventeenth- and early-eighteenth-century English writers responded to men's antimaritalism by invigorating demands that men marry and fulfill family duties. Today, American analysts link men's "flight from commitment" to an antimarital ethic that legitimizes freedom without family responsibility. Both liberals and conservatives criticize American men for failing "to invest time, money, and energy in family life" and advocate a revival of "family values" to encourage men to rebuild the family nest.[6]

From the founders' time to our time, American leaders have viewed mature manhood as a remedy for the male lust, licentiousness, selfishness, avarice, impulsiveness, aggression, and violence that foster disorder in the ranks of men. Manly merit still centers on individuals' ability to discipline their passions, elevate family interests above individual pleasures, and achieve social fit if not seek social fame in the service of the public good and posterity. Although the founders' rhetoric of liberty and equality fortified a Lockean individualism that gave rise to an ethic of self-made manhood, their devotion to consensual norms of manhood persists into the present to counteract both male individualism and women's claims to liberty and equality.

Manhood against Individualism

The founders' grammar of manhood favored manly merit, self-discipline, responsibility, civility, and procreativity for the public good. Did it also legitimize the actions of men who harnessed manly characteristics to individual self-interest? The backwoodsman, for example, could exhibit great self-control, family responsibility, and political artistry when he provoked border wars, murdered indigenous peoples, speculated in frontier land, and persuaded the U.S. government and military to support his violence and profiteering. Did the classical meaning of manhood as self-sacrifice and civic virtue give way to masculine individualism, rugged individualism, possessive individualism, or ideals of self-made manhood in early America? Joyce Appleby, John Diggins, and Joan Hoff think so. They argue that the founders stripped "virtue" of its classical civic meaning and reduced male virtue to the pursuit of self-interest.[7]

Unquestionably, the founders' rhetoric of liberty and equality helped promote individualism among white males. Rotundo emphasizes that the founders recognized "the growing claims of the self" but "only of the *male* self." This recognition helped catalyze the breakup of corporate families and traditional communities, on the one hand, and legitimize individual rights, entrepreneurship, contractual relations, and interest-based politics, on the other. Individualism was also manifested in American fraternal life. Men often bonded to optimize individual and aggregate utilities. They joined the self-help groups popularized by Franklin and the factions neutralized by Madisonian institutions to enhance their social standing, enrich their economic opportunities, and gain political leverage. Wilson Carey McWilliams suggests that the individualism at the core of American fraternities is what made them defective. Men committed themselves to fraternities only insofar as they recognized a congruence of interests; they failed to wed private desires to public ideals in ways that connected self-worth to enduring civic values. Sanford Lakoff adds that American men participated in republican politics only insofar as they connected self-interest to aggregate "public interest." They failed to join self-sacrifice to civic loyalty in support of the classical "common good."[8]

The founders granted white males' individualism its due. They dwelled on men's passions, avarice, and factionalism. Bernard Bailyn states that "federalists and antifederalists both agreed that man in his deepest nature was selfish and corrupt; that blind ambition most often overcomes even the most clear-eyed rationality; and that the lust for power was so overwhelming that no one should ever be entrusted with unqualified authority."[9] Simultaneously, their understanding of manhood and fraternity went beyond selfishness. The founders disputed the Bachelor's lustful, avaricious manhood and sought to restrain his passions and interests. They worried about the Family Man's parochialism, encouraged his devotion to neighbors, and pleaded for his loyalty to leaders committed to the public good. Liberal individualism began to flourish in the founding era, but the grammar of manhood counteracted it with an ethic of self-restraint and subordination in the service of order, stability, and posterity.

Throughout American history, norms of manhood encouraged males to restrain individualism and realize their social nature by committing themselves to family, friends, community, and nation. The founders did not portray male creatures solely in egomaniacal terms. They agreed that men who were individuated and isolated suffered great unhappiness. They also agreed that men's selfish passions were accompanied by a moral sensibility and natural sociability. The founders admired gregarious men who established informal networks and founded formal organizations that fostered mutual caring and community. For example, early American Freemasonry honored mobility in the marketplace but "also attempted to check the growth of an unrestricted pursuit of self-interest through its concept of itself as a brotherhood, an institution that promoted loyalty and benevolence." Fraternal orders relied on secret rituals to cultivate male bonding and benevolence. The rituals required initiates and members to demonstrate manly merit by making symbolic and tangible sacrifices for fraternity and the flag. "Rather than reinforcing the forms and ideologies of capitalist social organization," Mark Carnes suggests, "the rituals often subverted them."[10]

The enduring association of American manhood and fraternity with self-sacrifice and civic virtue is especially evident in American military thought. The founders believed that men were obligated by their birthright to support and serve in a military capacity to defend liberty and pass it on to their sons. From the early national period to the present, political, military, social, economic, and cultural elites have consistently urged young males to undergo trial by military ordeal to learn self-sacrifice, demonstrate civic virtue, and prepare to risk their lives for their families, friends, and fellow citizens. Elite urging has been especially intense at the beginnings of wars, but it has also been potent in peacetime. For example, early-twentieth-century civic leaders proposed Universal Military Training to transform a generation of ostensibly soft, selfish, effeminate boys into a national force of manly, patriotic soldiers. Despite periodic protests, virtually every generation of young American males has deferred to elites by adopting martial values, performing militia service, joining volunteer companies, enlisting in the regular army, or complying with conscription.[11]

To the extent that American manhood has counteracted individualism and its associated disorders, it has played a very conventional role. In *Manhood in the Making*, David Gilmore surveys rites of male passage that stretch from Europe through Africa and Asia across the Pacific Ocean to South and North America. The global similarities are staggering. Nearly everywhere, boys undergo trial by ordeal to develop and demonstrate manhood. They learn self-discipline, stoicism, and fortitude; they take on prescribed responsibilities and perform distinguished deeds; they prove competence through the conquest of women—all this and more to earn their ticket into adult male society. Once admitted, the struggle continues. They become fathers, providers, and protectors of families; and they assert independence from women, for example, by participating in fraternal rituals, war games, and wars. Gilmore argues that most cultures make a virtue of manhood to motivate young males to demonstrate a "selfless generosity" for their families and the public good. This ethic of selfless generosity binds men into relatively cohesive fraternities that enact, administer, and enforce the rules of public life.[12]

Gilmore is struck by the absence of systematic rites of male passage in the United States. Robert Moore and Douglas Gillette agree that "We no longer have a map to get us to maturity." Mark Gerzon worries that American males may be lost in the midst of uncertainty because, "There is no ritual—not sexual, economic, military, or generational—that can confirm masculinity." American manhood seems makeshift, diffuse, and ambiguous. How does a boy become a man? Should his father send him on Boy Scout camp-outs, emphasize academic achievement, push athletic prowess, or consign him to a drill sergeant? Should the boy focus on physical size and musculature, intelligence and wit, fearlessness in the face of danger, or future productivity and wealth? When he comes of age, should a young male cultivate mechanical skills, group leadership, managerial savvy, and then stoic dignity in the aging process? The answers have varied by time, place, religion, region, class, and race. The American road to manhood has crisscrossed traditional patriarchal authority, aristocratic gentility, republican simplicity, and liberal self-interest as well as filial obedience but also filial rebellion, courage and conquest in some circumstances but self-restraint and civility in others. America's exemplars of manhood have included sober New England Puritans, Georgia dirt farmers, Philadelphia artisans, western frontiersmen, southern cavaliers, northeastern entrepreneurs, small-town Babbitts, white urban professionals, and black professional athletes.[13] Does so much variety imply a lack of coherence?

Not necessarily. Three threads of consistency run through the variations. One is that manhood is never given; it must be earned. Each boy has to figure out how to achieve independence, assume and satisfy family responsibilities, and assert authority over women and other dependents in order to gain access to the differential payoffs of patriarchy. Each boy learns, "It takes work to become a man." Analogously, each male generation must measure up to prior generations. In the War of 1812, Michael Rogin remarks, "America's sons" sought to "vindicate the birthright of their revolutionary fathers . . . to acquire manly authority." Gerald Linderman attributes a post–Civil War "revival of the military spirit" to efforts by a new generation of males to earn its manhood by waging war against rampant individualism and routine civilian life.[14] In United States history, all white males were born with liberty but only meritorious white males acquired the respect, recognition, and reputation associated with *manly* liberty.

The second common thread is that manhood demands self-discipline. Peter Filene observes that American males achieve manhood "by earnest, often desperate suppression of instincts." They must control passions and master impulses to gain fraternal trust as husbands, fathers, neighbors, workers, businessmen, citizens, soldiers, and leaders. In addition, they need to strike a balance between self-interest and social regard. They achieve manly independence and integrity as ends in themselves but also as a means to earn a good name and reputation among worthy men. Moreover, they must continue to exhibit self-discipline and social consciousness throughout their entire life span. A man's place in the pecking order is always tenuous. He cannot rest on past laurels because competitors are always poised to raise themselves up by bringing him down. Even old men must struggle for manhood. Cotton Mather wrote that they had to measure up to manly standards of "sobriety, gravity, temperance, orthodoxy, charity, and patience" or suffer invective such as this: "For them that stagger with age, at the same time to stagger with drink; to see an old man reeling, spewing, stinking with the excesses of the tavern, 'tis too loathsome a thing to be mentioned without a very zealous detestation."[15]

The third unifying thread is that males must procreate to achieve full manhood. The founders' belief that manhood involved procreating a sober, responsible self reappears in "the great legend of American life" that men can "start over again," for example, by following self-improvement manuals and twelve-step programs that promise renewed health, virtue, wisdom, and happiness. The founders' consensus that manhood involved giving birth to families is especially evident among modern men who hire female surrogates to bear their genetic heirs. The founders' admiration for men who procreated communities and nations resurfaces among contemporary planners and developers who carve new suburbs out of old farmland, activists who establish community organizations, and subcultures that create their own lifestyle enclaves. The thread of male procreation is especially dense in mythopoetical masculinism. Robert Bly wants boys to tap into "male spirit" to achieve a "second birth" into manhood. Moore and Gillette want the modern man to find "procreative energy" to become "the Procreator"—a father of children and steward of the world whose "blood nourishes the earth as fertilizing semen" to bring "calm in the midst of chaos." Truly worthy men procreate "order through determined action."[16]

Why do modern American men weave these traditional threads of manhood into their personal, social, and political lives? One answer is that the founders set a powerful precedent when they used the language and norms of manhood to stabilize male identity, secure social order, and legitimize new governments amid the sweeping changes of the late eighteenth century. Since then, new generations of American males have forsaken some of the language of manhood but continue to rely on its consensual norms to give meaning to mortality, fit into fraternal society, fix their place in the pecking order, and share in the heroics of leaders seeking calm amidst chaos. The founders' commitment to manhood now constitutes the conservative core of contemporary liberalism.

Manhood and Mortality

By the eighteenth century, Phillipe Ariès argues, a profound change occurred in Western men's attitude toward death. Premodern men shared a sense of collective destiny. Death was familiar, not fearsome. Men were socialized to accept nature's order and expected to live on through their communities. With the rise of individualism, modern men began to put a premium on self and material interest. They saw death less as a natural part of their collective destiny and more as an assault on their individuality and accumulated treasure. Death became "a transgression" that ruptured the fabric of men's lives and plunged them "into an irrational, violent . . . world." How did men cope with impending rupture and chaos? They gave meaning to mortality by perpetuating the memory of the dead. Ariès observes, "Memory conferred on the dead a sort of immortality."[17]

American colonists refused to surrender to death. The common man sired sons to continue his seed, name, and memory into the next generation while the gentleman also performed notable deeds meant to be remembered by worthy friends and countrymen. This refusal outlasted the Revolution and nationhood. American men still hoped to cheat death by protecting and promoting family dynasties that honored the memories of dead patriarchs and paved the way for future ones. They sustained patriarchal memories by paying hyperbolic homage to family fathers and civic fathers. They initiated prolonged funeral watches in formal family parlors; the watches were occasions to honor dead patriarchs and the parlors were architectural testaments to the deceased's gentility and patrimony. They also generated memory-laden options for disposing of paternal corpses. Some sons cremated fathers, gathered the ashes into urns, and placed the urns on home altars; others invested in the American revival of the ancient Egyptian art of embalming to transform dead fathers into durable cadavers; still others buried fathers in new-style cemeteries that marked family plots with engraved stone monuments that proclaimed family surnames in perpetuity. Individual efforts to memorialize family dynasties were mirrored by public efforts to honor dead heroes with durable stone statues.[18]

Most American men sought to perpetuate family dynasties by fathering sons to carry their seeds, names, estates, and memories into the future. Jay Fliegelman notes that eighteenth-century Americans adopted Lockean parenting techniques that were especially conducive to men's search for immortality. A Lockean father educated his sons to steward the family dynasty. He used affection and discipline, praise and shame, and reason and emotion to teach boys appropriate manly virtues and abilities. When he died, the father would "be immortalized in his child," who would continue the family line. Alternatively, grandfathers hoped to immortalize themselves in their grandsons. For example, American men occasionally drew up wills that bypassed sons and sons-in-law in favor of grandsons. New Yorker David Haines "named his grandson and namesake" his primary heir, while one Chesapeake man hoped to protect his estate from a wasteful son-in-law by bequeathing it to as yet unborn grandsons.[19]

This fondness for male procreativity as a source of immortality was rooted in biblical imagery of male fecundity that reemerged in seventeenth-century England as political philosophy. Referring to Sir Robert Filmer's argument that "Eve . . . is not created *ab initio* but *from* Adam, who is thus in a sense her parent," Carole Pateman comments, "Filmer is able to treat all political right as the right of the father because the patriarchal father has the creative powers of both a mother and a father . . . who is complete in himself." English contract theorists refuted Filmer by transferring male procreativity from a single patriarchal father to the fraternity of patriarchal fathers who, by mutual consent, "give birth to an 'artificial' body, the body politic and civil society." A subtheme was that founding fathers immortalized themselves in their biological and political offspring. James Harrington suggested that a man became a father to "raise himself a pillar, a golden pillar for his monument . . . his own reviving flesh, and a kind of immortality." The founder of a republic created "beautiful order out of chaos" to raise an even grander monument to himself. John Locke also joined procreativity to immortality. He attacked "waste" and "spoilage" as squandered value but applauded labor and money for enabling men to procreate value, amass it without spoilage, and cheat death by bequeathing it to future generations. In turn, men safeguarded accumulated value by procreating a political society able to protect it.[20]

The American founders linked male procreativity and immortality when they praised men who founded and fostered family dynasties; acquired, settled, worked, and bequeathed land; established fraternal organizations and communities; and procreated new constitutions and governments. The founders' descendants continue to identify male procreativity with immortality. Modern Americans often pity bachelors who have no legitimate biological heirs to perpetuate their names but honor responsible fathers and doting grandfathers who procreate and provision new generations. They applaud citizens who earn reputable names and elect national leaders who promise to do memorable deeds. Indeed, American males of all classes and races are experts at the "Remember Me" game. Boys carve their names into school desktops and wet cement; youth gangs and tagger crews spray-paint their names onto neighborhood fences and highway overpasses; construction workers etch their names into steel infrastructures; rich men donate millions to have their names attached to college buildings and charitable foundations; and powerful politicians (such as the Kennedys and the Bushes) transmit clout across generations to affix their family names to political dynasties.

Why have American males been so concerned with memorializing themselves? Mary O'Brien suggests the possibility that men tend to be obsessed with immortality because they play a minor, temporary part in human reproduction. Men copulate, ejaculate, and then remain idle while women carry, bear, nurse, and nurture future generations. The result is that men feel separated from the birthing experience and from any affective sense of biological continuity. They are "isolated in their individual historicity." Seeking to escape this isolation, men commandeer culture, law, and coercion to reduce the uncertainty of their paternity and to build family dynasties that promise to fill them with a sense of historical continuity. Their desperation is evident in the extraordinary amount of time, resources, energy, and effort they invest in legitimizing patriarchal prerogative and fixing their places as fathers of posterity.[21]

Robert Jay Lifton proposes a related possibility. He believes that men have a deep psychological need "to maintain [them]selves as part of the great chain of being." To satisfy this need, men "require the symbolization of that continuity, imaginative forms of transcending death, in order to confront the fact that we die." Lifton identifies five symbolic modes of transcending death. In the biological/social mode, men seek continuity by identifying with their children, group, tribe, organization, culture, people, nation, or species. A religious mode assumes that men have an immortal soul and can achieve life after death. The creative mode enables men to endure through their works of art, literature, and science or through their influence on family and friends. The fourth mode involves men's identification with nature as an eternal force that precedes and postdates individual lives. Finally, an experiential mode refers to intense psychic experiences that temporarily free men from fear of death. J. Glenn Gray provides a useful example. He observes that combat soldiers sometimes experience a "sense of power and liberation" when risking their lives for comrades. It is as if "nothing less than the assurance of immortality . . . makes self-sacrifice at these moments so relatively easy."[22]

O'Brien defines the male quest for immortality in opposition to female maternalism, but Lifton is ambivalent. On the one hand, he observes that women who survive major historical discontinuities such as Nazi concentration camps and the atomic bombing of Hiroshima employ the same strategies as men to reaffirm life and reestablish a sense of continuity. On the other hand, he speculates that women's "close identification with organic life and its perpetuation" may produce in women an "organic" conservatism that steadies them during times of change. On this view, women's relative calm in the midst of crisis stands in contrast to men's anxiety over the ebb and flow of fortune.[23] Lifton does not resolve his ambivalence. However, he does allege that men are deeply threatened by disorders associated with change, crisis, and death, and that they engage in strenuous efforts to reestablish a symbolic sense of continuity and immortality.

These efforts often involve the procreation of surrogate families. Throughout American history, young men torn from their biological families to fight the nation's wars have been initiated into substitute military families (units) that include brothers (fellow soldiers) and father figures (officers) who promise to lead them to victory. Since the nineteenth century, young men migrating from farms to cities have joined extended families that formed in home-styled bordering houses, institutions such as the Young Men's Christian Association (YMCA), and fraternities such as the Order of Odd Fellows. Lifton perceives men's tendency to procreate surrogate families as especially intense during revolutions. A rebel might sustain a sense of continuity amid violence by identifying himself with "a vast 'family' reaching back to what he perceives to be the historical beginnings of his revolution and extending infinitely into the future." He participates in "a socially created family . . . as a mode of immortality." His family is often governed by a beloved father figure. Lifton suggests that Chinese revolutionaries perceived Mao Tse-tung to be a heroic patriarch who could transform "the most extreme threat of disintegration into an ordered certainty of mission" and convert "incapacitating death anxiety into a death-conquering calm of near invincibility." He believes, however, that Western men are more apt to feel a sense of "symbolic fatherlessness" and engage in endless experiments to reconcile patriarchal norms that give meaning, significance, and stability to their lives with the frightful openness and uncertainty of the future.[24]

An important element in the American founders' gendered legacy was a challenge to future generations of males to reconcile the relatively unchanging norms of manhood that ordered men's lives with the rhetoric of liberty and equality that justified openness but admitted uncertainties associated with social instability and political disarray in the ranks of men. Both the founders and their heirs addressed this challenge by employing criteria of manly merit to encourage self-restraint in the exercise of liberty and to establish stable hierarchies in civil society.

Manhood and Civil Society

The founders felt that most men's standing in civil society depended on their performances as family patriarchs and neighbors. Fatherhood was a social responsibility. A proper father, John Demos observes, raised his sons to "reflect credit" on him and his family's "good name." He also mastered local codes of civility to confirm membership and achieve respectability in his community.[25] Civility was a particularly useful marker of a man's standing in a society where formal ranks were being contested and abolished. It was an equal opportunity virtue. Theoretically, every white male who sought social recognition could learn the appropriate dispositions and exhibit the proper manners needed to climb the social ladder. At the same time, civility legitimized hierarchy. Some men never learned the basics; most men achieved adequacy; a select number picked up important subtleties; but only a few men mastered its intricacies. Because the common man had a chance to gain a "foothold in the ranks of polite society," he was less likely to resent subordination to social elites and more apt to respect social superiors as "models of manhood" worthy of emulation. Don Sabo reminds us that intermale hierarchy usually beckons low-ranking men "to climb its heights" rather than contest its inequalities.[26]

The founders' commitment to civility as a key criterion for social standing was symbolized by their elevation of George Washington to the highest rank of manhood and highest office in the land. Washington the child entered rules of civility into his copybook, and Washington the adult practiced those rules to attract extraordinary public esteem. Richard Bushman reports that great concern for civility resurfaced among nineteenth-century patricians hoping to save gentility from democracy as well as in nineteenth-century advice books that counseled aspirants to middle-class respectability to develop and practice pleasing dispositions that elevated character and improved business prospects. The ethic of civility endures in the twentieth century among upper-class men who cultivate country-club manners, entrepreneurs who seek social respectability, and professionals whose codes of ethics announce their commitment to employ expertise to serve rather than to exploit the public.[27]

The manly ethic of civility is especially important among minority males and other marginal men. Mitchell Duneier's study of "race, respectability, and masculinity" reveals the intricate codes of manhood, self-worth, and social standing that ordered relationships among a group of older, mostly African American men who frequented a restaurant on Chicago's South Side. These men articulated and adhered to masculine norms of speech, style, and action that honored personal responsibility, inner strength, expressiveness, pride, sincerity, honesty, genuineness, caring, and civility. The men who excelled at these virtues perceived themselves and were perceived by others in their circle as manly, meritorious, respectable, and dignified. They took great pride in being known as men of "higher self-worth," as "elevated" beings. In contrast, those men who failed to exhibit civil dispositions and manly conduct suffered personal pain and social disdain. They staked their personal honor on norms of manhood and punished themselves for falling short; they were accepted into the group on the basis of these norms but lost status and even membership for failing to live up to them.[28]

Relatedly, a group of elderly Jewish immigrants who belonged to a community center in Venice, California, created their own informal codes of civility. Barbara Myerhoff examines how members tried to maintain a sense of personal integrity and social dignity as they coped with the dependence associated with old age and with fears founded on proximity to death. "Their self-esteem," Myerhoff writes, "was based on the maintenance of honor, decorum, and dignity." Their particular code of honor included self-discipline, independence, articulateness, and generosity. For example, members took pride in being donors to needy causes but were deeply insulted by the merest hint that they themselves were needy. This insistence that they controlled their lives "enabled them to maintain their standing as people of honor" committed to the "American values of democracy and equality." Simultaneously, they greatly valued "individual merit," perceived "clear, important differences in human worth," were acutely attuned to small and large breaches in civility, and staked their dignity, membership, and reputations on earning and maintaining high social standing in the group.[29]

Duneier's study focuses on an all-male community where the prevailing codes emphasized manhood and civility as key sources of social standing. Myerhoff's study examines a community of men and women, emphasizing the importance that family played in determining people's standing. She suggests that "the old women had the deck stacked in their favor" because they kept closer ties with children and received the most credit when the children were highly educated, well married, and good parents. Still, men achieved social standing by asserting responsibility for and demonstrating achievement in perpetuating their family dynasties. One elderly man wrote an autobiography which he intended to be read at family gatherings after his death. He explained to his children that the book's purpose was "to draw out the thread of our family, in order that your children and grandchildren will have some understanding of their origins." The author gained social credit by bequeathing to his family "the concept of perpetual continuity."[30]

The norm of manly civility persists today as a putative source of fraternal cohesion. Moore and Gillette suggest that mature men are not selfish, materialistic, or aggressive. Instead, they are genuinely concerned about other people, cooperate with them, and sacrifice for them. Mature men *care*—about their children, other men, the community, the environment, the world, and posterity. Mature men who engage in legitimate state violence *care*—about the liberty and safety of their families and the friendship, camaraderie, and mutual aid of fellow citizens, police officers, or soldiers. Mature men fearful of social disorder and street violence *care*—about the triumph of civility over criminality. The point is not that American men are caring creatures but that they often associate mature manhood with concern and sacrifice for others. Garrison Keillor explains in *The Book of Guys*, "We try to become caring men, good husbands, great fathers, good citizens, despite the fact that guys are fundamentally unfaithful." The men most likely to achieve high standing in American society are not necessarily radical individualists, sexual predators, abusive husbands, ruthless capitalists, or highly authoritarian personalities. Instead, they tend to be men who subscribe to the very ethic of care that Carol Gilligan identifies with women.[31]

Manhood and Politics

Mainstream manhood is mundane. It involves settling into monogamous marriages, siring and raising children, earning money and paying bills. It is the daily grind of restraining lust outside marriage and exercising responsibility within it, winning bread and breeding heirs. Mainstream citizenship is passive. It entails listening to television news, obeying laws, paying taxes, and periodically voting. The one transcendent feature of both manhood and citizenship is an indirect association with heroism. Average American men can vicariously experience "the magnetic field of the deep masculine" by identifying with the procreative "Zeus energy" of heroic men and hegemonic leaders. They may imagine themselves heroes but, in politics, they mostly seek out heroic rulers to solve public problems and fulfill national promise. American men tend to couple mundane manhood and passive citizenship to compensatory hero worship.[32]

Since the founding era, few American men have sought to transform liberty into radical libertarianism or to push equality toward radical egalitarianism. American men have rarely used liberty as a pretext for contesting the legitimacy of the U.S. Constitution or promoted equality as a gateway to socialism. With important exceptions, they have mostly complied with laws and leaders, and occasionally offered enthusiastic support to presidents who exercised extraordinary power and prerogative. Eugene Debs recognized and regretted American men's tendency to sacrifice democratic self-government for passive quiescence to leaders. He regularly refused to assume official Socialist Party leadership and gave this explanation: "Too long have the workers of the world waited for some Moses to lead them out of bondage. He has not come; he will never come. I would not lead you out if I could; for if you could be led out, you could be led back again."[33] Ironically, Debs's refusal, like Washington's reticence to accept public office, made his leadership that much more influential, lasting, and memorable.

Does this record of political passivity imply that the founders' obsessive fears of disorderly men were exaggerated? Louis Hartz thinks so. He argues that early Americans and their leaders were "united on a liberal way of life" that focused on individual rights and economic opportunities. The founders' attempt to ensure order by installing a powerful national government was political overkill. Hartz states, "The American majority has been an amiable shepherd dog kept forever on a lion's leash." Gordon Wood disagrees. He suggests that the founders' fears were warranted but their new science of politics suppressed much of the disorder. The founders implemented a Constitution that freed men's acquisitive appetites but harnessed their political ambitions. Henceforth, American men pursued their economic interests with little reason to seek political power or resist political leadership.[34] Both explanations are incomplete because they do not recognize that the founders' hegemonic norms of manhood helped stabilize liberal citizenship and authorize exceptional leaders to override institutional restraints.

Early American liberalism contained a conservative core requirement that mature men give up the Bachelor's pleasures for the Family Man's responsibilities. This was crucial for establishing and maintaining order in the ranks of men. The Bachelor sought liberty without responsibility whereas the Family Man defended liberty and exercised it with self-restraint. The Bachelor transformed liberty into licentiousness but the Family Man practiced a sober productivity and fraternal civility. The Bachelor knew no authority but his own desires while the Family Man recognized, admired, and followed the Better Sort who managed the Republic and the Heroic Man who guided it into the future. Ultimately, the Family Man was a political moderate who could be trusted to practice disciplined individualism and deferent citizenship. His moderate disposition, in turn, created a cushion of legitimacy that enabled great leaders to wield prerogative regardless of adverse public opinion or legal restraints.

The Family Man's mundane manhood and passive citizenship acquired transcendent meaning through hero worship. The Family Man shared in manly heroism not by emulating it but by honoring it, for example, in Fourth of July orations that commemorated pioneering fathers. The Family Man engaged in political procreativity not by exemplifying it but by adoring it, for example, in election sermons that traced modern citizenship back to heroic founders of cities, constitutions, and republics. This version of hero worship encouraged men to find political meaning primarily in the past rather than to take heroic initiative in the present. By 1783, the founders were enjoining men to "venerate the memories and long perpetuate the names of those who guided the helm throughout the storm." After 1789, Michael Lienesch notes, the founders sought to secure political stability by suggesting that "heroic politics existed only in the past, the duty of Americans being to revere the founders, remembering their illustrious deeds, applauding their magnificent government, and cherishing their hallowed Constitution."[35]

Nineteenth-century males did not resign themselves to a mixture of mundane manhood and reverence for dead political leaders. They also worshiped living heroes such as the Jacksonian frontiersman and the Gilded Age entrepreneur. These new ideals incorporated old norms such as manly liberty and procreativity but lacked the key characteristic that elevated manhood from the secular to the sacred: self-sacrifice for the public good. The frontiersman and the entrepreneur were possessive individualists who, at best, made a self-interested, circuitous, and suspect contribution to the public good. Only the citizen soldier could claim the civic virtue associated with unselfish patriotism—but he was about to be replaced by the professional soldier. By the end of "the Masculine Century," many commentators feared, American manhood not only was routinized, bureaucratized, and effeminized but also was lacking in redeeming heroic value.[36]

The turn of the twentieth century witnessed a conjuncture of political radicalism and renewed emphasis on heroism. American elites dreaded the prospect of millions of American and immigrant men exchanging citizen passivity for the class conflict manifested in anarchist, populist, and socialist activism against the capitalist order. Elites deployed economic policy, political co-optation, and military coercion to control activists but they also initiated efforts to educate and channel young men away from political engagement into a sort of subdued heroism. They called on boys to recapture the frontiersman's fortitude by participating in planned Boy Scout outings; they counseled youth to exhibit the entrepreneur's competitiveness in organized sports; they urged young men to practice martial virtue by enrolling in military training programs. National elites were convinced that long-term stability in the ranks of men required that young men infuse greater meaning into manhood by participating in managed heroics.[37]

William James and Randolph Bourne agreed that American men craved transcendent political meaning. However, they expressed pacifist fears that the glorification of heroism often reinforced and legitimized young men's most aggressive, violent, warlike tendencies. Their solution was to devise a moral equivalent to war that would engage young men in self-sacrifice, develop their procreative abilities, and allow them to experience real heroism by way of public participation and service. They proposed that young men enlist in a domestic army and devote several years of their lives to solving the nation's problems. Their proposal was quickly forgotten amid public enthusiasm for President Woodrow Wilson's decision to bring the United States into a world war that invited a new generation of young males to "enact and repossess" the martial manliness of their fathers, forefathers, and founding fathers.[38]

American men's hero worship is now manifested in a desperate and often fruitless search for great political leaders. The founders set a precedent when they encouraged contemporaries to suspend their suspicions of political authority and submit to the exceptional leadership of the procreative men who bloodied the British Empire, gave birth to the Constitution, sired a new republic, and nursed it through its infancy. Since then, American men have submitted to patriarchal presidents (often military heroes) who promised to unite manly "restraint and responsibility" with "masculine, potent caring" as a way to resolve national crises and realize historic opportunities.[39] Today, American men still search for great political leaders only to suffer a sense of disappointment and betrayal. But rather than invigorate liberty and equality by emphasizing democratic self-government over leadership, most American men appear to prefer to seek out new political heroes who promise, once again, to infuse manly virtue into public life.

Remember the Ladies

The American founders died suspended in time and space. They did not know if their republic would undergo classical declension into corruption, followed by anarchy and tyranny, or whether their innovative government would endure into posterity. Thomas Jefferson expressed optimism just before dying. Unable to travel to Washington, D.C., to celebrate the fiftieth anniversary of the Declaration of Independence, he regretted missing the opportunity to meet with "the remnant of that host of worthies who joined with us that day in the bold and doubtful election we were to make for our country between submission or the sword." However, he was gratified by the "consolatory fact that our fellow citizens after half a century of experience and prosperity continue to approve the choice we made."[40] The founders were convinced that democratic disorder in the ranks of men was the primary threat to the Republic and they were proud that their procreative efforts secured sufficient hegemony to restore and reinforce order in the ranks of men.

Simultaneously, the founders believed that public order required the rule of men over women. Eighteenth-century America's complex, diverse, and contested culture of manhood magnified familial and social instability. In part, the founders addressed problems of male disorder and gender conflict by urging men to assume familial responsibility for governing women. They defined manhood against womanhood, assessed male worth in opposition to female vices, expressed misogynist attitudes that demanded male governance, and effectively depoliticized patriarchal rule over women. Most founders did not consider women in their political deliberations. Instead, they presumed an exclusive unity of manhood, citizenship, and leadership that precluded women from public life. The few founders who wrote about women and politics usually did so to degrade and dismiss women or to use women to make a point about men. Overall, the founders showed almost no interest in confronting issues involving women's freedom and equality, or their citizenship and leadership. Not surprisingly, they ignored Mary Wollstonecraft's *Vindication of the Rights of Woman*, or criticized the author's reputed immoral conduct, or dismissed her ideas as invitations to chaos.[41]

The founders perpetuated patriarchalism by promoting a misogynist ideology which held that a mature man affirmed his selfhood by mastering female depravity and governing dependent women. The very concept of selfhood was gendered. "When influential thinkers of the late eighteenth century pondered the growing claims of the self," Rotundo writes, "they thought only of the *male* self." A few thinkers such as Judith Sargent Murray spoke in favor of women's autonomy, but their voices were subdued by patriarchal laws and customs that required women to sacrifice subjectivity for the good of their families and nation. This normative conjuncture of male selfhood and female self-sacrifice was justified by social contract theories that expanded men's rights, economic opportunities, and political participation and by what Carole Pateman calls the implicit sexual contract that reinforced female domesticity and subordination. The result, Joan Hoff argues, was that the founders created an enduring republic that recognized male autonomy but required women's selfless devotion to men.[42]

Nonetheless, many founders were ambivalent about the war between the sexes. They relied on men to defend liberty but praised women for their "manly exertions" and "patriotic zeal" in the cause of liberty. They enjoined men to practice civility in society but appreciated women who excelled at the "disposition to please," which elevated both "men and women above the brutes." Furthermore, some founders were convinced that men did not monopolize rationality and women were not wholly consumed by passion. They recognized women's potential for reason, promoted female education, and speculated on women's intellectual equality with men. Meanwhile, most founders dwelled on men's desires, impulses, avarice, and deceitfulness. Even relative optimists such as Benjamin Franklin and Thomas Jefferson worried about men's tendency to submit to lust, alcohol, gambling, profligacy, luxury, factionalism, and other vices. In a complex culture of manhood where gender boundaries blurred, gender opposition became a somewhat slippery foundation for patriarchy.[43]

One of the most innovative aspects of the founders' gendered legacy was their expropriation for manhood of traditional female vices and virtues. The founders attributed disorderly passions and procreative potentials to both men and women. Their distrust of the Bachelor as a symbol for disorderly men was a variation of traditional patriarchal fears of disorderly women. Their support for the Family Man as a sober citizen was an adaptation of the conventional belief that marriage subdued female passions. Their praise for the procreative leadership of the Better Sort and the Heroic Man represented a male usurpation of women's unique ability to give birth. Men were just like women—*but even more so.* This quantitative difference was decisive. If men were more disorderly than women, then disorderly men posed the greater danger to the Republic and deserved the highest political priority. If men were more procreative than women, then procreative men positioned themselves as the most qualified people to restore social order and secure political stability. The founders' legacy to posterity included the belief that disorderly men were the main problem of politics and procreative men were the nation's main problem solvers.

The founders inherited the traditional portrait of women as lustful, manipulative, dangerous creatures. However, they expressed a heightened awareness that women's vices were regularly reproduced among men. Most founders recognized that both women and men were disposed to seduce and were vulnerable to seduction. Noah Webster criticized lustful women who manipulated men's passions and deceitful libertines who preyed on female innocence. He worried that the example of "artless females" who were victimized by rogue lovers was being repeated among male citizens who were seduced by silver-tongued demagogues. Most founders also recognized that women and men shared other failings. Benjamin Franklin condemned women's intemperance and men's "more frequent" intemperance. He cursed women's fickleness and berated men's "wavering and inconstant" disposition. John Adams criticized women and men who exhibited affinities toward "luxury" and related "dissipations." Both sexes needed an education in virtue to resist luxury, but not the sort of education that produced the equally "contemptible characters" of the "femme savant" and male "pedant."[44] Overall, the founders believed that both sexes were composed of disorderly creatures.

However, these disorderly creatures were not equally subversive of social stability and political peace. The female "coquette," for example, was a minor irritant and secondary source of social conflict. Her selfishness, vanity, and flirtations threatened her own well-being more than anything else. Hannah Webster Foster's novel *The Coquette* told the story of a self-described "young, gay, volatile" woman who refused a virtuous suitor for "a designing libertine," who eventually impregnated and abandoned her to a premature death. By contrast, the founders believed that the male rogue epitomized men's "ambitious, vindictive, and rapacious" nature. His passions, impulses, and interests threatened not only his own health and happiness or the fortunes of a few families but also larger social bonds and legitimate authority. Recall John Adams's reply to Abigail's request to "remember the ladies." John ridiculed Abigail's concern for women but expressed grave fear that the male disorders brought on by the revolutionary struggle had "loosened the bands of government everywhere."[45]

The founders' front-line remedy for disorderly men was an adaptation of the traditional prescription for disorderly women: marriage. Both the Family Man and the Goodwife encountered religious, cultural, and legal pressures to channel lust into marriage, contribute to the family economy, share responsibility for child rearing, and practice civility in community affairs. Patriarchal family life afforded husbands the authority to manage their wives' passions and authorized pious wives to monitor their husbands' morals. During and after the Revolution, the founders thickened both men's and women's marital responsibilities by adding a layer of civic duty. Husbands were to defend their rights, families, and country while wives were to serve as republican mothers who educated sons to become "virtuous citizens of the republic."[46] The founders encouraged men and women to enter into family life, but their foremost concern was to get young males settled into marriage, family responsibility, and fraternal society to ensure family patriarchy, social order, and sober citizenship.

In turn, the founders hoped to shield sober citizens from social conflict and political disarray by expropriating women's procreativity. Their grammar of manhood declared that male procreativity superseded women's reproductive powers. Procreative men sired sons; women simply carried them. Procreative men produced and protected liberty, mixed their blood with the land to generate moral value and economic wealth, and established social bonds that created civil society; women simply enjoyed the fruits of men's liberty, labor, and society. Procreative men framed constitutions, established governments, and ran them; women simply lived under them. The founders believed that a few heroic men monopolized the extraordinary procreativity needed to father a republic and transmit it to posterity; they used the language and concepts of manhood to encourage most other men and require all women to acquiesce to their leadership.

More than two hundred years later, American politics still privileges problems associated with disorderly men. These problems include domestic crime and international conflict. The main perpetrators of violence in both arenas are disorderly men—from thieves and murderers to terrorists and dictators. American leaders give priority to addressing these problems, often in the name of protecting innocent women. A usual result is to trivialize matters related to women's liberty and equality. When innocent bystanders are getting killed in drive-by shootings and American soldiers are put in harm's way, issues involving domestic abuse or reproductive rights readily become back-burner items. Equally important, American politics still favors male procreativity as a primary source of public policy. Men's preferred means to address national problems is to identify and rely on a few heroic men to assert hegemonic leadership, for example, to conquer crime and win war. Manly leaders who exhibit a proper combination of resolution and tenderness, integrity and civility, and self-discipline and selfless generosity can count on most citizens to comply with their initiatives. To the extent that men are still seen as the principal problem and problem solvers in American public life, the founders succeeded beyond all expectations to establish an enduring republic of men.

Notes

NOTES TO THE INTRODUCTION

1. Susan Juster, *Disorderly Women: Sexual Politics and Evangelicalism in Revolutionary New England* (Ithaca: Cornell University Press, 1994), 138.

2. John Witherspoon, quoted in Jan Lewis, "The Republican Wife: Virtue and Seduction in the Early Republic," *William and Mary Quarterly*, 3d ser., 44 (October 1987): 709; Carroll Smith-Rosenberg in Linda K. Kerber, Nancy F. Cott, Lynn Hunt, Carroll Smith-Rosenberg, and Christine Stansell, "Forum: Beyond Roles, Beyond Spheres: Thinking about Gender in the Early Republic," *William and Mary Quarterly*, 3d ser., 64 (July 1989): 573.

3. Thomas Paine, "Common Sense," in *The Life and Major Writings of Thomas Paine*, ed. Philip S. Foner (New York: Citadel Press, 1961), 23; Stanley Griswold, "Overcoming Evil with Good" (1801), in *Political Sermons of the American Founding Era, 1730–1805*, ed. Ellis Sandoz (Indianapolis: Liberty Press, 1991), 1552; Samuel Sherwood, "Scriptural Instructions to Civil Rulers" (1774), in Ibid., 377–78; John Witherspoon, "The Dominion of Providence over the Passions of Men" (1776), in Ibid., 556.

NOTES TO CHAPTER 1

1. Judith Sargent Murray, "Sketch of the Present Situation in America" (1794), in *Selected Writings of Judith Sargent Murray*, ed. Sharon M. Harris (New York: Oxford University Press, 1995), 52.

2. E. Anthony Rotundo, "Patriarchs and Participants: A Historical Perspective on Fatherhood in the United States," in *Beyond Patriarchy: Essays by Men on Pleasure, Power, and Change*, ed. Michael Kaufman (Toronto: Oxford University Press, 1987), 65–67; idem, *American Manhood: Transformations in Masculinity from the Revolution to the Modern Era* (New York: Basic Books, 1993), 11–14; Melvin Yazawa, *From Colonies to Commonwealth: Familial Ideology and the Beginnings of the American Republic* (Baltimore: Johns Hopkins University Press, 1985), 46; John Demos, *Past, Present, and Personal: The Family and the Life Course in American History* (New York: Oxford University Press, 1986), 27–28, 44–45; idem, *A Little Commonwealth: Family Life in Plymouth Colony* (Oxford: Oxford University Press, 1970), part 2.

3. Juster, *Disorderly Women*, 35–38; anonymous Virginian, quoted in Mary Beth

Norton, *Liberty's Daughters: The Revolutionary Experience of American Women, 1750–1800* (Boston: Little, Brown & Co., 1980), 43; Nancy F. Cott, "Eighteenth-Century Family and Social Life Revealed in Massachusetts Divorce Records," in *A Heritage of Her Own: Toward a New Social History of American Women,* ed. Nancy F. Cott and Elizabeth H. Pleck (New York: Simon & Schuster, 1979), 120; see also Edmund Morgan, "The Puritans and Sex," *New England Quarterly* 15 (1942): 591–607.

4. Mary Noyes Silliman, quoted in Joy Day Buel and Richard Buel, Jr., *The Way of Duty: A Woman and Her Family in Revolutionary America* (New York: Norton, 1984), 230–31; Benjamin Franklin, "Observations Concerning the Increase of Mankind, Peopling of Countries, &c." (1751), in *Writings,* ed. J. A. Leon Lemay (New York: Library of America, 1987), 368; George Washington to Marquis de Lafayette, July 25, 1785, in *George Washington: A Collection,* ed. W. B. Allen (Indianapolis: Liberty Press, 1988), 304; Thomas Jefferson to Jean Baptiste Say, February 1, 1804, in *The Portable Thomas Jefferson,* ed. Merrill D. Peterson (New York: Viking Press, 1975), 498; see also Norton, *Liberty's Daughters,* 67.

5. John Gregory and *Pennsylvania Magazine* quoted in Jay Fliegelman, *Prodigals and Pilgrims: The American Revolution against Patriarchal Authority, 1750–1800* (Cambridge: Cambridge University Press, 1982), 44, 124–25; Hannah Webster Foster, *The Coquette; or, the History of Eliza Wharton* (1797), in *The Heath Anthology of American Literature,* ed. Paul Lauter, 2 vols., 2d ed. (Lexington, Mass.: D. C. Heath & Co., 1994), 1:1160; Judith Sargent Murray, "The Story of Margaretta" (1792–94), in Harris, ed., *Selected Writings,* 174–75.

6. Laurel Thatcher Ulrich, "Vertuous Women Found: New England Ministerial Literature, 1668–1735," in Cott and Pleck, eds., *A Heritage of Her Own,* 68; Benjamin Franklin, "Reply to a Piece of Advice" (1735), in Lemay, ed., *Writings,* 248–50; see also Glenna Matthews, *The Rise of Public Woman: Woman's Power and Women's Place in the United States, 1630–1970* (New York: Oxford University Press, 1992), chaps. 1–2.

7. Demos, *Past, Present, and Personal,* 46, 153–54; Carol Shammas, Marylynn Salmon, and Michel Dahlin, *Inheritance in America: From Colonial Times to the Present* (New Brunswick: Rutgers University Press, 1987), 56–57; artisans quoted in Gordon S. Wood, *The Radicalism of the American Revolution* (New York: Knopf, 1992), 246; see also Fliegelman, *Prodigals and Pilgrims,* 204.

8. Wood, *Radicalism,* 43.

9. Fliegelman, *Prodigals and Pilgrims,* 1; see also Lawrence Stone, *The Family, Sex, and Marriage in England, 1500–1800* (New York: Harper & Row, 1977), chap. 6.

10. Gordon J. Schochet, *The Authoritarian Family and Political Attitudes in Seventeenth-Century England: Patriarchalism in Political Thought* (New Brunswick, N.J.: Transaction Books, 1988), 14–15, 57, 65–67; Antonia Fraser, *The Weaker Vessel* (New York: Random House, 1984), 41, 60–63, 71–72, 148; see also John Toland, *The Militia Reform'd; or an Easy Scheme of Furnishing England with a Constant Land Force capable to prevent or to subdue any Forein Power, and to maintain perpetual Quiet at Home, without endangering the Publick Liberty* (London: John Darby, 1698), 83–84.

11. See Algernon Sidney, *Discourses Concerning Government,* 2d ed. (London: John Darby, 1704), 13, 38, 62–63, 227–28; James Tyrrell, *Patriarcha non Monarcha: The Patriarch Unmonarch'd* (London: Richard Janeway, 1681), chap. 1; John Locke, *Two Treatises of Government,* ed. Peter Laslett (Cambridge: Cambridge University Press, 1988), book 1, paras. 29, 47, 61; book 2, esp. paras. 82–83; see also Melissa Butler, "Early Liberal Roots of Feminism: John Locke and the Attack on Patriarchy," *American Political Science Review* 72 (March 1978): 135–50; Mary Lyndon Shanley, "Marriage Contract and Social Contract in Seventeenth-Century English Political Thought," *Western Political Quarterly* 32, 1 (March 1979): 79–91.

12. Mary Astell, "Reflections Upon Marriage," in *The First English Feminist: Reflections upon Marriage and Other Writings by Mary Astell,* ed. Bridget Hill (New York: St. Martin's Press, 1986), 75–76; Lady Mary Chudleigh, *The Ladies Defence, or, the Bride-Woman's Counselor Answer'd* (London: John Deeve, 1701), 3; Stone, *Family, Sex, and Marriage,* 655–56.

13. James Harrington, *The Commonwealth of Oceana* (London: J. Streater, 1656), 208–9; John Locke, *Some Thoughts Concerning Education,* in *The Educational Writings of John Locke,* ed. James Axtell (Cambridge: Cambridge University Press, 1968), 145, 213; see also Nathan Tarcov, *Locke's Education for Liberty* (Chicago: University of Chicago Press, 1984), 98.

14. Schochet, *Authoritarian Family,* 72; James Otis, Jr., "The Rights of the British Colonies Asserted and Proved" (1764), in *Pamphlets of the American Revolution, 1750–1776,* ed. Bernard Bailyn, 2 vols. (Cambridge: Harvard University Press, 1965), 1:420; Thomas Paine, "An Occasional Letter on the Female Sex" (1775), in *Against the Tide: Pro-Feminist Men in the United States, 1776–1990: A Documentary History,* ed. Michael S. Kimmel and Thomas F. Mosmiller (Boston: Beacon Press, 1992), 63–66; Abigail Adams to John Adams, March 31, 1776, in *Familiar Letters of John Adams and His Wife Abigail Adams during the Revolution,* ed. Charles Francis Adams (Freeport, N.Y.: Books for Libraries Press, 1970), 148–50.

15. Kenneth Lockridge, *On the Sources of Patriarchal Rage: The Commonplace Books of William Byrd and Thomas Jefferson and the Gendering of Power in the Eighteenth Century* (New York: New York University Press, 1992), 84, 88, 108–9; see also Smith-Rosenberg, in Kerber et al., "Forum: Beyond Roles, Beyond Spheres," 573; Norton, *Liberty's Daughters,* 125, 225.

16. Anonymous, "Verse Written by a Young Lady, on Women Born to be Controll'd" (1743), in Lauter, ed., *Heath Anthology,* 1:701–2; Annis Boudinot Stockton, "A Satire on Fashionable Pompoons Worn by the Ladies in the Year 1759" (1759), in *Second to None: A Documentary History of American Women,* ed. Ruth Barnes Moynihan, Cynthia Russett, and Laurie Crumpacker, 2 vols. (Lincoln: University of Nebraska Press, 1993), 1:150–51; Judith Sargent Murray, "Observations on Female Abilities" (1792–94) and "Story of Margaretta," in Harris, ed., *Selected Writings,* 38, 223, 233; see also Lewis, "Republican Wife," 693, 707, 709, 711–12; Juster, *Disorderly Women,* 187.

17. Rotundo, "Patriarchs and Participants," in Kaufman, ed., *Beyond Patriarchy,*

67; Kenneth A. Lockridge, *A New England Town: The First One Hundred Years* (New York: Norton, 1970), 102; Demos, *Past, Present, and Personal*, 99; Matthews, *Rise of Public Woman*, 33–34; Lewis, "Republican Wife," 696; Wood, *Radicalism*, 145–168; see also Robert A. Gross, *The Minutemen and Their World* (New York: Hill & Wang, 1976), 76–89.

18. Demos, *Past, Present, and Personal*, 49–52; Rotundo, *American Manhood*, 23.

19. Lockridge, *Sources of Patriarchal Rage*, 68, 81–82, 112–13; Nancy F. Cott, in Kerber et al., "Forum: Beyond Roles, Beyond Spheres," 568; Mary H. Blewett, *Men, Women, and Work: Class, Gender, and Protest in the New England Shoe Industry, 1780–1910* (Urbana: University of Illinois Press, 1988), 17; Grace Galloway, "Journal of Grace Growden Galloway," in Moynihan, Russett, and Crumpacker, eds., *Second to None*, 1:173.

20. R. W. K. Hinton, "Husbands, Fathers and Conquerors," *Political Studies* 15, 3 (October 1967): 294.

21. Michael S. Kimmel, *Manhood in America: A Cultural History* (New York: Free Press, 1996), 16–18; Wood, *Radicalism*, part 1, esp. 32; Richard Bushman, *The Refinement of America: Persons, Houses, Cities* (New York: Random House, 1992), 207.

22. Bushman, *Refinement*, xix, 84, 207–8; John Perkins, "Theory of Agency: or, An Essay on the Nature, Source, and Extent of Moral Freedom" (1771), in *American Political Writings during the Founding Era, 1760–1805*, ed. Charles S. Hyneman and Donald S. Lutz, 2 vols. (Indianapolis: Liberty Press, 1983), 1:145; Timothy Dwight, quoted in Bushman, *Refinement*, 194–95.

23. G. J. Barker-Benfield, *The Culture of Sensibility: Sex and Society in Eighteenth-Century Britain* (Chicago: University of Chicago Press, 1992), 117; Kimmel, *Manhood in America*, 21; Buel and Buel, *Way of Duty*, 48; Royall Tyler, "The Contrast, A Comedy in Five Acts" (1790), in Lauter, ed., *Heath Anthology*, 1:1111; Jay Fliegelman, *Declaring Independence: Jefferson, Natural Language, and the Culture of Performance* (Stanford: Stanford University Press, 1993), 37.

24. Kimmel, *Manhood in America*, 16; Mary Ann Clawson, *Constructing Brotherhood: Class, Gender, and Fraternalism* (Princeton: Princeton University Press, 1989), 14, 23, 52; Gary B. Nash, *Race, Class, and Politics: Essays on American and Colonial Society* (Urbana: University of Illinois Press, 1986), chap. 9, esp. 251.

25. Tyler, "The Contrast" (1790), in Lauter, ed., *Heath Anthology*, 1:1113–14, 1117, 1133–34, 1141; Murray, "Observations on Female Abilities," in *Selected Writings*, 39; see also Lewis, "Republican Wife," 689–721; Norton, *Liberty's Daughters*, 254–55; Benjamin Rush, "A Plan for the Establishment of Public Schools and Diffusion of Knowledge in Pennsylvania, to which are Added, Thoughts upon the Mode of Education, Proper in a Republic, Addressed to the Legislature and Citizens of the State" (1786) and "Thoughts Upon Female Education, Accommodated to the Present State of Society, Manners, and Government in the United States of America" (1787), in *Essays on Education in the Early Republic*, ed. Frederick Rudolph (Cambridge: Harvard University Press, 1965), 2–23, 27–40.

26. Lockridge, *Sources of Patriarchal Rage,* 112; Juster, *Disorderly Women,* chaps. 4–5; Caroline Robbins, *The Eighteenth-Century Commonwealthman: Studies in the Transmission, Development and Circumstances of English Liberal Thought from the Restoration of Charles II until the War with the Thirteen Colonies* (Cambridge: Harvard University Press, 1961), 16. Compare Gordon S. Wood, *The Creation of the American Republic, 1776–1787* (New York: Norton, 1969); Joyce Appleby, *Capitalism and a New Social Order: The Republican Visions of the 1790s* (New York: New York University Press, 1984); and John P. Diggins, *The Lost Soul of American Politics* (New York: Basic Books, 1984).

27. Rotundo, *American Manhood,* 17–20; Kimmel, *Manhood in America,* 45; Bushman, *Refinement,* 402–3.

28. George Mason to George Mason, Jr., January 8, 1783, in *The Papers of George Mason, 1779–1786,* ed. Robert A. Rutland, 3 vols. (Chapel Hill: University of North Carolina Press, 1970) 2:762; Mary P. Ryan, *Cradle of the Middle Class: The Family in Oneida County, New York, 1790–1865* (Cambridge: Cambridge University Press, 1981), chap. 1; Joan Hoff, *Law, Gender, and Injustice: A Legal History of U.S. Women* (New York: New York University Press, 1991), chap. 1; Ruth H. Bloch, "The Gendered Meanings of Virtue in Revolutionary America," *Signs: Journal of Women in Culture and Society* 13, 11 (1987): 56; Rotundo, *American Manhood,* 20–21; Clawson, *Constructing Brotherhood,* 72–73.

29. Kimmel, *Manhood in America,* 21; Rotundo, *American Manhood,* 19–20; Appleby, *Capitalism and a New Social Order,* 104 and chap. 4; Louis Hartz, *The Liberal Tradition in America* (New York: Harcourt, Brace and World, 1955), 111–12.

30. R. W. Connell, *Masculinities* (Berkeley and Los Angeles: University of California Press, 1995), 198.

31. See Nash, *Race, Class, and Politics,* 248.

32. Joan R. Gundersen, "Independence, Citizenship, and the American Revolution," *Signs: Journal of Women in Culture and Society* 13, 11 (1987): 77; Stonington Association (1787), quoted in Juster, *Disorderly Women,* 117; Judith Sargent Murray, "On the Equality of the Sexes" (1790), in Lauter, ed., *Heath Anthology,* 1:1011–16.

33. Nancy Hartsock, "The Barracks Community in Western Political Thought: Prolegomena to a Feminist Critique of War and Politics," in *Women and Men's Wars,* ed. Judith H. Stiehm (Oxford: Pergamon, 1983), 283–84; Hanna Fenichel Pitkin, *Fortune Is a Woman: Gender and Politics in the Thought of Niccolo Machiavelli* (Berkeley and Los Angeles: University of California Press, 1984), 109, 117; Carole Pateman, *The Sexual Contract* (Stanford, Calif.: Stanford University Press, 1988), chap. 1; idem, *The Disorder of Women: Democracy, Feminism and Political Theory* (Stanford: Stanford University Press, 1989), 4.

34. Smith-Rosenberg, in Kerber et al., "Forum: Beyond Roles, Beyond Spheres," 573; Linda Kerber, "'History Can Do It No Justice': Women and the Reinterpretation of the American Revolution," in *Women in the Age of the American Revolution,* ed. Ronald Hoffman and Peter Albert (Charlottesville: University Press of Virginia, 1989),

24–25, 30–31; Bloch, "Gendered Meanings of Virtue," 44–45, 56; Philip Greven, *The Protestant Temperament: Patterns of Child-Rearing, Religious Experience, and Self in Early America* (New York: Knopf, 1977), 351–52; Juster, *Disorderly Women*, 142–43; Gundersen, "Independence," 75, 77; Christine Stansell, *City of Women: Sex and Class in New York: 1789–1860* (Urbana: University of Illinois Press, 1987), 21; Judith Shklar, *American Citizenship: The Quest for Inclusion* (Cambridge: Harvard University Press, 1991), 15–16; Hoff, *Law, Gender, and Injustice*, 4, 38–39, 117, and chaps. 1–3; Joyce Appleby, *Liberalism and Republicanism in the Historical Imagination* (Cambridge: Harvard University Press, 1992), 29; Lewis, "Republican Wife," 689–721; see also Linda K. Kerber, *Women of the Republic: Intellect and Ideology in Revolutionary America* (Chapel Hill: University of North Carolina Press, 1980), 199–200, 229.

35. Rotundo, *American Manhood*, 17–20; Kimmel, *Manhood in America*, 7, 14; David G. Pugh, *Sons of Liberty: The Masculine Mind in Nineteenth-Century America* (Westport, Conn.: Greenwood Press, 1983), xvi–xvii; Michael Paul Rogin, *Fathers and Children: Andrew Jackson and the Subjugation of the American Indian* (New York: Random House, 1975), 30: Joe L. Dubbert, *A Man's Place: Masculinity in Transition* (Englewood Cliffs, N.J.: Prentice-Hall, 1979), 11, 13, 17; Michael S. Kimmel, "The Contemporary 'Crisis' of Masculinity in Historical Perspective," in *The Making of Masculinities: The New Men's Studies*, ed. Harry S. Brod (Boston: Allen & Unwin, 1987), 140–42; Peter G. Filene, *Him/Her/Self: Sex Roles in Modern America*, 2d ed. (Baltimore: Johns Hopkins University Press, 1986), chap. 3.

36. Christine Stansell, in Kerber et al., "Forum: Beyond Roles, Beyond Spheres," 569; Alexander Hamilton, *Federalist* No. 6, in Alexander Hamilton, James Madison, and John Jay, *The Federalist Papers*, ed. Clinton Rossiter (New York: New American Library, 1961), 54–55; John Adams to James Sullivan, May 26, 1776, in *Free Government in the Making: Readings in American Political Thought*, ed. Alpheus Thomas Mason and Gordon E. Baker, 4th ed. (New York: Oxford University Press, 1985), 120–21; John Adams, "A Defence of the Constitutions of Government of the United States of America" (1787), in *The Political Writings of John Adams*, ed. George Peek (Indianapolis: Bobbs-Merrill, 1954), 124, 147; Anna G. Jónasdóttir, *Why Women Are Oppressed* (Philadelphia: Temple University Press, 1994), 117–18.

37. Genevieve Lloyd, *The Man of Reason: "Male" and "Female" in Western Philosophy*, 2d ed. (Minneapolis: University of Minnesota Press, 1993), viii, xviii, 103–4; Pateman, *Disorder of Women*, 4, 21.

38. Theophilus Parsons, "The Essex Result" (1778), in Hyneman and Lutz, eds., *American Political Writings*, 1:497.

39. Christine Di Stefano, *Configurations of Masculinity: A Feminist Perspective on Modern Political Theory* (Ithaca: Cornell University Press, 1991), 143; Lockridge, *Sources of Patriarchal Rage*, 83–84, 96, 98.

40. Kerber, *Women of the Republic*, 31; Samuel Williams, "The Natural and Civil History of Vermont" (1794), in Hyneman and Lutz, eds., *American Political Writings*, 2:956; John Adams to Abigail Adams, June 3, 1778, in Adams, ed., *Familiar Letters*, 334;

Mercy Otis Warren, *History of the Rise, Progress and Termination of the American Revolution, interspersed with Biographical, Political and Moral Observations* (1805), ed. Lester H. Cohen, 2 vols. (Indianapolis: Liberty Press, 1988), 1:212.

41. George Washington to Nathanael Greene, October 6, 1781, in *Affectionately Yours, George Washington: A Self-Portrait in Letters of Friendship*, ed. Thomas J. Fleming (New York: Norton, 1967), 155; Michael Grossberg, "Institutionalizing Masculinity: The Law as a Masculine Profession," in *Meanings for Manhood: Constructions of Masculinity in Victorian America*, ed. Mark C. Carnes and Clyde Griffin (Chicago: University of Chicago Press, 1990), 135; Oxenbridge Thatcher, "The Sentiments of a British American" (1764), in Bailyn, ed., *Pamphlets*, 1:496; Landon Carter, quoted in Fliegelman, *Declaring Independence*, 109; Paine, "Common Sense," in *The Life and Major Writings*, 19, 25; idem, "American Crisis II," in Ibid., 62; idem, "American Crisis III," in Ibid., 78–79; idem, "American Crisis VII," in Ibid., 147, 154; idem, "American Crisis XII," in Ibid., 227.

42. Shklar, *American Citizenship*, 2, 15, 17.

43. James Dana, "The African Slave Trade" (1791), in Sandoz, ed., *Political Sermons*, 1052–54; David Ramsay, *The History of the American Revolution* (1789), 2 vols. (Indianapolis: Liberty Press, 1990), 1:29–30; Timothy Ford, "The Constitutionalist: Or, An Inquiry How Far It Is Expedient and Proper to Alter the Constitution of South Carolina" (1794), in Hyneman and Lutz, eds., *American Political Writings*, 2:934; John Taylor, *Arator: Being a Series of Agricultural Essays, Practical and Political in Sixty-Four Numbers* (1803), ed. M. E. Bradford (Indianapolis: Liberty Press 1977), 124; J. Hector St. John de Crèvecoeur, *Letters from an American Farmer* (New York: Penguin Books, 1981), 68–69, 168–71; see also Doreen Alvarez Saar, "The Heritage of Ethnicity in Crèvecouer's *Letters from an American Farmer*," in *A Mixed Race: Ethnicity in Early America*, ed. Frank Shuffelton (New York: Oxford University Press, 1993), 245, 251–53.

44. Noah Webster, "The Revolution in France" (1794), in Sandoz, ed., *Political Sermons*, 1269–70; David Daggett and Elbridge Gerry, quoted in Yazawa, *From Colonies to Commonwealth*, 108–9.

45. Noah Webster, "An Oration on the Anniversary of the Declaration of Independence" (1802), in Hyneman and Lutz, eds., *American Political Writings*, 2:1234; Benjamin Franklin, "On Constancy" (1734), in Lemay, ed., *Writings*, 225–26; idem, "On Drunkenness" (1733), in Ibid., 213–14; Foster, *The Coquette* (1797), in Lauter, ed., *Heath Anthology*, 1:1150–68; Hamilton, *Federalist* No. 6, 54, 56–57; John Adams to Abigail Adams, April 14, 1776, in Mason and Baker, eds., *Free Government*, 119–20; see also Fliegelman, *Declaring Independence*, 32, 38, 130.

46. Lockridge, *Sources of Patriarchal Rage*, 81–82; Joel Barlow, "The Hasty Pudding" (1793), in Lauter, ed., *Heath Anthology*, 1:1092; Nancy Hartsock, *Money, Sex, and Power: Toward a Feminist Historical Materialism* (New York: Longman, 1983), 196–97; Pateman, *Sexual Contract*, 102; idem, *Disorder of Women*, 38; idem, "Introduction: The Theoretical Subversiveness of Feminism," in *Feminist Challenges: Social and Political Theory*, ed. Carole Pateman and Elizabeth Gross (Boston: Northeastern University Press, 1986), 7.

47. Jonathan Mayhew, "The Snare Broken" (1766), in Sandoz, ed., *Political Sermons*, 241, 249; Thomas Jefferson, "Second Inaugural Address" (1805), in Peterson, ed., *The Portable Thomas Jefferson*, 320–21; Fisher Ames, "The Dangers of American Liberty" (1805), in Hyneman and Lutz, eds., *American Political Writings*, 2:1318–19.

48. Benjamin Franklin, "Celia Single" (1732), in Lemay, ed., *Writings*, 189–90; see also Mark E. Kann, *On the Man Question: Gender and Civic Virtue in America* (Philadelphia: Temple University Press, 1991), esp. the conclusion titled "Fortune Is a Man," 295–316.

49. Thomas Jefferson to François de Barbé-Marbois, December 5, 1783, in *Jefferson Himself: The Personal Narrative of a Many-Sided American*, ed. Bernard Mayo (Charlottesville: University Press of Virginia, 1970), 43; Thomas Jefferson to Maria Cosway, October 12, 1786, in Ibid., 129–40.

50. Wood, *Radicalism*, 27–28, 46.

51. Bernard Bailyn, *The Ideological Origins of the American Revolution* (Cambridge: Harvard University Press, 1967), 305.

52. Otis, "Rights of the British Colonies" (1764), in Bailyn, *Pamphlets*, 1:436, 444, 447.

53. Ramsay, *History*, 1:172, 2:637; John Adams to Abigail Adams, July 7, 1774, in Adams, ed., *Familiar Letters*, 20; George Washington, "General Orders, July 10, 1776," in *A Biography in His Own Words*, ed. Ralph K. Andrist (New York: Harper & Row, 1972), 153.

54. John Adams to Abigail Adams, April 14, 1776, in Adams, ed., *Familiar Letters*, 153–55; John Adams to John Taylor (1814), in Peek, ed., *Political Writings*, 206.

55. See Terence Ball and J. G. A. Pocock, "Introduction," in *Conceptual Change and the Constitution*, ed. Terence Ball and J. G. A. Pocock (Lawrence: University of Kansas Press, 1988), 1; Appleby, *Capitalism and a New Social Order*, 16–23; Fliegelman, *Declaring Independence*, 28–35.

56. Juster, *Disorderly Women*, 141–42

57. Lockridge, *Sources of Patriarchal Rage*, 96–98.

58. Matthews, *Rise of Public Woman*, 4; see also Fliegelman, *Declaring Independence*, 130.

59. Pateman, *Sexual Contract*, 102–3; Noah Webster, "On the Education of Youth in America" (1790), in Rudolph, ed., *Essays on Education*, 69.

60. Antonio Gramsci, "State and Civil Society," in *Selections from the Prison Notebooks*, ed. Quintin Hoare and Geoffrey Nowell Smith (New York: International Publishers, 1971), 258–59, 263; Raymond Williams, *Marxism and Literature* (Oxford: Oxford University Press, 1977), 108–14.

61. R. W. Connell, *Gender and Power: Society, the Person and Sexual Politics* (Stanford: Stanford University Press, 1987), 110, 183; idem, *Masculinities*, 77–80; Kimmel, *Manhood in America*, 7; David Leverenz, *Manhood and the American Renaissance* (Ithaca: Cornell University Press, 1989), 72–73; Mark Gerzon, *A Choice of Heroes: The Changing Face of American Manhood* (Boston: Houghton Mifflin, 1982), 43.

NOTES TO CHAPTER 2

1. Benjamin Franklin, "The Autobiography," in *The Autobiography and Other Writings*, ed. L. Jesse Lemisch (New York: New American Library, 1961), 18; Paine, "Common Sense," in *The Life and Major Writings*, 40; John Adams, "Dissertation on the Canon and Feudal Law" (1765), in Peek, ed., *Political Writings*, 8, 16; idem, "Defence of the Constitutions" (1787), in Ibid., 114; Thomas Jefferson, "Declaration of Independence" (1776), in Peterson, ed., *The Portable Thomas Jefferson*, 236, 240.

2. Paine, "Common Sense,"in *The Life and Major Writings*, 41; Abigail Adams to John Adams, October 20, 1777, in Adams, ed., *Familiar Letters*, 317.

3. Patrick Henry, "Speeches of Patrick Henry, June 5, 1788," in *The Anti-Federalist Papers and the Constitutional Convention Debates*, ed. Ralph Ketcham (New York: New American Library, 1986), 200; James Otis, Jr., quoted in Warren, *History*, 1:29; Benjamin Franklin, "The Trial and Reprieve of Prouse and Mitchel" (1729), in Lemay, ed., *Writings*, 140; George Washington, "Farewell Orders to the Armies of the United States, November 2, 1783," in Allen, ed., *George Washington*, 268–69; Perkins, "Theory of Agency" (1771), in Hyneman and Lutz, eds., *American Political Writings*, 1:146; James Kent, "An Introductory Lecture to a Course of Law Lectures" (1794), in Ibid., 2:944, 949; James Madison, *Federalist* No. 40, 253–54; Samuel Cooper, "A Sermon on the Day of the Commencement of the Constitution" (1780), in Sandoz, ed., *Political Sermons*, 645; Joel Barlow, "A Letter to the National Convention of France on the Defects in the Constitution of 1791" (1792), in Hyneman and Lutz, eds., *American Political Writings*, 2:834.

4. George Washington to John Hancock, September 16, 1776, in Andrist, ed., *A Biography*, 159; "The Liberty Song" (1768), in Lauter, ed., *Heath Anthology*, 1:918; Anna Young Smith, "An Elegy to the Memory of our American Volunteers, who Fell in Engagement Between the Massachusetts-Bay Militia, and the British Troops" (1775), in Ibid., 1:694; Joel Barlow, "The Prospect of Peace" (1778), in Ibid., 1:1084; Milcah Martha Moore, "The Female Patriots, Address'd to the Daughters of Liberty in America" (1768), in Ibid., 1:683; Greven, *Protestant Temperament*, 352.

5. Gerda Lerner, *The Creation of Patriarchy* (New York: Oxford University Press, 1986), 201, also 44–45, 178; Jónasdóttir, *Why Women Are Oppressed*, 30; Richard Ames, *The Folly of Love; or, an Essay upon Satyr against Woman* (1691), reprinted in *Satires on Women*, ed. Felicity Nussbaum, Augustan Reprint Society, no. 180 (Los Angeles: William Andrews Clark Memorial Library, 1976), 71; Pateman, *Sexual Contract*, 88–89; Lockridge, *Sources of Patriarchal Rage*, 14, 19, 25, 81–83.

6. John Leland, "The Connecticut Dissenters' Strong Box: No. 1" (1802), in Hyneman and Lutz, eds., *American Political Writings*, 2:1190; Adams, "Defence of the Constitutions" (1787), in Peek, ed., *Political Writings*, 46.

7. Washington to Lafayette, July 25, 1785, in Allen, ed., *George Washington*, 304; grandfather quoted in Demos, *Past, Present, and Personal*, 46.

8. Mayhew, "The Snare Broken" (1766), in Sandoz, ed., *Political Sermons*, 240,

247; Thomas Fitch, "Reasons Why the British Colonies in America should not be Charged with Internal Taxes" (1764), in Bailyn, ed., *Pamphlets*, 1:399; Adams, "Dissertation on the Canon" (1765), in Peek, ed., *Political Writings*, 12–13.

9. Sheldon Wolin, *The Presence of the Past: Essays on the State and the Constitution* (Baltimore: Johns Hopkins University Press, 1989), 137, 140; Warren, *History*, 1:59–61.

10. Silas Downer, "Discourse at the Dedication of the Tree of Liberty" (1768), in Hyneman and Lutz, eds., *American Political Writings*, 1:107.

11. Daniel Shute, "An Election Sermon" (1768), in Hyneman and Lutz, eds., *American Political Writings*, 1:135; John Allen, "An Oration Upon the Beauties of Liberty" (1773), in Sandoz, ed., *Political Sermons*, 310, 322–23; Moses Mather, "America's Appeal to the Impartial World" (1775), in Ibid., 445.

12. Thomas Jefferson, "The Declaration on the Causes and Necessity of Taking up Arms" (July 6, 1775), in Mayo, ed., *Jefferson Himself*, 55; Cooper, "A Sermon" (1780), in Sandoz, ed., *Political Sermons*, 656; see also "Cato I" (1787), in *The Debate on the Constitution: Federalist and Antifederalist Speeches, Articles and Letters during the Struggle over Ratification*, ed. Bernard Bailyn, 2 vols. (New York: Library of America, 1993), 1:32; Simeon Howard, "A Sermon Preached to the Ancient and Honorable Artillery Company in Boston" (1773), in Hyneman and Lutz, eds., *American Political Writings*, 1:202.

13. Douglass Adair, "Fame and the Founding Fathers," in *Fame and the Founding Fathers: Essays by Douglass Adair*, ed. Trevor Colbourn (New York: Norton, 1974), 7; Griswold, "Overcoming Evil" (1801), in Sandoz, ed., *Political Sermons*, 1551.

14. Franklin, "Reply to a Piece of Advice" (1735), in Lemay, ed., *Writings*, 249; idem, "Causes of American Discontents Before 1768" (1768), in Ibid., 611; Murray, "Observations on Female Abilities," in Harris, ed., *Selected Writings*, 24, 28.

15. Franklin, "Observations Concerning the Increase of Mankind" (1751), in Lemay, ed., *Writings*, 368; Washington to Lafayette, July 25, 1785, in Allen, ed., *George Washington*, 304; Jefferson to Jean Baptiste Say, February 1, 1804, in Peterson, ed., *The Portable Thomas Jefferson*, 498.

16. Benjamin Franklin, "On the Tenure of the Manor of East Greenwich" (1766), in Lemay, ed., *Writings*, 572; Thomas Jefferson, "A Summary View of the Rights of British America" (1774), in Peterson, ed., *The Portable Thomas Jefferson*, 4–5; George Duffield, "A Sermon Preached on a Day of Thanksgiving" (1783), in Sandoz, ed., *Political Sermons*, 782–83.

17. George Washington to Marquis de Chastellux, April 25, 1788, in Allen, ed., *George Washington*, 394; Taylor, *Arator*, 96–97, 315; see also Gross, *Minutemen*, 80; Wood, *Radicalism*, 178.

18. Thomas Jefferson, "Notes on the State of Virginia" (1781), in Peterson, ed., *The Portable Thomas Jefferson*, 217; idem, "Second Inaugural Address" (1805), in Ibid., 318; Taylor, *Arator*, 67.

19. Garry Wills, *Cincinnatus: George Washington and the Enlightenment* (Garden City, N.Y.: Doubleday, 1984), 23; see also Warren, *History*, 1:34; Adams, "Defence of the Constitutions" (1787), in Peek, ed., *Political Writings*, 135–36.

20. Anonymous, "A Letter to the People of Pennsylvania; Occasioned by the Assembly's Passing that Important Act for Constituting the Judges of the Supreme Court and Common-Pleas During Good Behavior" (1760), in Bailyn, ed., *Pamphlets,* 1:270–71.

21. Daniel Dulany, "Considerations on the Propriety of Imposing Taxes in the British Colonies" (1765), in Bailyn, ed., *Pamphlets,* 1:614.

22. James Madison and James Wilson, "Citizenship for Immigrants" (1787), in Ketcham, ed., *Anti-Federalist Papers,* 157–58; Shklar, *American Citizenship,* 3.

23. Kerber, *Women of the Republic,* chap. 4; Gross, *Minutemen,* 102.

24. Michael Lienesch, *New Order of the Ages: Time, the Constitution, and the Making of Modern American Political Thought* (Princeton: Princeton University Press, 1988), 82; Caleb Lownes, "An Account of the Alteration and Present State of the Penal Laws of Pennsylvania" (1793), in *Reform of Criminal Law in Pennsylvania: Selected Inquiries, 1787–1819* (New York: Arno Press Reprint, 1972), 93.

25. See Pateman, *Sexual Contract,* 77–78.

26. Samuel Adams, quoted in A. J. Langguth, *Patriots: The Men Who Started the American Revolution* (New York: Simon & Schuster, 1988), 98; Mather, "America's Appeal" (1775), in Sandoz, ed., *Political Sermons,* 483; Oxenbridge Thatcher quoted in Langguth, *Patriots,* 71; Sherwood, "Scriptural Instructions" (1774), in Sandoz, ed., *Political Sermons,* 378; Ramsay, *History,* 1:183.

27. James Otis, Jr., "A Vindication of the British Colonies" (1765), in Bailyn, ed., *Pamphlets,* 1:565; John Dickinson, "Letters from a Farmer in Pennsylvania" (1767), in Mason and Baker, eds., *Free Government,* 98; Jefferson, "Summary View" (1774), in Peterson, ed., *The Portable Thomas Jefferson,* 21.

28. George Washington to Brian Fairfax, August 24, 1774, in Fleming, ed., *Affectionately Yours,* 48; Witherspoon, "Dominion of Providence" (1776), in Sandoz, ed., *Political Sermons,* 537; Joseph Warren, quoted in Langguth, *Patriots,* 252; Paine, "Common Sense," in *The Life and Major Writings,* 22–23.

29. Paine, "American Crisis II," in *The Life and Major Writings,* 162; Abigail Adams to John Adams, July 13, 1776, in Adams, ed., *Familiar Letters,* 210; Thomas Jefferson, "Rough Draft of the Declaration of Independence," in Carl Becker, *The Declaration of Independence: A Study in the History of Political Ideas* (New York: Random House, 1970), 148–49; George Washington, "General Orders, July 2, 1776," in Allen, ed., *George Washington,* 71; George Washington to John Augustine Washington, May 31, 1776, in Ibid., 69; George Washington to John Banister, April 21, 1778, in Ibid., 101.

30. Wilson Carey McWilliams, *The Idea of Fraternity in America* (Berkeley and Los Angeles: University of California Press, 1973), 92–93; Ramsay, *History,* 1:112; Jefferson, "Notes on the State of Virginia" (1781), in Peterson, ed., *The Portable Thomas Jefferson,* 213.

31. Ramsay, *History,* 1:221–22; David Tappan, "A Sermon for the Day of General Election" (1792), in Sandoz, ed., *Political Sermons,* 1109.

32. James Winthrop, "Agrippa IX" (1787), in Bailyn, ed., *Debate on the Constitu-*

tion, 1:628; Crèvecoeur, *Letters from an American Farmer*, 77–78; A Constant Customer, "Letter from a Gentleman in the Country to His Friend" (1773), in Hyneman and Lutz, eds., *American Political Writings*, 1:183; anonymous, "Rudiments of Law and Government Deduced from the Law of Nature" (1783), in Ibid., 1:584.

33. James Madison, *Federalist* No. 14, 103–4; "Cato V," in Ketcham, ed., *Anti-Federalist Papers*, 318–19; James Madison, "Debates in the House of Representatives" (1789), in *Creating the Bill of Rights: The Documentary Record from the First Federal Congress*, ed. Helen E. Veit, Kenneth R. Bowling, and Charlene Bangs Bickford (Baltimore: Johns Hopkins University Press, 1991), 78; Peres Fobes, "An Election Sermon" (1795), in Hyneman and Lutz, eds., *American Political Writings*, 2:1010–11.

34. Webster, "Revolution in France" (1794), in Sandoz, ed., *Political Sermons*, 1259–60; Thomas Jefferson to Anne Willing Bingham, May 11, 1788, in Moynihan, Russett, and Crumpacker, eds., *Second to None*, 1:184–85.

35. George Washington to David Humphreys, December 26, 1786, in Allen, ed., *George Washington*, 351; Thomas Jefferson to Ezra Stiles, December 24, 1786, in *The Political Writings of Thomas Jefferson*, ed. Edward Dumbauld (Indianapolis: Bobbs-Merrill, 1955), 69.

36. Thomas Jefferson to William Short, January 3, 1793, in Mayo, ed., *Jefferson Himself*, 185.

37. Crèvecouer, *Letters from an American Farmer*, 70, 90; George Washington, "General Orders, March 1, 1778," in Allen, ed., *George Washington*, 96; idem, "General Orders, April 18, 1783," in Ibid., 237.

38. Madison, *Federalist* No. 40, 248–49; Hamilton, *Federalist* No. 71, 432; see also Adair, "Fame and the Founding Fathers," 12.

39. George Washington, "Speech to the Officers of the Army, March 15, 1783," in Allen, ed., *George Washington*, 217–22.

40. John Adams to Thomas Jefferson, May 11, 1794, in John Adams, Abigail Adams, and Thomas Jefferson, *The Adams-Jefferson Letters: The Complete Correspondence between Thomas Jefferson and Abigail and John Adams*, ed. Lester J. Cappon, 2 vols. (Chapel Hill: University of North Carolina Press, 1959), 1:255; Alexander Hamilton to John Jay, May, 7, 1800, in *A Biography in His Own Words*, ed. Mary-Jo Kline (New York: Harper & Row, 1973), 377; Gary J. Schmitt, "Jefferson and Executive Power: Revisionism and the 'Revolution of 1800,'" in *American Models of Revolutionary Leadership: George Washington and Other Founders*, ed. Daniel J. Elazar and Ellis Katz (Lanham, Md.: University Press of America, 1992), 167.

41. William Emerson, "An Oration in Commemoration of the Anniversary of American Independence" (1802), in Sandoz, ed., *Political Sermons*, 1568.

42. See Reid Mitchell, *The Vacant Chair: The Northern Soldier Leaves Home* (New York: Oxford University Press, 1993), 116; Clawson, *Constructing Brotherhood*, 185–86.

43. John Tucker, "An Election Sermon" (1771), in Hyneman and Lutz, eds., *American Political Writings*, 1:173.

44. Mather, "America's Appeal" (1775), in Sandoz, ed., *Political Sermons*, 488.

45. Samuel Miller, "A Sermon on the Anniversary of the Independence of America, July 4, 1793," in Sandoz, ed., *Political Sermons*, 1153; John Adams to Abigail Adams, June 16, 1776, in Adams, ed., *Familiar Letters*, 185; Warren, *History*, 2:505, 600; Zabdiel Adams, "An Election Sermon" (1782), in Hyneman and Lutz, eds., *American Political Writings*, 1:563; George Washington to George William Fairfax, July 10, 1783, in Fleming, ed., *Affectionately Yours*, 184; George Washington to Benjamin Harrison, January 18, 1784, in Andrist, ed., *A Biography*, 252; "An Old State Soldier" (1788), in Bailyn, ed., *Debate on the Constitution*, 2:34.

46. Jeremiah Hill to George Thatcher, February 26, 1788, in Bailyn, ed., *Debate on the Constitution*, 2:241; Simeon Baldwin, "Oration at New Haven, Connecticut, July 4, 1788," in Ibid., 2:524; Mercy Otis Warren, "Observations on the Constitution" (1788), in Ibid., 2:293, 301–2.

47. Murray, "Sketch of the Present Situation" (1794), in Harris, ed., *Selected Writings*, 53–54; Bishop James Madison, "Manifestations of the Beneficence of Divine Providence Towards America" (1795), in Sandoz, ed., *Political Sermons*, 1314; Fobes, "Election Sermon" (1795), in Hyneman and Lutz, eds., *American Political Writings*, 2:1004; Jonathan Maxey, "An Oration" (1799), in Ibid., 2:1044; Webster, "Oration" (1802), in Ibid., 2:1221; Ames, "Dangers of American Liberty" (1805), in Ibid., 2:1301, 1304.

48. Hannah Arendt, *The Human Condition* (Chicago: University of Chicago Press, 1958), 8–9; Adair, "Fame and the Founding Fathers," 21; Samuel McClintock, "A Sermon on Occasion of the Commencement of the New Hampshire Constitution" (1784), in Sandoz, ed., *Political Sermons*, 802; Hartsock, *Money, Sex, and Power*, 197; Murray, "Equality of the Sexes" (1790), in Lauter, ed., *Heath Anthology*, 1:1012–13.

49. Warren, *History*, 1:80.

50. See Klaus Theweleit, *Male Fantasies*, trans. Stephen Conway, Erica Carter, and Chris Turner, 2 vols. (Minneapolis: University of Minnesota Press, 1987, 1989), 2:185.

51. See Nancy F. Cott, "Passionlessness: An Interpretation of Victorian Sexual Ideology, 1790–1850," in Cott and Pleck, eds., *Heritage of Her Own*, 162–81.

NOTES TO CHAPTER 3

1. James Winthrop, "Agrippa XVIII" (1788), in Bailyn, ed., *Debate on the Constitution*, 2:157.

2. Astell, "Reflections Upon Marriage," in *The First English Feminist*, 94; Aphra Behn, "To Alexis in Answer to his Poem against Fruition," in *Kissing the Rod*, ed. Germain Greer, Susan Hastings, Jeslyn Medoff, and Melinda Sansone (New York: Farrar, Straus & Giroux, 1988), 259; anonymous, *A Farther Essay Relating to the Female Sex* (London: A. Roper & E. Wilkinson, 1696), 105–15; Barker-Benfield, *Culture of Sensibility*, chap. 2; and Robert Gould, *Love given o're or, a Satire against the Pride, Lust, and Inconstance, &tc. of Woman* (London: Andrew Green, 1682), in Nussbaum, ed., *Satires on Women*, 12.

3. Astell, "Reflections," in *The First English Feminist*, 75; anonymous, *An Essay in Defence of the Female Sex* (London: A. Roper & E. Wilkinson, 1696), 127–29; anonymous, *Mundus Foppensis: or, the Fop Display'd* (London: John Harris, 1691), in *Mundus Foppensis (1691) and The Levellers (1703)*, ed. Michael S. Kimmel, Augustan Reprint Society, no. 248 (Los Angeles: William Andrews Clark Memorial Library, 1988), 11–13.

4. Anonymous, *The Levellers: A Dialogue between two young Ladies, concerning Matrimony, Proposing an Act for Enforcing Marriage, for the Equality of Matches, and Taxing Single Persons, With the Danger of Celebacy to a Nation* (1703), in Kimmel, ed., *Mundus Foppensis and the Levellers*, 422–23.

5. Locke, *Some Thoughts Concerning Education*; anonymous, *The Levellers*, in Kimmel, ed., *Mundus Foppensis and the Levellers*, 419, 420–22.

6. Third Earl of Shaftesbury, quoted in Barker-Benfield, *Culture of Sensibility*, 113–15.

7. Barker-Benfield, *Culture of Sensibility*, 46; David Hume, *A Treatise of Human Nature*, ed. L. A. Selby-Bigge (Oxford: Oxford University Press, 1968), book 3, pt. 2, sec. 12, 570–73.

8. John Trenchard, *An Argument Shewing That a Standing Army Is Inconsistent with a Free Government, and Absolutely Destructive to the Constitution of the English Monarchy* (London, 1697), iii.

9. William Prynne, quoted in Lois G. Schwoerer, *"No Standing Armies!" The Anti-Army Ideology of Seventeenth-Century England* (Baltimore: Johns Hopkins University Press, 1974), 62; Trenchard, *Argument*, 28–29; Toland, *Militia Reform'd*, 76; Andrew Fletcher of Saltoun, *A Discourse of Government with relation to Militias* (Edinburgh, 1698), 33–34; see also J. R. Western, *The English Militia in the Eighteenth Century* (London: Routledge & Kegan Paul, 1965), 269.

10. Anonymous, *Essay in Defence of the Female Sex*, 92–93, 115; Toland, *Militia Reform'd*, 7–8, 17; see also Barker-Benfield, *Culture of Sensibility*, 47, 80.

11. Toland, *Militia Reform'd*, 83–84.

12. Sir George Ferrars, quoted in Barker-Benfield, *Culture of Sensibility*, 49; Sir Edwin Sandys quoted in Mary Ryan, *Womanhood in America: From Colonial Times to the Present*, 3d ed. (New York: Franklin Watts, 1983), 32; anonymous missionary quoted in Barker-Benfield, *Culture of Sensibility*, 49; see also Mimi Abramovitz, *Regulating the Lives of Women: Social Welfare Policy from Colonial Times to the Present* (Boston: South End Press, 1988), 46, 53–54.

13. Benjamin Franklin, "The Speech of Polly Baker" (1747), in Lemay, ed., *Writings*, 305–8; Gross, *Minutemen*, 100, 181–82.

14. John Adams to Abigail Adams, July 29, 1776, in Adams, ed., *Familiar Letters*, 205–6; Abigail Adams to John Adams, August 14, 1776, in Ibid., 214; Abigail Adams to John Adams, July 31, 1777, in Ibid., 286–87; John Adams to Abigail Adams, August 11, 1777, in Ibid., 290.

15. Tyler, "The Contrast" (1790), in Lauter, *The Heath Anthology*, esp. 1:1111, 1129, 1131, 1133–34; Joel Barlow, "The Prospect of Peace" (1778), in Ibid., 1:1087–88; Judith

Sargent Murray, "Desultory Thoughts upon the Utility of Encouraging a Degree of Self-Complacency, Especially in Female Bosoms" (1784), in Harris, ed., *Selected Writings*, 46–47.

16. George Washington to Robin Washington (1748), in Fleming, ed., *Affectionately Yours*, 15; George Washington to Benedict Calvert (1773), in Ibid., 42–43; George Washington to Bushrod Washington, January 15, 1783, in Ibid., 165–66; George Washington to George Steptoe Washington, March 23, 1789, in Ibid., 218–21; George Washington to David Stuart, January 22, 1789, in Ibid., 264; George Washington to George Washington Parke Custis, June 13, 1798, in Ibid., 269; James Madison to William Bradford, November 9, 1772, in *A Biography in His Own Words*, ed. Merrill D. Peterson (New York: Harper & Row, 1974), 23–24; John Adams to Thomas Jefferson, October 9, 1787, in Cappon, ed., *Adams-Jefferson Letters*, 1:203.

17. Anonymous, "Untitled" (1763), in Hyneman and Lutz, eds., *American Political Writings*, 1:33–37; Samuel Wales, "The Dangers of Our National Prosperity: and the Way to Avoid Them" (1785), in Sandoz, ed., *Political Sermons*, 849; Fliegelman, *Declaring Independence*, 37; see also Abigail Adams to Thomas Jefferson, October 7, 1785, in Cappon, ed., *Adams-Jefferson Letters*, 1:80.

18. Benjamin Franklin to Jane Mecom (June 1748), in Lemay, ed., *Writings*, 437; Benjamin Franklin, "A Letter from Father Abraham to His Beloved Son" (1758), in Ibid., 517; Benjamin Franklin to John Alleyne, August 9, 1768, in Ibid., 836–37; Benjamin Franklin, "Poor Richard's Almanack" (1733–1757), in Ibid., 1188, 1233, 1283; Jeremiah Atwater, "A Sermon" (1801), in Hyneman and Lutz, eds., *American Political Writings*, 2:1183; anonymous, "Untitled" (1763), in Ibid., 1:35–36.

19. Benjamin Rush, quoted in Fliegelman, *Declaring Independence*, 138; Franklin, "Autobiography," 81, 193; idem, "Old Mistresses Apologue" (1745), in Lemay, ed., *Writings*, 302.

20. Thomas Jefferson to John Adams, October 28, 1813, in Peterson, ed., *The Portable Thomas Jefferson*, 533–34; Thomas Jefferson to Thomas Jefferson Randolph, November 24, 1808, in Ibid., 511, 514; Thomas Jefferson to John Barrister, October 15, 1785, in Ibid., 393–94; Thomas Jefferson to Charles Bellini, Sept 30, 1785, in Mayo, ed., *Jefferson Himself*, 112; Thomas Jefferson to Abigail Adams, August 30, 1787, in Cappon, ed., *Adams-Jefferson Letters*, 1:193; Bernard Bailyn, *Faces of the Revolution: Personalities and Themes in the Struggle for American Independence* (New York: Random House, 1992), 28; Washington to David Stuart, January 22, 1798, in Fleming, ed., *Affectionately Yours*, 264.

21. Paine, "Common Sense," in *The Life and Major Writings*, 9; Jefferson to John Barrister, October 15, 1785, in Peterson, ed., *The Portable Thomas Jefferson*, 393–94; Charles Carroll, quoted in Sally D. Mason, "Mama, Rachel, and Molly: Three Generations of Carroll Women," in Hoffman and Albert, eds., *Women in the Age of the American Revolution*, 245; Adams to John Taylor (1814), in Peek, ed., *Political Writings*, 206; Webster, "Education of Youth in America" (1790), in Rudolph, *Essays on Education*, 69.

22. Jacob Rush, "The Nature and Importance of an Oath—the Charge to a Jury" (1796), in Hyneman and Lutz, eds., *American Political Writings*, 2:1020–21; Alexander Hamilton, *Observations on Certain Documents . . . in which the Charge of Speculation against Alexander Hamilton . . . is Fully Refuted* (1797), in Kline, ed., *A Biography*, 355–56; Tunis Wortman, "A Solemn Address to Christians and Patriots" (1800), in Sandoz, ed., *Political Sermons*, 1499; Bloch, "Gendered Meanings of Virtue," 52.

23. Daniel Williams, "The Gratification of That Corrupt and Lawless Passion: Character Types and Themes in Early New England Rape Narratives," in Shuffelton, ed., *Mixed Race*, 196; Stephanie Coontz, *The Social Origins of Private Life: A History of American Families 1600–1900* (London: Verso, 1988), 83, 126–27; Abramovitz, *Regulating the Lives of Women*, 53–54, 94, 96; Samuel Walker, *Popular Justice: A History of American Criminal Justice* (New York: Oxford University Press, 1980), 16; Kermit Hall, *The Magic Mirror: Law in American History* (New York: Oxford University Press, 1989), 33; see also Mary Beth Norton, *Founding Mothers and Fathers: Gendered Power and the Forming of American Society* (New York: Knopf, 1996), prologue.

24. Norton, *Liberty's Daughters*, 43; Judith Sargent Murray, *The Gleaner* (Schenectady, N.Y.: Union College Press, 1992), 309–12; Benjamin Rush, *My Dearest Julia: The Love Letters of Dr. Benjamin Rush* (New York: Neale Watson Academic Publications, 1979), 3, 5–6, 20–21, 28, 36; see also Carl Degler, *At Odds: Women and the Family in America from the Revolution to the Present* (Oxford: Oxford University Press, 1980), 5–9.

25. Nathanael Emmons, "A Discourse Delivered on the National Fast" (1799), in Hyneman and Lutz, eds., *American Political Writings*, 2:1034–38.

26. Hall, *Magic Mirror*, 33; Marybeth Hamilton Arnold, "The Life of a Citizen in the Hands of a Woman: Sexual Assault in New York City, 1790 to 1820," in *Passion and Power: Sexuality in History*, ed. Kathy Peiss and Christina Simmons (Philadelphia: Temple University Press, 1989), 41–42, 47; Stansell, *City of Women*, 23–27.

27. Arnold, "Life of a Citizen," in Peiss and Simmons, eds., *Passion and Power*, 35; Josiah Quincy, quoted in Fliegelman, *Declaring Independence*, 75; John Adams to Abigail Adams, July 5, 1774, in Adams, ed., *Familiar Letters*, 13; Ramsay, *History*, 1:304–5; William Bradford, *An Enquiry How Far the Punishment of Death is Necessary in Pennsylvania*, in *Reform of Criminal Law*, 29; see also Stansell, *City of Women*, 25; Walker, *Popular Justice*, 13–14; Buel and Buel, *Way of Duty*, 125.

28. Bradford, *Enquiry*, 29–30; Barlow, "Letter to the National Convention" (1792), in Hyneman and Lutz, eds., *American Political Writings*, 2:834; see also Walker, *Popular Justice*, 33, 48.

29. Bradford, *Enquiry*, 29–30, 63; see also Pauline Schloesser, "Republican Motherhood, Modern Patriarchy, and the Question of Woman Citizenship in Post-Revolutionary America" (paper presented at the Annual Meeting of the American Political Science Association, Washington, D.C., August 29–September 1, 1991), 9; Walker, *Popular Justice*, 16.

30. "Davis vs. Maryland, 1810," in *Gay American History: Lesbians and Gay Men in*

the U.S.A., ed. Jonathan Katz (New York: Harper & Row, 1976), 26 and pt. 1; John Winthrop, quoted in John D'Emilio and Estelle Freedman, *Intimate Matters: A History of Sexuality in America* (New York: Harper & Row, 1988), 30; Jonathan Edwards, Jr., "The Necessity of the Belief in Christianity" (1794), in Sandoz, ed., *Political Sermons*, 1201.

31. Bradford, *Enquiry*, 20–21.

32. Hall, *Magic Mirror*, 29–30; Gross, *Minutemen*, 90.

33. Madison, "Notes from the Constitutional Convention," in Mason and Baker, eds., *Free Government*, 194; Franklin, "Trial and Reprieve of Prouse and Mitchel" (1729), in Lemay, ed., *Writings*, 139; idem, "A Mock Petition to the House of Commons" (1766), in Ibid., 583; idem, "A Conversation on Slavery" (1770), in Ibid., 650; Raymond A. Mohl, "Poverty, Pauperism, and Social Order in the Preindustrial American City, 1780–1840," in *Law and Order in American History*, ed. Joseph M. Hawes (Port Washington, N.Y.: Kennikat Press, 1979), 31–32; see also Juster, *Disorderly Women*, 25; Walker, *Popular Justice*, 15; Stansell, *City of Women*, 5–6.

34. Crèvecoeur, *Letters from an American Farmer*, 72, 78–79; George Washington to James Duane, September 7, 1783, in Allen, ed., *George Washington*, 260–63; Franklin, "Autobiography," 132–33; Thomas Jefferson to Brother Handsome Lake, November 3, 1802, in Peterson, ed., *The Portable Thomas Jefferson*, 305–7.

35. Saar, "Heritage of Ethnicity," in Shuffelton, *A Mixed Race*, 251; Washington to James Duane, September 7, 1783, in Allen, ed., *George Washington*, 266; Crèvecoeur, *Letters from an American Farmer*, 79.

36. Ramsay, *History*, 1:23; Anonymous, "Rudiments of Law and Government" (1783), in Hyneman and Lutz, eds., *American Political Writings*, 1:584; David Rice, "Slavery Inconsistent with Justice and Good Policy" (1792), in Ibid., 2:867–74; Theodore Dwight, "An Oration Spoken Before the Connecticut Society for the Promotion of Freedom and the Relief of Persons Unlawfully Holden in Bondage" (1794), in Ibid., 2:891–92.

37. Dwight, "Oration" (1794), in Hyneman and Lutz, eds., *American Political Writings*, 2:891–92; Jefferson, "Notes on the State of Virginia" (1781), in Peterson, ed., *The Portable Thomas Jefferson*, 214–15; Rice, "Slavery Inconsistent with Justice" (1792), in Hyneman and Lutz, eds., *American Political Writings*, 2:868; Taylor, *Arator*, 122–24.

38. Witherspoon, "Dominion of Providence" (1776), in Sandoz, ed., *Political Sermons*, 537; Gross, *Minutemen*, 94, 96; Dana, "African Slave Trade" (1791), in Sandoz, ed., *Political Sermons*, 1049; Wortman, "Solemn Address" (1800), in Ibid., 1508–9; anonymous, "Rudiments of Law and Government" (1783), in Hyneman and Lutz, eds., *American Political Writings*, 1:584; Rice, "Slavery Inconsistent with Justice" (1792), in Ibid., 2:874; Taylor, *Arator*, 178.

39. Jefferson, "Notes on the State of Virginia" (1781), in Peterson, ed., *The Portable Thomas Jefferson*, 94–95, 187–89, 192–93; Frank Shuffelton, "Thomas Jefferson: Race, Culture, and the Failure of the Anthropological Method," in Shuffelton, ed., *Mixed Race*, 268–70.

40. Rice, "Slavery Inconsistent with Justice" (1792), in Hynemann and Lutz, eds.,

American Political Writings, 2:861; Williams, "Gratification of That Corrupt and Lawless Passion," in Shuffelton, *A Mixed Race*, 198–200; Walker, *Popular Justice*, 33–34.

41. Levi Hart, "Liberty Described and Recommended: in a Sermon Preached to the Corporation of Freemen in Farmington" (1775), in Hyneman and Lutz, eds., *American Political Writings*, 1:314; Benjamin Rush, *An Address to the Inhabitants of the British Settlements on the Slavery of Negroes in America* (1773; New York: Arno Press Reprint, 1969), 16; idem, *Vindication of the Address to the Inhabitants of the British Settlements, on the Slavery of Negroes in America in Answer to a Pamphlet entitled, "Slavery not Forbidden in Scripture; Or a Defence of the West-Indian Planters from the Aspersions thrown out against them by the Author of the Address"* (1773), in Ibid., 41–43; Crèvecoeur, *Letters from an American Farmer*, 169–70.

42. Jefferson, "Notes on the State of Virginia" (1781), in Peterson, ed., *The Portable Thomas Jefferson*, 186; Taylor, *Arator*, 125, 180–83.

43. See Terence Ball, "The Myth of Adam and the American Identity," in *Reappraising Political Theory* (New York: Oxford University Press, 1994), chap. 12; Fliegelman, *Prodigals and Pilgrims*, esp. chap. 6; Walker, *Popular Justice*, 24.

44. Hall, *Magic Mirror*, 55; Langguth, *Patriots*, 119; Don Higginbotham, *The War of American Independence: Military Attitudes, Policies, and Practices, 1763–1789* (Boston: Northeastern University Press, 1983), 43; Warren, *History*, 1:244.

45. Allen, "Oration" (1773), in Sandoz, ed., *Political Sermons*, 313; Witherspoon, "Dominion of Providence" (1776), in Ibid., 556; Franklin, "Conversation on Slavery" (1770), in LeMay, ed. *Writings*, 652; idem, "The King's Own Regulars" (1775), in Ibid., 739–40; idem, "Information to Those Who Would Remove to America" (1784), in Ibid., 981; Howard, "Sermon" (1773), in Hyneman and Lutz, *American Political Writings*, 1:198; Warren, *History*, 1:36.

46. Warren, *History*, 1:184–85, 191; Phillips Payson, "A Sermon" (1778), in Hyneman and Lutz, eds., *American Political Writings*, 1:534–35; Paine, "American Crisis I," in *The Life and Major Writings*, 57.

47. Howard, "Sermon" (1773), in Hyneman and Lutz, eds., *American Political Writings*, 1:201, 205; Buel and Buel, *Way of Duty*, 144; Laurel Thatcher Ulrich, "'Daughters of Liberty': Religious Women in Revolutionary New England," in Hoffman and Albert, eds., *Women in the Age of the American Revolution*, 211–43; Higginbotham, *War of American Independence*, 262.

48. George Washington to John Hancock, September 2, 1776 in Andrist, ed., *A Biography*, 157; George Washington, "Letter to Congress, September 24, 1776," in *American Military Thought*, ed. Walter Millis (Indianapolis: Bobbs-Merrill Co., 1966), 12; Russell F. Weigley, *History of the United States Army*, enlarged ed. (Bloomington: Indiana University Press, 1984), 30; "Caractacus," Benjamin Rush, and Samuel Adams, cited in Higginbotham, *War of American Independence*, 92, 205–6.

49. Gross, *Minutemen*, 151–52; Benjamin Franklin, quoted in Higginbotham, *War of American Independence*, 439; William Manning, *The Key of Liberty*, ed. Michael Merrill and Sean Wilentz (Cambridge: Harvard University Press, 1993), 142.

50. "Letters from the 'Federal Farmer' III" (1787), in *The Origins of the American Constitution: A Documentary History*, ed. Michael Kammen (New York: Penguin Books, 1986), 284; "John DeWitt, Essay III" (1787), in Ketcham, ed., *Anti-Federalist Papers*, 312–13; anonymous, "Untitled" (1788), in Bailyn, ed., *Debate on the Constitution*, 2:243.

51. John Humble, "Untitled" (1787), in Bailyn, ed., *Debate on the Constitution*, 1:225; Benjamin Workman, "Philadelphiensis IV" (1787), in Ibid., 1:496; John Dawson, "An Address to the Virginia Ratifying Convention" (1788), in Ibid., 2:749; "The Impartial Examiner I, Part 2" (1788), in Ibid., 2:253; see also "Brutus IX" (1788), in Ibid., 2:43.

52. Hamilton, *Federalist* No. 24, 161; *Federalist* No. 28, 180.

53. Ramsay, *History*, 1:199; 2:504–5, 624, 637; Dana, "African Slave Trade" (1791), in Sandoz, ed., *Political Sermons*, 1049.

54. Cesare Beccaria, *On Crimes and Punishments and Other Writings*, ed. Richard Bellamy, trans. Richard Davies (Cambridge: Cambridge University Press, 1995), 67; Franklin, "Trial and Reprieve," in Lemay, ed., *Writings*, 140.

55. Warren, *History*, 2:404–6; George Washington to John Laurens, October 13, 1780, in Fleming, ed., *Affectionately Yours*, 143; John André, quoted in Langguth, *Patriots*, 508; Alexander Hamilton to John Laurens, October 11, 1780, in Kline, ed., *A Biography*, 91–92.

56. Benjamin Rush, *An Enquiry into the Effects of Public Punishments Upon Criminals and Upon Society* (1787), in *Reform of Criminal Law*, 5; idem, *Considerations on the Injustice and Impolicy of Punishing Murder by Death* (1792), in Ibid., 12; see also Michael Meranze, *Laboratories of Virtue: Punishment, Revolution, and Authority in Philadelphia, 1760–1835* (Chapel Hill: University of North Carolina Press, 1996), 69–70.

57. Rush, *Enquiry*, 4, 8, 10, 14; Caleb Lownes, "Account of the Alteration and Present State of the Penal Laws of Pennsylvania" (1793), in Ibid., 77; John Howard, *The State of Prisons* (1777), in Walker, *Popular Justice*, 42; Benevolus, "Poverty" (1789), in Hyneman and Lutz, eds., *American Political Writings*, 2:714.

58. Thomas Jefferson to Maria Cosway, October 12, 1786, in Peterson, ed., *The Portable Thomas Jefferson*, 403, 408; Otis, "Rights of the British Colonies" (1764), in Bailyn, ed., *Pamphlets*, 1:425–26; John Dickinson, "Observations on the Constitution Proposed by the Federal Convention, III" (1788), in Bailyn, ed., *The Debate on the Constitution*, 2:409; Samuel Quarrier to President Thomas Jefferson, February 13, 1802, in *To His Excellency Thomas Jefferson: Letters to a President*, ed. Jack McLaughlin (New York: Avon Books, 1991), 150.

59. Rush, *Enquiry*, 14; see Joseph M. Hawes, "Prison in Early Nineteenth Century America: The Process of Convict Reformation," in Hawes, ed., *Law and Order*, 41; Walker, *Popular Justice*, 42.

60. Anonymous, "Rudiments of Law and Government" (1783), in Hyneman and Lutz, eds., *American Political Writings*, 1:591–92; Alexander Hamilton to Rufus King,

October 1794, in Kline, ed., *A Biography*, 327; see also Beccaria, *On Crimes and Punishments*, 58.

61. Samuel P. Huntington, *The Soldier and the State: The Theory and Politics of Civil-Military Relations* (Cambridge: Harvard University Press, 1957), 144; Edward M. Coffman, *The Old Army: A Portrait of the American Army in Peacetime, 1784–1898* (New York: Oxford University Press, 1986), chap. 1; Charles Lofgren, *"Government from Reflection and Choice": Constitutional Essays on War, Foreign Relations, and Federalism* (New York: Oxford University Press, 1986), chap. 2; see also Kann, *On the Man Question*, chap. 10.

62. Washington to George Steptoe Washington, March 23, 1789, in Fleming, ed., *Affectionately Yours*, 218–19; Atwater, "A Sermon" (1801), in Hyneman and Lutz, eds., *American Political Writings*, 2:1175.

63. Amicus Republicae, "Address to the Public, Containing Some Remarks on the Present Political State of the American Republicks, etc." (1786), in Hyneman and Lutz, eds., *American Political Writings*, 1:653–655; see also Michael Grossberg, *Governing the Hearth: Law and the Family in Nineteenth-Century America* (Chapel Hill: University of North Carolina Press, 1985), 47, 49; Hall, *Magic Mirror*, 152.

64. Washington, "General Orders, March 1, 1778," in Allen, ed., *George Washington*, 95; George Rogers Clark to George Mason, November 19, 1779, in Rutland, ed., *Papers of George Mason*, 2:583; Alexander Hamilton to Elias Boudinot, July 5, 1778, in Kline, ed., *A Biography*, 65, 70; David Ramsay, "Oration at Charleston, South Carolina" (1788), in Bailyn, ed., *Debate on the Constitution*, 2:506; Edmund Randolph, "Address to the Virginia Legislature," October 10, 1787, in Ibid., 1:604; Baldwin, "Oration" (1788), in Ibid., 2:522; Tench Coxe, "An American Citizen I" (1787), in Ibid., 1:23; idem, "An American Citizen II" (1787), in Ibid., 1:25–26; "Civic Rusticus" (1788), in Ibid., 1:357; Noah Webster, "A Citizen of America" (1787), in Ibid., 1:132; Arthur Lee, "Cincinnatus V" (1787), in Ibid., 1:118; Warren, "Observations on the Constitution" (1788), in Ibid., 2:288; Webster, "Citizen of America" (1787), in Ibid., 1:133; Pelatiah Webster, "A Citizen of Philadelphia" (1787), in Ibid., 1:182; Robert R. Livingston, "Address to the New York Ratifying Convention" (1788), in Ibid., 2:837; James Iredell, "Address to the North Carolina Ratifying Convention" (1788), in Ibid., 2:899.

NOTES TO CHAPTER 4

1. Francis Bacon, quoted in Jónasdóttir, *Why Women Are Oppressed*, 18.

2. Webster, "Education of Youth in America," in Rudolph, ed., *Essays on Education*, 53.

3. Alexander Hamilton, "On Marriage" (1771), in Kline, ed., *A Biography*, 17; Alexander Hamilton to Catherine Livingston, April 11, 1777, in Ibid., 54; Alexander Hamilton to Margarita Schuyler, February, 1780, in Ibid., 78–79.

4. Murray, "Story of Margaretta," in Harris, ed., *Selected Writings*, 225; Alice Izard to Margaret Manigault, May 29, 1801, in Moynihan, Russett, and Crumpacker, eds.,

Second to None, 1:202; anonymous, "The Maid's Soliloquy" (1751), in Lauter, ed., *Heath Anthology*, 1:703; Lewis, "Republican Wife," 694–96, 699, 701–2, 706–7.

5. Washington to Marquis de Chastellux, April 25, 1788, in Allen, ed., *George Washington*, 393; Franklin, "Reply to a Piece of Advice" (1735), in Lemay, ed., *Writings*, 249–50; idem, "On Drunkenness" (1733), in Ibid., 213–14; Webster, "Citizen of America" (1787), in Bailyn, ed., *Debate on the Constitution*, 1:149; see also Norton, *Founding Mothers and Fathers*, 136.

6. George Savile, Marquis of Halifax, "Advice to a Daughter," in Moynihan, Russett, and Crumpacker, eds., *Second to None*, 1:130–31; Judith Sargent Murray, "On the Equality of the Sexes" (1790), in Lauter, ed., *Heath Anthology*, 1:1016; Mary Fish Noyes, "Portrait of a Good Husband" (1773), in Buel and Buel, *Way of Duty*, 80; anonymous, "Impromptus, on Reading an Essay on Education, By a Lady" (1773), in Lauter, ed., *Heath Anthology*, 1:704; see also "Letters from Eliza Southgate to Her Cousin Moses Porter" (1800–1802), in *Roots of Bitterness: Documents of the Social History of American Women*, ed. Nancy F. Cott (New York: Dutton, 1972), 109.

7. Benjamin Franklin, "Rules and Maxims for Promoting Matrimonial Happiness" (1729), in Lemay, ed., *Writings*, 152; idem, "Reply to a Piece of Advice" (1735), in Ibid., 250; "Autobiography," 81, 92, 109–10; see also Rush, "Thoughts Upon Female Education," in Rudolph, ed., *Essays on Education*, 29.

8. Downer, "Discourse" (1768), in Hyneman and Lutz, eds., *American Political Writings*, 1:106; Jefferson, "Summary View" (1774), in Peterson, ed., *The Portable Thomas Jefferson*, 13; Peter Thacher, "A Sermon Preached before the Artillary Company" (1793), in Sandoz, ed., *Political Sermons*, 1145; George Washington to Lund Washington, November 26, 1775, in Fleming, ed., *Affectionately Yours*, 60.

9. George Washington to Eleanor Parke Custis, January 16, 1795, in Fleming, ed., *Affectionately Yours*, 244; Franklin, "Autobiography," 161–62, 283; John Adams, "Discourses on Davila" (1789), in Peek, ed., *Political Writings*, 179; John Adams to Abigail Adams, April 12, 1778, in Adams, ed., *Familiar Letters*, 329; Adams to John Taylor (1814), in Peek, ed., *Political Writings*, 200.

10. Barlow, "Letter to the National Convention" (1792), in Hyneman and Lutz, eds., *American Political Writings*, 2:824; Williams, "Natural and Civil History of Vermont" (1794), in Ibid., 2:952; Webster, "Revolution in France" (1794), in Sandoz, ed., *Political Sermons*, 1264; see also anonymous, "Rudiments of Law and Government" (1783), in Hyneman and Lutz, eds., *American Political Writings*, 1:597.

11. William Byrd's *Commonplace Book*, quoted in Lockridge, *Sources of Patriarchal Rage*, 14; Murray, "Sketch of the Present Situation of America" (1794), in Harris, ed., *Selected Writings*, 56; Coontz, *Social Origins of Private Life*, 155; An Impartial Citizen, "A Dissertation Upon the Constitutional Freedom of the Press" (1801), in Hyneman and Lutz, eds., *American Political Writings*, 2:1139, 1168; see also Cott, "Eighteenth-Century Family and Social Life," in Cott and Pleck, eds., *A Heritage of Her Own*, 120, 127; Norton, *Liberty's Daughters*, 43.

12. Demos, *Past, Present, and Personal*, 47; Norton, *Founding Mothers and Fathers*,

76; Fliegelman, *Prodigals and Pilgrims*, 204; George Mason, in Madison, "Notes from the Constitutional Convention," in Mason and Baker, eds., *Free Government*, 191.

13. Mason to George Mason, Jr., January 8, 1783, in Rutland, ed., *Papers of George Mason*, 2:762; Ava Baron, "Acquiring Manly Competence: The Demise of Apprenticeship and the Remasculinization of Printers' Work," in Carnes and Griffin, eds., *Meanings for Manhood*, 162–63; Nash, *Race, Class, and Politics*, 246, 248–49; see also Franklin, "Autobiography," 109–10; Bernard Bailyn, *Education in the Forming of American Society* (New York: Vintage Books, 1960), 17.

14. Thomas Paine, "The Rights of Man" (1791–92), in *The Life and Major Writings*, 288–89; Thomas Jefferson to James Madison, October 28, 1785, in Peterson, ed., *The Portable Thomas Jefferson*, 396.

15. Buel and Buel, *Way of Duty*, 241; Nathanael Emmons, "The Dignity of Man" (1787), in Sandoz, ed., *Political Sermons*, 907; Ramsay, *History*, 2:630.

16. Charles Cotesworth Pinckney, "Address to the South Carolina Ratifying Convention" (1788), in Bailyn, ed., *Debate on the Constitution*, 2:579–80.

17. Thomas Jefferson, "Autobiography," in Mayo, ed., *Jefferson Himself*, 77–78; idem, "Draft Constitution for Virginia" (1776), in Peterson, ed., *The Portable Thomas Jefferson*, 249; Benjamin Franklin to Jonathan Shipley, February 24, 1786, in Lemisch, ed., *Autobiography and Other Writings*, 317; see also Kann, *On the Man Question*, 196.

18. Bradford, *Enquiry*, in *Reform of Criminal Law*, 7–8; Adams, "Defence of the Constitutions" (1787), in Peek, ed., *Political Writings*, 149; Robert Coram, "Political Inquiries to which is Added a Plan for the General Establishment of Schools throughout the United States" (1791), in Rudolph, ed., *Essays on Education*, 143.

19. "From the 'Federal Farmer' to the 'Republican,' Letter V" (1787), in Bailyn, ed., *Debate on the Constitution*, 1:282; "'The Republican' to the People" (1788), in Ibid., 1: 712; Webster, "Citizen of America" (1787), in Ibid., 1:157–58.

20. Franklin, "Autobiography," 24, 95; compare Wood, *Radicalism*, 129.

21. Yazawa, *From Colonies to Commonwealth*, 49–50, 74; Demos, *Past, Present and Personal*, 46; Thomas Jefferson, "Report of the Commissioners for the University of Virginia" (1818), in Peterson, ed., *The Portable Thomas Jefferson*, 345; John Dickinson, "Observations on the Constitution Proposed by the Federal Convention VIII" (1788), in Bailyn, ed., *Debate on the Constitution*, 2:427; "Plough Jogger" (1788), in Ibid., 2:415; Thacher, "A Sermon" (1793), in Sandoz, ed., *Political Sermons*, 1146; see also Fliegelman, *Prodigals and Pilgrims*, 5, 12.

22. John Adams, "Thoughts on Government" (1776), in Peek, ed., *Political Writings*, 91; John Adams to Abigail Adams, August 28, 1774, in Adams, ed., *Familiar Letters*, 28; John Adams to Abigail Adams, April 15, 1776, in Ibid., 159; Thomas Jefferson to Peter Carr, August 19, 1785, in Peterson, ed., *The Portable Thomas Jefferson*, 381; Mason, "Mama, Rachel, and Molly," in Hoffman and Albert, eds., *Women in the Age of the American Revolution*, 286; Fliegelman, *Prodigals and Pilgrims*, 33.

23. Emmons, "Dignity of Man" (1787), in Sandoz, ed., *Political Sermons*, 905–6.

24. Jefferson to Adams, October 28, 1813, in Peterson, ed., *The Portable Thomas*

Jefferson, 534; Adams, "Defence of the Constitutions" (1787), in Peek, ed., *Political Writings*, 135–37.

25. John Adams to Thomas Jefferson, December 13, 1785, in Cappon, ed., *Adams-Jefferson Letters*, 107; Thomas Jefferson to John Adams, December 27, 1785, in Ibid., 112.

26. George Mason to Patrick Henry, May 6, 1783, in Rutland, ed., *Papers of George Mason*, 2:772–73; Thomas Jefferson to John Adams, February 7, 1786, in Cappon, ed., *Adams-Jefferson Letters*, 1:119; Thomas Jefferson to John Adams, November 13, 1787, in Ibid., 1:211.

27. Benjamin Franklin, "Proposals Relating to the Education of Youth in Pennsylvania" (1749), in Lemay, ed., *Writings*, 342; "Letter from Father Abraham" (1758), in Ibid., 513–14; "Poor Richard's Almanack," in Ibid., 1281; "Autobiography," 72–74 104, 112–13.

28. Jefferson to Thomas Jefferson Randolph, November 24, 1808, in Peterson, ed., *The Portable Thomas Jefferson*, 512–14; Thomas Jefferson to John Saunderson, August 31, 1820, in Mayo, ed., *Jefferson Himself*, 7; Jefferson to Charles Bellini, September 30, 1785, in Ibid., 113.

29. George Washington, "The Rules of Civility and Decent Behavior in Company and Conversation" (1741), in Allen, ed., *George Washington*, 6–13; George Washington to Joseph Reed, December 15, 1775, in Fleming, ed., *Affectionately Yours*, 71; idem, "Farewell Orders" (1783), in Allen, ed., *George Washington*, 268–69.

30. Warren, *History*, 1:128.

31. Paine, "Common Sense," in *The Life and Major Writings*, 17; "An Officer of the Late Continental Army" (1787), in Bailyn, ed., *Debate on the Constitution*, 1:104; Paine, "American Crisis II," in *The Life and Major Writings*, 69; "Cato I" (1787), in Bailyn, ed., *Debate on the Constitution*, 1:32.

32. Howard, "Sermon" (1773), in Hyneman and Lutz, eds., *American Political Writings*, 1:202; The Preceptor, "Social Duties of the Political Kind" (1772), in Ibid., 1:180; George Mason, "Opposition to a Unitary Executive" (1787), in Ketcham, ed., *Anti-Federalist Papers*, 47.

33. Gross, *Minutemen*, 71; John Adams to Abigail Adams, February 21, 1777, in Adams, ed., *Familiar Letters*, 248; Paine, "American Crisis I," in *The Life and Major Writings*, 50; idem, "American Crisis II," in Ibid., 63; Thomas Jefferson, "Fifth Annual Message to Congress" (1805), in Peterson, ed., *The Portable Thomas Jefferson*, 324.

34. Webster, "Oration" (1802), in Hyneman and Lutz, eds., *American Political Writings*, 2:1237–38; George Washington to David Stuart, December 30, 1798, in Andrist, ed., *A Biography*, 399–400.

35. Paine, "American Crisis XII," in *The Life and Major Writings*, 224, 227; Thomas Jefferson to John Breckinridge, August 12, 1803, in Peterson, ed., *The Portable Thomas Jefferson*, 497; see also Gross, *Minutemen*, 75; and Wills, *Cincinnatus*, 23, where the author argues that Washington gained authority by his willingness to let go of it.

36. Bailyn, *Education*, 36; Jefferson, "Report of the Commissioners," in Peterson,

ed., *The Portable Thomas Jefferson*, 336–37; Thomas Jefferson to James Madison, September 6, 1789, in Ibid., 445, 449; Thomas Jefferson to Samuel Kerchival, July 12, 1816, in Ibid., 559; Paine, "Rights of Man," in *The Life and Major Writings*, 251; idem, "Common Sense," in Ibid., 21, 45; idem, "American Crisis VII," in Ibid., 154; see Demos, *Past, Present, and Personal*, 102, 205; Gross, *Minutemen*, 89.

37. McClintock, "Sermon" (1784), in Sandoz, ed., *Political Sermons*, 801–2; Madison, *Federalist* No. 14, 104; Noah Webster, "Giles Hickory I" (1787), in Bailyn, ed., *Debate on the Constitution*, 1:671.

38. James Madison to Thomas Jefferson, October 24, 1787, in Kammen, ed., *Origins*, 70; Madison, "Notes from the Constitutional Convention," in Mason and Baker, eds., *Free Government*, 196; idem, "Debates in the House," in Veit, Bowling, and Bickford, eds., *Creating the Bill of Rights*, 79–80, 86; James Madison to Thomas Jefferson, May 8, 1793, in Peterson, ed., *A Biography*, 196.

39. "John DeWitt I" (1787), in Ketcham, ed., *Anti-Federalist Papers*, 192; "John DeWitt II" (1787), in Ibid., 194; Patrick Henry, "Opening Address to the Virginia Ratifying Convention" (1788), in Bailyn, ed., *Debate on the Constitution*, 2:596; Alexander Hamilton quoted in Madison, "Notes from the Constitutional Convention," in Mason and Baker, eds., *Free Government*, 196; Adams, "Defence of the Constitutions" (1787), in Peek, ed., *Political Writings*, 121; Lienesch, *New Order of the Ages*, 162.

40. Lienesch, *New Order of the Ages*, 209; Ramsay, *History*, 1:331; Thomas Jefferson to Edward Carrington, January 16, 1787, in Peterson, ed., *The Portable Thomas Jefferson*, 415; Thomas Jefferson, "Kentucky Resolutions" (1798), in Ibid., 287; Thomas Jefferson to John Adams, August 2, 1788, in Cappon, ed., *Adams-Jefferson Letters*, 1:230.

41. Adams to Jefferson, May 11, 1794, in Cappon, ed., *Adams-Jefferson Letters*, 1:255.

42. Paine, "Rights of Man," in *The Life and Major Writings*, 372–73; Warren, *History*, 2:520.

43. Franklin, "On Constancy" (1734), in Lemay, ed., *Writings*, 225–26; Franklin to John Alleyne, August 9, 1768, in Ibid., 836–37; idem, "Information to Those Who would Remove to America" (1784), in Ibid., 979; Samuel West, "On the Right to Rebel Against Governors: Election Day Sermon" (1776), in Hyneman and Lutz, eds., *American Political Writings*, 1:439; Paine, "Rights of Man," in *The Life and Major Writings*, 338.

44. Thomas Jefferson to Edmund Pendleton, August 26, 1776, in Peterson, ed., *The Portable Thomas Jefferson*, 356–57; Mason, quoted in Madison, "Notes from the Constitutional Convention," in Ketcham, ed., *Anti-Federalist Papers*, 147.

45. Franklin, quoted in Madison, "Notes from the Constitutional Convention," in Ketcham, ed., *Anti-Federalist Papers*, 148; Madison, "Notes from the Constitutional Convention," in Ibid., 152.

46. Bloch, "Gendered Meanings of Virtue," 47; Rush, "Plan for the Establishment of Public Schools" (1786), in Rudolph, ed., *Essays on Education*, 6.

47. Fisher Ames, "Address to the Massachusetts Ratifying Convention" (1788), in Bailyn, ed., *Debate on the Constitution*, 1:894–95 (emphasis added); see also "Old State Soldier" (1788), in Ibid., 2:37.

48. John Jay, *Federalist* No. 64, 395; Iredell, "Address to the North Carolina Convention" (1788), in Bailyn, ed., *Debate on the Constitution,* 2:866; Hamilton, *Federalist* No. 29, 186; Zachariah Johnston, "Address to the Virginia Ratifying Convention" (1788), in Bailyn, ed., *Debate on the Constitution,* 2:752, 754.

49. Alexander Hamilton, "Address to the New York Ratifying Convention" (1788), in Bailyn, ed., *Debate on the Constitution,* 2:835; James Wilson, "Address to the Pennsylvania Ratifying Convention" (1787), in Ibid., 1:825.

50. Ramsay, *History,* 2:666; Timothy Pickering to Charles Tillinghast, December 24, 1787, in Bailyn, ed., *Debate on the Constitution,* 1:304.

51. Kerber, "'History Can Do It No Justice,'" in Hoffman and Albert, eds., *Women in the Age of the American Revolution,* 32–33; idem, *Women of the Republic,* 199–200; Hoff, *Law, Gender, and Injustice,* 38.

52. "Cato III" (1787), in Bailyn, ed., *Debate on the Constitution,* 1:218; Hamilton, *Federalist* No. 17, 119.

53. Nash, *Race, Class, and Politics,* 257–58; Joseph Lathrop, "A Miscellaneous Collection of Original Pieces" (1786), in Hyneman and Lutz, eds., *American Political Writings,* 1:660; see also Wood, *Radicalism,* 246.

54. Joel Barlow, "To His Fellow Citizens of the United States, Letter II: On Certain Political Measures Proposed to their Consideration" (1801), in Hyneman and Lutz, eds., *American Political Writings,* 2:1121.

55. Rush, "Plan for the Establishment of Public Schools" (1786), in Rudolph, ed., *Essays on Education,* 14; George Washington to Joseph Jones, March 18, 1783, in Allen, ed., *George Washington,* 228; George Washington to Theodorick Bland, April 4, 1783, in Ibid., 232.

56. Melancton Smith, "Address to the New York Ratifying Convention" (1788), in Bailyn, ed., *Debate on the Constitution,* 2:762; "Brutus III" (1787), in Ibid., 1:321–22; Adams, "Defence of the Constitutions" (1787), in Peek, ed., *Political Writings,* 147; Adams to Abigail Adams, October 29, 1775, in Adams, ed., *Familiar Letters,* 120.

57. Adams to Jefferson, October 9, 1787, in Cappon, ed., *Adams-Jefferson Letters,* 1:202.

58. See Lienesch, *New Order of the Ages,* 172–74.

59. Tyler, "The Contrast" (1790), in Lauter, ed., *Heath Anthology,* 1:1117.

60. Nancy F. Cott, "On Men's History and Women's History," in Carnes and Griffin, eds., *Meanings for Manhood,* 211.

NOTES TO CHAPTER 5

1. Mary O'Brien, *The Politics of Reproduction* (Boston: Routledge & Kegan Paul, 1981), 54; Pateman, *Disorder of Women,* 7; Juster, *Disorderly Women,* 211; Lockridge, *Sources of Patriarchal Rage,* 68, 105–6.

2. Tyler, "The Contrast" (1790), in Lauter, ed., *Heath Anthology,* 1:1111; Ann Fairfax Withington, *Toward a More Perfect Union: Virtue and the Formation of American*

Republics (New York: Oxford University Press, 1991), 31; Murray, "Sketch of the Present Situation" (1794), in Harris, ed., *Selected Writings*, 53–54; anonymous visitor quoted in Bushman, *Refinement*, 182.

3. Franklin to Jane Mecom (June 1748), in Lemay, ed., *Writings*, 438; Clark to Mason, November 19, 1779, in Rutland, ed., *Papers of George Mason*, 2:555; Kent, "Introductory Lecture" (1794), in Hyneman and Lutz, eds., *American Political Writings*, 2:949; Adams, "Discourses on Davila" (1789), in Peek, ed., *Political Writings*, 176.

4. Mayhew, "The Snare Broken" (1766), in Sandoz, ed., *Political Sermons*, 255, 260–61; Witherspoon, "Dominion of Providence" (1776), in Ibid, 552; McClintock, "Sermon" (1784), in Ibid., 800; Ramsay, *History*, 1:123, 132; Warren, *History*, 1:84.

5. Greven, *Protestant Temperament*, 351–52; Withington, *Toward a More Perfect Union*, xiii–xiv, 16–17, 55, 134, 184, 208, 212, 215.

6. Withington, *Toward a More Perfect Union*, 217, 224, 229, 235–36, 242.

7. Paine, "Common Sense," in *The Life and Major Writings*, 4–5; Shute, "Election Sermon" (1768), in Hyneman and Lutz, eds., *American Political Writings*, 1:111; anonymous, "Rudiments of Law and Government" (1783), in Ibid., 1:568; Ford, "The Constitutionalist" (1794), in Ibid., 2:911; Alexander Hamilton to John Jay, November 26, 1775, in Kline, ed., *A Biography*, 45.

8. Ramsay, *History*, 1:112, 176, 305; Higginbotham, *War of American Independence*, 263; see also Henry Cummings, "A Sermon Preached at Lexington on the 19th of April" (1781), in Sandoz, ed., *Political Sermons*, 671; Wales, "Dangers of Our National Prosperity" (1785), in Ibid., 850.

9. James Madison to George Nicholas, May 17, 1788, in Bailyn, ed., *Debate on the Constitution*, 2:444; Ramsay, *History*, 2:631; Thomas Paine, "Common Sense," in *The Life and Major Writings*, 36; Jefferson to George Washington, April 16, 1784, in Peterson, ed., *The Portable Thomas Jefferson*, 368–69; Jay, *Federalist* No. 2, 38; Madison, *Federalist* No. 14, 103–4.

10. Thomas Jefferson to Benjamin Franklin, John Adams, and John Jay, October 5, 1781, in Cappon, ed., *Adams-Jefferson Letters*, 1:11; Pelatiah Webster, "Citizen of Philadelphia" (1787), in Bailyn, ed., *The Debate on the Constitution*, 1:567.

11. Wales, "Dangers of Our National Prosperity" (1785), in Sandoz, ed., *Political Sermons*, 850; Jefferson, "Notes on the State of Virginia" (1781), in Peterson, ed., *The Portable Thomas Jefferson*, 213; Jefferson to Washington, April 16, 1784, in Ibid., 368–69; Payson, "A Sermon" (1778), in Hyneman and Lutz, eds., *American Political Writings*, 1:527; George Mason to Patrick Henry, May 6, 1783, in Rutland, ed., *Papers of George Mason*, 2:770; see also McWilliams, *The Idea of Fraternity in America*, 92–93.

12. George Washington to John Jay, August 15, 1786, in Allen, ed., *George Washington*, 333; Washington, "Farewell Orders" (1783), in Ibid., 268–69; Alexander Hamilton, "Treasury Department Instructions," June 4, 1791, in Kline, ed., *A Biography*, 247.

13. Anonymous, untitled article from the *Boston Gazette* (1763), in Hyneman and Lutz, eds., *American Political Writings*, 1:33; An Impartial Citizen, "Dissertation" (1801), in Ibid., 2:1134–35; Webster, "Revolution in France" (1794), in Sandoz, ed., *Po-*

litical Sermons, 1268; Thomas Jefferson to Edward Rutledge, June 24, 1797, in Mayo, ed., *Jefferson Himself*, 210; Madison, "Debates in the House," in Veit, Bowling, and Bickford, eds., *Creating the Bill of Rights*, 73.

14. *United States Magazine*, quoted in Fliegelman, *Declaring Independence*, 112–13; *The Polite Philosopher*, quoted in Bushman, *Refinement*, 182, see also 29.

15. Bushman, *Refinement*, 43, 84, 411; Forrest McDonald, "Washington, Cato, and Honor: A Model for Revolutionary Leadership," in Elazar and Katz, eds., *American Models*, 55; The Preceptor, "Social Duties" (1772), in Hyneman and Lutz, eds., *American Political Writings*, 1:178–79; Perkins, "Theory of Agency" (1771), in Ibid., 1:145; Adams, "Thoughts on Government" (1776), in Peek, ed., *Political Writings*, 91.

16. Bushman, *Refinement*, 404.

17. Miller, "Sermon" (1793), in Sandoz, ed., *Political Sermons*, 1157; George Washington to Alexander Hamilton, October 3, 1788, in Fleming, ed., *Affectionately Yours*, 213; Washington to James Craik, September 8, 1789, in Ibid., 223; Alexander Hamilton to James McHenry, January 27–February 11, 1798, in Kline, ed., *A Biography*, 358; Edmund Randolph to the Virginia Legislature, October 10, 1787, in Bailyn, ed., *Debate on the Constitution*, 1:597; John Stevens, Jr., "Americanus VII" (1788), in Ibid., 2:58.

18. Madison, *Federalist* No. 10, 82–83; Franklin, "Poor Richard's Almanack," in Lemay, ed., *Writings*, 1290; Atwater, "Sermon" (1801), in Hyneman and Lutz, eds., *American Political Writings*, 2:1178; Landon Carter to George Washington, October 1776, in Fliegelman, *Declaring Independence*, 109; Wales, "Dangers of Our National Prosperity" (1785), in Sandoz, ed., *Political Sermons*, 851; Webster, "Oration" (1802), in Hyneman and Lutz, eds., *American Political Writings*, 2:1233, 1237; idem, "Revolution in France" (1794), in Sandoz, ed., *Political Sermons*, 1280; see also Wood, *Radicalism*, 58, 71, 194–95.

19. Madison to Jefferson, October 24, 1787, in Kammen, ed., *Origins*, 71; Murray, "Sketch of the Present Situation" (1794), in Harris, ed., *Selected Writings*, 62–63; Fobes, "Election Sermon" (1795), in Hyneman and Lutz, eds., *American Political Writings*, 2:993; Webster, "Oration" (1802), in Ibid., 2:1229; see also Timothy Ford, "The Constitutionalist" (1794), in Ibid., 2:926–28; Maxey, "Oration" (1799), in Ibid., 2:1048.

20. Norton, *Founding Mothers and Fathers*, 207, 210; Martin Howard, Jr., "A Letter from a Gentleman at Halifax" (1765), in Bailyn, ed., *Pamphlets*, 1:542; Thomas Jefferson to Abigail Adams, November 1786, in Cappon, ed., *Adams-Jefferson Letters*, 1:157; Abigail Adams to Thomas Jefferson, August 8, 1804, in Ibid., 1:276–77.

21. George Mason to George Washington, March 19, 1783, in Rutland, ed., *Papers of George Mason* , 2:763–65; Alexander Hamilton, "Account of a Duel between John Laurens and Charles Lee" (1778), in Kline, ed., *A Biography*, 70.

22. George Washington to Lund Washington, September 30, 1776, in Fleming, ed., *Affectionately Yours*, 93; Parsons, "Essex Result" (1778), in Hyneman and Lutz, eds., *American Political Writings*, 1:503–4, 519.

23. Benjamin Franklin, "An Account of the Supremest Court of Judicature in

Pennsylvania, vis. the Court of the Press" (1789), in Lemay, ed., *Writings*, 1152; George Washington to John Augustine Washington, May 1778, in Fleming, ed., *Affectionately Yours*, 126; Wortman, "Solemn Address" (1800), in Sandoz, ed., *Political Sermons*, 1527; Alexander Addison, "Analysis of the Report of the Committee of the Virginia Assembly" (1800), in Hyneman and Lutz, eds., *American Political Writings*, 2:1096–97; see Fobes, "Election Sermon" (1795), in Ibid., 2:1010–11; An Impartial Citizen, "Dissertation" (1801), in Ibid., 2:1132–34.

24. An Impartial Citizen, "Dissertation" (1801), in Hyneman and Lutz, eds., *American Political Writings*, 2:1168; Benjamin Franklin to George Whatley, May 23, 1785, in Lemay, ed., *Writings*, 1105; Benjamin Franklin to George Washington, March 5, 1780, in Ibid., 1019; Murray, quoted in "Introduction," in Harris, ed., *Selected Writings*, xliii.

25. Withington, *Toward a More Perfect Union*, 149–56, 242–43.

26. Charles Pinckney, "Qualifications for Suffrage" (1787), in Ketcham, ed., *Anti-Federalist Papers*, 149; Webster, "Oration" (1802), in Hyneman and Lutz, eds., *American Political Writings*, 2:1223; Pelatiah Webster, "Citizen of Philadelphia" (1787), in Bailyn, ed., *Debate on the Constitution*, 1:181; Annis Boudinot Stockton, "The Vision, an Ode to Washington" (1789), in Lauter, ed., *Heath Anthology*, 1:679; see also Iredell, "Address to the North Carolina Convention" (1788), in Bailyn, *Debate on the Constitution*, 2:883; Parsons, "Essex Result" (1778), in Hyneman and Lutz, eds., *American Political Writings*, 1:519.

27. Elizur Goodrich, "The Principles of Civil Union and Happiness Considered and Recommended" (1787), in Sandoz, ed., *Political Sermons*, 919–22; Wood, *Radicalism*, 276.

28. Hamilton, *Federalist* No. 36, 217; "Address to the New York Convention" (1788), in Bailyn, *Debate on the Constitution*, 2:770–71; Livingston, "Address to the New York Convention" (1788), in Ibid., 2: 778–79.

29. Smith, "Address to the New York Convention" (1788), in Bailyn, ed., *Debate on the Constitution*, 2:760–62; "From the 'Federal Farmer' to the 'Republican,' Letter III" (1787), in Ibid., 1:260; "Brutus III" (1787), in Ibid., 1:321.

30. Wilson, "Address to the Pennsylvania Convention" (1787), in Bailyn, ed., *Debate on the Constitution*, 1:825; Richard Henry Lee to George Mason, October 1, 1787, in Ibid., 1:45; Livingston, "Address to the New York Convention" (1788), in Ibid., 2:778–79.

31. Samuel Bryan, "Centinel I" (1787), in Bailyn, ed., *Debate on the Constitution*, 1: 53; "Officer of the Late Continental Army" (1787), in Ibid., 1:103; Luther Martin, "The Genuine Information I" (1787), in Ibid., 1: 638; Smith, "Address to the New York Convention" (1788), in Ibid., 2:761.

32. Anonymous, "A Revolution Effected by Good Sense and Deliberation" (1787), in Bailyn, ed., *Debate on the Constitution*, 1:13; Webster, "Citizen of America" (1787), in Ibid., 1:162; James Madison to Edmund Randolph, January 10, 1788, in Ibid., 1:745.

33. Thomas B. Wait to George Thatcher, January 8, 1788, in Bailyn, ed., *Debate on*

the Constitution, 1: 727; Samuel Bryan, "Centinel II" (1787), in Ibid., 1:78–79; idem, "Centinel VIII" (1788), in Ibid., 1:688; idem, "Centinel XII" (1788), in Ibid., 2:81.

34. Webster, "Revolution in France" (1794), in Sandoz, ed., *Political Sermons,* 1279, 1288–91; John Adams to Thomas Jefferson, July 29, 1791, in Cappon, ed., *Adams-Jefferson Letters,* 1:249; John Adams to Samuel Adams (1790), in *Political Thought in America: An Anthology,* ed. Michael Levy (Homewood, Ill.: Dorsey, 1982), 75–76; Wortman, "Solemn Address" (1800), in Sandoz, ed., *Political Sermons,* 1519.

35. Manning, *Key of Liberty,* 129, 136, 138, 139.

36. Jefferson to Adams, October 28, 1813, in Peterson, ed., *The Portable Thomas Jefferson,* 534; Jefferson to Washington, April 16, 1784, in Ibid., 368–69.

37. Alexander Hamilton to George Washington, May 5, 1789, in Kline, ed., *A Biography,* 217.

38. Paine, "American Crisis VII," in *The Life and Major Writings,* 154, Hoff, *Law, Gender, and Injustice,* 80–81; Ramsay, *History,* 1:30; Tappan, "Sermon" (1792), in Sandoz, ed., *Political Sermons,* 1113; Bishop James Madison, "Manifestations" (1795), in Ibid., 1312; Adams, "Discourses on Davila" (1789), in Peek, ed., *Political Writings,* 176–77.

39. Adams, "Discourses on Davila" (1789), in Peek, ed., *Political Writings,* 192; Warren, *History,* 1:3; Stevens, "Americanus V" (1787), in Bailyn, ed., *Debate on the Constitution,* 1:489–90; anonymous, "Ambition" (1789), in Hyneman and Lutz, eds., *American Political Writings,* 2:713; Paine, "American Crisis I," in *The Life and Major Writings,* 52–53; idem, "American Crisis IV," in Ibid., 103; idem, "Occasional Letter on the Female Sex" (1775), in Kimmel and Mosmiller, eds., *Against the Tide,* 65–66; "Brutus X" (1788), in Bailyn, ed., *Debate on the Constitution,* 2:88; see also Jefferson to Cosway, October 12, 1786, in Peterson, ed., *The Portable Thomas Jefferson,* 405.

40. Murray, "Desultory Thoughts" (1784), in Harris, ed., *Selected Writings,* 45; Murray to Miss Palfrey, November 24, 1776, in Moynihan, Russett, and Crumpacker, ed., *Second to None,* 1:190.

41. Adair, "Fame and the Founding Fathers," 8, 10–12; Ramsay, *History,* 1:106; George Washington to Thomas Jefferson, February 10, 1783, in Fleming, ed., *Affectionately Yours,* 172; Wills, *Cincinnatus,* 128–29, 165; Emerson, "Oration" (1802), in Sandoz, ed., *Political Sermons,* 1568; see also Wood, *Radicalism,* 207.

42. James Madison to Thomas Jefferson, June 13, 1793, in Peterson, ed., *A Biography,* 196; James Madison to Thomas Jefferson, June 19, 1793, in Ibid., 197; Duffield, "Sermon" (1783), in Sandoz, ed., *Political Sermons,* 784–85.

43. Shute, "Election Sermon" (1768), in Hyneman and Lutz, eds., *American Political Writings,* 1:131; Payson, "A Sermon" (1778), in Ibid., 1:538; Madison, *Federalist* No. 57, 351–52; Gouverneur Morris, "Election and Term of Office of the National Executive" (1787), in Ketcham, ed., *Anti-Federalist Papers,* 117; Hamilton, *Federalist* No. 72, 437; Fobes, "Election Sermon" (1795), in Hyneman and Lutz, eds., *American Political Writings,* 2:1010.

44. Duffield, "Sermon" (1783), in Sandoz, ed., *Political Sermons,* 785; "A Cumber-

land County Mutual Improvement Society Addresses the Pennsylvania Minority" (1788), in Bailyn, ed., *Debate on the Constitution*, 1:564.

45. Baldwin, "Oration" (1788), in Bailyn, ed., *Debate on the Constitution*, 2:516–18, 523.

46. Stevens, "Americanus V" (1787), in Ibid., 1:492–93.

47. Jefferson, "Notes on the State of Virginia" (1781), in Peterson, ed., *The Portable Thomas Jefferson*, 196.

48. Ramsay, *History*, 1:288; Warren, "Observations on the Constitution" (1788), in Bailyn, ed., *Debate on the Constitution*, 2:286; Warren, *History*, 2:401.

49. Benjamin Franklin to Lord Howe, July 20, 1776, in Lemay, ed., *Writings*, 994; Ramsay, *History*, 2:550; Henry Laurens, quoted in Ibid., 2:594; see also Washington, "General Orders, July 2, 1776," in Allen, ed., *George Washington*, 71.

50. James Madison to William Bradford, April 1, 1774, in Peterson, ed., *A Biography*, 30; Gouverneur Morris, "Eulogy" (1804), in Kline, ed., *A Biography*, 407; McClintock, "Sermon" (1784), in Sandoz, ed., *Political Sermons*, 809–10.

51. Barker-Benfield, *Culture of Sensibility*, 88–91; Baron, "Acquiring Manly Competence," in Carnes and Griffin, *Meanings for Manhood*, 153; Grossberg, "Institutionalizing Masculinity," in Ibid., 136; see also Franklin, "Autobiography," 72–74.

52. Adams, "Discourses on Davila" (1789), in Peek, ed., *Political Writings*, 177; Benjamin Franklin, quoted in Clawson, *Constructing Brotherhood*, 77, 112–15.

53. Clawson, *Constructing Brotherhood*, 15, 23, 52, 72–73, 184–85, 259; Wood, *Radicalism*, 223; see also Higginbotham, *War of American Independence*, 440.

54. Minor Myers, Jr., *Liberty without Anarchy: A History of the Society of the Cincinnati* (Charlottesville: University Press of Virginia, 1983), x, 17, 85–86, 93, 98, 137.

55. Benjamin Franklin to Sarah Bache, January 26, 1784, in Lemay, ed., *Writings*, 1084–85; Warren, *History*, 2:615; Myers, *Liberty without Anarchy*, 94, 124; Thomas Jefferson to James Madison, December 28, 1794, in Mayo, ed., *Jefferson Himself*, 197; Manning, *Key of Liberty*, 123, 138, 145; see also an anonymous article from the 1788 *Independent Gazetteer* in Bailyn, ed., *Debate on the Constitution*, 2:243.

56. Jefferson to Madison, December 28, 1794, in *Jefferson Himself*, 197; Appleby, *Capitalism and a New Social Order*, 57; Henry F. May, *The Enlightenment in America* (Oxford: Oxford University Press, 1976), 229–30; Manning, *Key of Liberty*, 157, 160–62, 165.

57. David Osgood, "The Wonderful Works of God are to be Remembered" (1794), in Sandoz, ed., *Political Sermons*, 1129–32; Webster, "Revolution in France" (1794), in Ibid., 1278; Alexander Hamilton, "Letters of Pacificus," July 17, 1793, in Kline, ed., *A Biography*, 308; George Washington to Henry Lee, July 21, 1793, in Andrist, ed., *A Biography*, 350–51; George Washington to Henry Lee, August 26, 1794, in Ibid., 356; George Washington to Alexander Hamilton, July 29, 1795, in Ibid., 365.

58. See George Washington to Burgess Ball, September 25, 1794, in Allen, ed., *George Washington*, 597; Thomas Jefferson, "First Inaugural Address" (1801), in Peterson, ed., *The Portable Thomas Jefferson*, 291–92.

59. Madison, *Federalist* No. 10, 82–83; *Federalist* No. 40, 253–54; Randolph, "Address to the Virginia Convention" (1788), in Bailyn, ed., *Debate on the Constitution*, 2:717.

60. Madison, *Federalist* No. 57, 352; Hamilton, *Federalist* No. 35, 214–16.

61. David Howell, "Solon, Junior" (1788), in Bailyn, ed., *Debate on the Constitution*, 2:534–35.

NOTES TO CHAPTER 6

1. Paine, "Common Sense," in *The Life and Major Writings*, 29; Alexander Hamilton to Robert Morris, August 13, 1782, in Kline, ed., *A Biography*, 118; "Officer of the Late Continental Army" (1787), in Bailyn, ed., *Debate on the Constitution*, 1:97; Adams to Taylor (1814), in Peek, ed., *Political Writings*, 209; "Plough Jogger" (1788), in Bailyn, ed., *Debate on the Constitution*, 2:415; George Washington to George Mason, March 27, 1779, in Rutland, ed., *Papers of George Mason*, 2:493.

2. Murray, "Observations on Female Abilities," in Harris, ed., *Selected Writings*, 18, 23–24, 28; Paine, "American Crisis I," in *The Life and Major Writings*, 51; Teresa Brennan and Carole Pateman, "'Mere Auxiliaries to the Commonwealth': Women and the Origins of Liberalism," *Political Studies* 27, 2 (June 1979): 183–200.

3. Henry St. John, Lord Bolingbroke, *The Idea of a Patriot King*, in *The Works of Lord Bolingbroke*, 4 vols. (Philadelphia: Carey & Hart, 1841), 2:374, 377, 391–92, 395–97, 401, 407, 419, 422–23, 426, 428; see also Connell, *Gender and Power*, 183–85.

4. Dulany, "Considerations" (1765), in Bailyn, ed., *Pamphlets*, 1:620–21; Fitch, "Reasons" (1764), in Ibid., 1:394–95; Continental Congress, "Address to the Inhabitants of Great Britain" (1775), in Ramsay, *History*, 1:177–78.

5. Richard Bland, "The Colonel Dismounted" (1764), in Bailyn, ed., *Pamphlets*, 1:324; Thatcher, "Sentiments of a British American" (1764), in Ibid., 1:491; Warren, *History*, 1:61; Ramsay, *History*, 1:93, 97; Joseph Reed quoted in Higginbotham, *War of American Independence*, 101.

6. Ralph Ketcham, *Presidents above Party: The First American Presidency, 1789–1829* (Chapel Hill: University of North Carolina Press, 1984), x–xi, 73, 76; George Washington to Joseph Reed, July 4, 1780, in Allen, ed., *George Washington*, 150–51.

7. Katherine Auspitz, "Civic Virtue: Interested and Disinterested Citizens," in *Civility and Citizenship in Liberal Democratic Societies*, ed. Edward C. Banfield (New York: Paragon House, 1992), 19; Alexander Hamilton to Elizabeth Hamilton, July 13, 1781, in Kline, ed., *A Biography*, 98; Washington to Nathanael Greene, October 6, 1781, in Fleming, ed., *Affectionately Yours*, 155.

8. Appleby, *Liberalism and Republicanism*, 218–19.

9. George Washington to Benjamin Lincoln, June 29, 1788, in Fleming, ed., *Affectionately Yours*, 209; see also Michael Walzer, *Exodus and Revolution* (New York: Basic Books, 1985), esp. 51–53.

10. John Adams, "Constitution of Massachusetts" (1780), in Peek, ed., *Political*

Writings, 98; Thomas Jefferson to John Colvin, September 10, 1810, cited in Ketcham, *Presidents above Party*, 172; Thomas Jefferson to John Breckinridge, August 12, 1803, in Mayo, ed., *Jefferson Himself*, 250; Thomas Jefferson, "Second Inaugural Address" (1805), in Ibid., 249.

11. See Connell, *Gender and Power*, 184–85.

12. Paine, "American Crisis V," in *The Life and Major Writings*, 116; George Washington to Alexander Hamilton, October 29, 1795, in Allen, ed., *George Washington*, 615; Alexander Hamilton to Edward Carrington, May 26, 1792, in Mason and Baker, eds., *Free Government*, 309.

13. Edmund Randolph, quoted in Ketcham, ed., *Anti-Federalist Papers*, 69; George Washington to the Secretary of Foreign Affairs, March 10, 1787, in Allen, ed., *George Washington*, 358; George Washington to Alexander Hamilton quoted in Clinton Rossiter, "Introduction," in Hamilton, Madison, and Jay, *Federalist Papers*, vi–vii.

14. Jay, *Federalist* No. 64, 393.

15. Madison, *Federalist* No. 40, 252–55; idem, *Federalist* No. 43, 279; James Madison to Edmund Randolph, January 10, 1788, in Kammen, ed., *Origins*, 97.

16. Alexander Hamilton, in Ketcham, ed., *Anti-Federalist Papers*, 71; idem, "Speech to the New York Assembly" (January 19, 1787), in Kline, ed., *A Biography*, 161; idem, *Federalist* No. 25, 167; idem, *Federalist* No. 34, 207.

17. Madison, *Federalist* No. 41, 257; idem, *Federalist* No. 63, 384–85; Hamilton, *Federalist* No. 71, 434–35.

18. Warren, "Observations on the Constitution" (1788), in Bailyn, ed., *Debate on the Constitution*, 2:296; Richard Henry Lee to Edmund Pendleton, May 26, 1788, in Ibid., 2:463; Lienesch, *New Order of the Ages*, 148; Henry, "Address to the Virginia Convention" (1788), in Bailyn, ed., *Debate on the Constitution*, 2:626.

19. Goodrich, "Principles of Civil Union" (1787), in Sandoz, ed., *Political Sermons*, 919.

20. Yazawa, *From Colonies to Commonwealth*, 3–4, 112; Wood, *Radicalism*, 149–50, 187; Fliegelman, *Prodigals and Pilgrims*, 267; see also Ketcham, *Presidents above Party*, 224–25; Gross, *Minutemen*, 191.

21. Gad Hitchcock, "An Election Sermon" (1774), in Hyneman and Lutz, eds., *American Political Writings*, 1:299; Payson, "A Sermon" (1778), in Ibid., 1:537; Cooper, "A Sermon" (1780), in Sandoz, ed., *Political Sermons*, 643, 652–53; McClintock, "Sermon" (1784), in Ibid., 802, 806–7; Samuel Langdon, "The Republic of the Israelites as Example to the American States" (1788), in Ibid., 959, 965; Israel Evans, "A Sermon delivered at the Annual Election" (1791), in Ibid., 1070; Timothy Stone, "An Election Sermon" (1792), in Hyneman and Lutz, eds., *American Political Writings*, 2:846, 854; Murray, "Sketches of the Present Situation" (1794), in Harris, ed., *Selected Writings*, 66; Fobes, "Election Sermon" (1795), in Hyneman and Lutz, ed., *American Political Writings*, 2:996; Samuel Kendal, "Religion the Only Sure Basis of Free Government" (1804), in Ibid., 2:1262.

22. Wilson, "Address to the Pennsylvania Convention" (1787), in Bailyn, ed., *De-*

bate on the Constitution, 1:825; Zephaniah Swift Moore, "An Oration on the Anniversary of the Independence of the United States of America" (1802), in Hyneman and Lutz, eds., *American Political Writings,* 2:1214; Addison, "Analysis of the Report of the Committee of the Virginia Assembly" (1800), in Ibid., 2:1063; Stockton, "The Vision, an Ode to Washington" (1789), in Lauter, ed., *The Heath Anthology,* 1:679; Webster, "Revolution in France" (1794), in Sandoz, ed., *Political Sermons,* 1290 (emphasis added).

23. Henry Holcombe, "A Sermon Occasioned by the Death of Washington" (1800), in Sandoz, ed., *Political Sermons,* 1409–11.

24. George Washington to Henry Laurens, January 31, 1778, in Fleming, ed., *Affectionately Yours,* 119; Fobes, "Election Sermon" (1795), in Sandoz, ed., *Political Sermons,* 1009; James Madison to Thomas Jefferson, October 17, 1788, in Kammen, ed., *Origins,* 371; James Madison to Edmund Randolph, June 15, 1789, in Veit, Bowling, and Bickford, eds., *Creating the Bill of Rights,* 250; Edmund Randolph to James Madison, June 30, 1789, in Ibid., 256.

25. Langdon, "Republic of the Israelites" (1788), in Sandoz, ed., *Political Sermons,* 957, 959.

26. Mitchell, *Vacant Chair,* 52, 116.

27. Norton, *Founding Mothers and Fathers,* 15; "Philanthrop" (1787), in Bailyn, ed., *Debate on the Constitution,* 1:327; Warren, *History,* 1:212; John Smalley, "On the Evils of a Weak Government" (1800), in Sandoz, ed., *Political Sermons,* 1422–25, 1430–33.

28. Griswold, "Overcoming Evil" (1801), in Sandoz, ed., *Political Sermons,* 1551–52; see also Ketcham, *Presidents above Party,* 216.

29. Abigail Adams to Thomas Jefferson, September 10, 1787, in Cappon, ed., *Adams-Jefferson Letters,* 1:198; Tucker, "Election Sermon" (1774), in Hyneman and Lutz, eds., *American Political Writings,* 1:167; Hitchcock, "Election Sermon" (1774), in Ibid., 1:293; Jay, *Federalist* No. 2, 39; James Madison, "Vices of the Political System of the United States" (1787), in Mason and Baker, eds., *Free Government,* 160.

30. Hamilton, *Federalist* No. 68, 414; Adams, "Thoughts on Government," in Mason and Baker, eds., *Free Government,* 143; Goodrich, "Principles of Civil Union" (1787), in Sandoz, ed., *Political Sermons,* 919–20; Moore, "Oration" (1802), in Hyneman and Lutz, eds., *American Political Writings,* 2:1217; Zabdiel Adams, "Election Sermon" (1782), in Ibid., 1:552.

31. Stephen Peabody, "Sermon before the General Court of New Hampshire at the Annual Election" (1797), in Sandoz, ed., *Political Sermons,* 1326–29, 1333; Wortman, "Solemn Address" (1800), in Ibid., 1527; Emmons, "Dignity of Man" (1787), in Ibid., 898; Franklin, "Autobiography," 131; "Speech at the Constitutional Convention" (1787), in Lemay, ed., *Writings,* 1133.

32. Madison, *Federalist* No. 57, 350; John Adams to Thomas Jefferson, February 5, 1795, in Cappon, ed., *Adams-Jefferson Letters,* 1:256; Adams, "Defence of the Constitutions" (1787), in Peek, ed., *Political Writings,* 158; Livingston, "Address to the New York Convention" (1788), in Bailyn, ed., *Debate on the Constitution,* 2:794.

33. Webster, "Oration" (1802), in Hyneman and Lutz, eds., *American Political Writings*, 2:1231; George Washington to Bushrod Washington, September 30, 1786, in Allen, ed., *George Washington*, 335–36.

34. Barlow, "Letter to the National Convention" (1792), in Hyneman and Lutz, eds., *American Political Writings*, 2:832; Roger Sherman, "Congressional Debates," in Veit, Bowling, and Bickford, eds., *Creating the Bill of Rights*, 151; see also Thomas Hartley, "Congressional Debates," in Ibid., 151, 161–62.

35. Madison, "Congressional Debates," in Veit, Bowling and Bickford, eds., *Creating the Bill of Rights*, 155; Jeremiah Wadsworth, "Congressional Debates," in Ibid., 156.

36. Smalley, "Evils of a Weak Government" (1800), in Sandoz, ed., *Political Sermons*, 1422; John Adams to Abigail Adams, December 2, 1781, in Adams, ed., *Familiar Letters*, 396; Thomas Jefferson to Elbridge Gerry, January 26, 1799, in Peterson, ed., *The Portable Thomas Jefferson*, 477.

37. Wales, "Dangers of our National Prosperity" (1785), in Sandoz, ed., *Political Sermons*, 851; John Mitchell Mason, "The Voice of Warning to Christians" (1800), in Ibid., 1451–52; Henry, "Speeches" (1788), in Ketcham, ed., *Anti-Federalist Papers*, 200; Fobes, "Election Sermon" (1795), in Hyneman and Lutz, eds., *American Political Writings*, 2:998; Atwater, "A Sermon" (1801), in Ibid., 2:1183; Ames, "Dangers of American Liberty" (1805), in Ibid., 2:1320.

38. James Madison, "Public Opinion" (1791), in Peterson, ed., *A Biography*, 187; Washington, "First Inaugural Message" (1790), in Allen, ed., *George Washington*, 469.

39. Locke, *Two Treatises*, bk. II, para. 160; idem, "Old England's Legal Constitution," in *The Life of John Locke*, ed. H. R. Fox Bourne, 2 vols. (New York: Harper & Brothers, 1876), 2:322–23; Bolingbroke, *Idea of a Patriot King*, 2:396, 413, 424–25.

40. Hitchcock, "Election Sermon" (1774), in Hyneman and Lutz, eds., *American Political Writings*, 1:298–99; Jefferson, "Summary View" (1774), in Peterson, ed., *The Portable Thomas Jefferson*, 21.

41. Edmund Randolph, "Debate at the Constitutional Convention" (1787), in Ketcham, ed., *Anti-Federalist Papers*, 69; idem, "Address to the Virginia Legislature" (1787), in Bailyn, ed., *Debate on the Constitution*, 2:602; James Madison to George Washington, April 16, 1787, in Peterson, ed., *A Biography*, 108–9.

42. Howell, "Solon, Junior" (1788), in Bailyn, ed., *Debate on the Constitution*, 2:534; see also Sheldon Wolin, "The Idea of the State in America," in *The Problem of Authority in America*, ed. John P. Diggins and Mark E. Kann (Philadelphia: Temple University Press, 1981), 50–51.

43. Madison to Jefferson, June 13, 1793, in Peterson, ed., *A Biography*, 196; Warren, *History*, 2:579, 591.

44. Judith N. Shklar, *Ordinary Vices* (Cambridge: Harvard University Press, 1984), 145, 177, 184, 220; Murray Edelman, *Political Language: Words That Succeed and Policies That Fail* (New York: Academic Press, 1977), chap. 1.

45. Alexander Hamilton, "Opinion on the Constitutionality of the Bank of the United States" (1791), in Mason and Baker, eds., *Free Government*, 303; Alexander

Hamilton to James Duane, September 3, 1780, in Kline, ed., *A Biography*, 87; idem, *Federalist* No. 71, 432–34; Washington, "General Orders, July 2, 1776," in Allen, ed., *George Washington*, 71; George Washington to John Hancock, September 2, 1776, in Andrist, ed., *A Biography*, 157.

46. Paine, "American Crisis V," in *The Life and Major Writings*, 115–16, 125.

47. Alexander Hamilton, "Letter to his Father published in the *Royal Danish American Gazette*, October 3, 1772," in Kline, ed., *A Biography*, 23; idem, *Federalist* No. 74, 448; Washington, "Seventh Annual Address" (1795), in Allen, ed., *George Washington*, 502.

48. John Thayer, "A Discourse Delivered at the Roman Catholic Church in Boston" (1798), in Sandoz, ed., *Political Sermons*, 1344–45; George Washington, "Fragments of the Discarded First Inaugural Address" (April 1789), in Allen, ed., *George Washington*, 446; Coxe, "American Citizen II" (1787), in Bailyn, ed., *Debate on the Constitution*, 1:25–26.

49. Webster, "Citizen of America" (1787), in Bailyn, ed., *Debate on the Constitution*, 1:149; Emmons, "Discourse" (1799), in Hyneman and Lutz, eds., *American Political Writings*, 2:1033–35; Adams, "Defence of the Constitutions" (1787), in Peek, ed., *Political Writings*, 114.

50. Evans, "Sermon Delivered at Annual Election" (1791), in Sandoz, ed., *Political Sermons*, 1066–67; Fobes, "Election Sermon" (1795), in Hyneman and Lutz, eds., *American Political Writings*, 2:998.

51. "Brutus IV" (1787), in Bailyn, ed., *Debate on the Constitution*, 1:426–27.

52. Madison, *Federalist* No. 49, 316; idem, *Federalist* No. 46, 294–95; idem, *Federalist* No. 40, 253–54; idem, *Federalist* No. 57, 353; idem, "Speech Before the House of Representatives" (June 8, 1789), in Mason and Baker, eds., *Free Government*, 292.

53. Hamilton, *Federalist* No. 27, 176.

54. Paine, "American Crisis II," in *The Life and Major Writings*, 62; Warren, *History*, 2:668.

55. Washington to Hamilton, October 29, 1795, in Allen, ed., *George Washington*, 615; Washington to Hamilton, May 8, 1796, in Ibid., 631; see also Hamilton to Edward Carrington, May 26, 1792, in Mason and Baker, eds., *Free Government*, 309.

56. Alexander Hamilton, "The Continentalist" (1781–1782), in Mason and Baker, eds., *Free Government*, 148; Thomas Paine, "American Crisis XIII," in *Life and Major Writings*, 231–32; Jefferson to John Adams, July 11, 1786, in Cappon, ed., *Adams-Jefferson Letters*, 1:142; Jay, *Federalist* No. 4, 49–50.

57. Alexander Hamilton to George Washington, May 2, 1793, in Kline, ed., *A Biography*, 284.

58. Madison, *Federalist* No. 62, 380–82; Hamilton, *Federalist* No. 11, 87, 91; idem, *Federalist* No. 15, 106; idem, *Federalist* No. 30, 189, 191.

59. James Madison to Thomas Jefferson, February 18 or 19, 1798, in Peterson, ed., *A Biography*, 218–19; James Madison to Thomas Jefferson, May 13, 1798, in Ibid., 221; see also Ketcham, *Presidents above Party*, 172.

60. James Madison, "Address to the People" (January 23, 1799), in Peterson, ed., *A Biography*, 227; "'The Republican' to the People" (1788), in Bailyn, ed., *Debate on the Constitution*, 1:710–11; George Washington to Charles Thomson, January 22, 1784, in Fleming, ed., *Affectionately Yours*, 187; John Adams to Abigail Adams, July 2, 1774, in Adams, ed., *Familiar Letters*, 9; see also Anne Norton, *Republic of Signs: Liberal Theory and American Popular Culture* (Chicago: University of Chicago Press, 1993), 9; Wolin, *Presence of the Past*, 9.

61. Abigail Adams to John Adams, May 9, 1776, in Adams, ed., *Familiar Letters*, 170; William Pitt, quoted in Warren, *History*, 2:506.

NOTES TO CHAPTER 7

1. Rotundo, *American Manhood*, chap. 2.

2. Barrie Thorne, *Gender Play: Girls and Boys in School* (New Brunswick, N.J.: Rutgers University Press, 1993), 92–93.

3. Joseph H. Pleck, "Men's Power with Women, Other Men, and Society," in *Men's Lives*, ed. Michael Kimmel and Michael Messner (New York: Macmillan Publishing Co., 1989), 25; Connell, *Gender and Power*, 110.

4. William J. Goode, "Why Men Resist," in Kimmel and Messner, eds., *Men's Lives*, 45, 49. Judith H. Stiehm reminds us that men who monopolize the means of protection often institute "a protection racket"; see her *Bring Me Men and Women: Mandated Change at the U.S. Air Force Academy* (Berkeley and Los Angeles: University of California Press, 1981), 299.

5. Gerzon, *Choice of Heroes*, 43, 93; Leverenz, *Manhood and the American Renaissance*, 72–73.

6. Barbara Ehrenreich, *The Hearts of Men: American Dreams and the Flight from Commitment* (Garden City, N.Y.: Anchor/Doubleday, 1984), 11, 13, 47, 50–51; David Popenoe, "Family Decline in America," in *Rebuilding the Nest: A New Commitment to the American Family*, ed. David Blankenhorn, Steven Bayme, and Jean Bethke Elshtain (Milwaukee: Family Service of America, 1990), 43, 45, 48; Dennis K. Orthne, "The Family in Transition," in Ibid., 95; Jean Bethke Elshtain, "The Family and Civic Life," in Ibid., 127–28.

7. See Appleby, *Capitalism and a New Social Order*, 15; Diggins, *Lost Soul of American Politics*, 66; Hoff, *Law, Gender, and Injustice*, chap. 1.

8. Rotundo, *American Manhood*, 17; McWilliams, *Idea of Fraternity in America*, 92; Sanford Lakoff, "From the Common Good to the Public Interest" (paper presented to the Western Political Science Association annual meeting, Anaheim, California, March 1987); see also Rogin, *Fathers and Children*, 92–93; Robert Booth Fowler, *The Dance with Community: The Contemporary Debate in American Political Thought* (Lawrence: University Press of Kansas, 1991), esp. chap. 3.

9. Bailyn, *Faces of the Revolution*, 259–60.

10. Clawson, *Constructing Brotherhood*, 72–73; Mark C. Carnes, *Secret Ritual and Manhood in Victorian America* (New Haven: Yale University Press, 1989), 32.

11. See Kann, *On the Man Question,* chap. 10.

12. David D. Gilmore, *Manhood in the Making: Cultural Concepts of Masculinity* (New Haven: Yale University Press, 1990), 17–21, 87–89, 108–10, 124.

13. Robert Moore and Douglas Gillette, *The King Within: Accessing the King in the Male Psyche* (New York: Avon Books, 1992), 26; Gerzon, *Choice of Heroes,* 173–74; Demos, *Past, Present, and Personal,* 205; Fliegelman, *Prodigals and Pilgrims,* 67; Dubbert, *A Man's Place,* 32–33; Filene, *Him/Her/Self,* 70–71, 141.

14. Moore and Gillette, *King Within,* 234; Rogin, *Fathers and Children,* 141; Gerald F. Linderman, *Embattled Courage: The Experience of Combat in the American Civil War* (New York: Free Press, 1987), epilogue.

15. Filene, *Him/Her/Self,* 70; Cotton Mather, quoted in Demos, *Past, Present, and Personal,* 145; see also Kimmel, *Manhood in America,* 45–50.

16. Frances Fitzgerald, *Cities on a Hill: A Journey through Contemporary American Cultures* (New York: Simon & Schuster, 1981), 23; Robert Bly, *Iron John: A Book about Men* (Reading, Mass.: Addison-Wesley, 1990), 8, 14, 16; Moore and Gillette, *King Within,* 126, 132, 149, 156.

17. Phillipe Ariès, *Western Attitudes toward Death: From the Middle Ages to the Present,* trans. Patricia Ranum (Baltimore: Johns Hopkins University Press, 1974), 59, 72.

18. See Bushman, *Refinement,* 120–22; Warren, *History,* 2:520; Jessica Mitford, *The American Way of Death* (New York: Fawcett Crest, 1978), 191, 194; David C. Sloane, *The Last Great Necessity: Cemeteries in American History* (Baltimore: Johns Hopkins University Press, 1991), 30–32; Ariès, *Western Attitudes toward Death,* 78–79.

19. Fliegelman, *Prodigals and Pilgrims,* 14, 50–51, 204; David E. Narrett, "Men's Wills and Women's Property Rights in Colonial New York," in Hoffman and Albert, eds., *Women in the Age of the American Revolution,* 129–30; Lois Carr Green, "Inheritance in Colonial Chesapeake," in Ibid., 168; Mason, "Mama, Rachel, and Molly," in Ibid., 265, 280–82; Shammas, Salmon, and Dahlin, *Inheritance in America,* 76.

20. Pateman, *Disorder,* 38; idem, *Sexual Contract,* 102; Harrington, *The Commonwealth of Oceana,* 62, 81, 103; see also Kann, *On the Man Question* , pt. 2.

21. O'Brien, *Politics of Reproduction,* 52–53, 62; see also Judith H. Stiehm, "Government and the Family: Justice and Acceptance," in *Changing Images of the Family,* ed. Virginia Tufte and Barbara Myerhoff (New Haven: Yale University Press, 1979), 369.

22. Robert Jay Lifton, *The Future of Immortality and Other Essays for a Nuclear Age* (New York: Basic Books, 1987), 3, 13–15; J. Glenn Gray, *The Warriors: Reflections on Men in Battle* (New York: Harper & Row, 1967), 46.

23. Robert Jay Lifton, "Woman as Knower," in *History and Human Survival* (New York: Random House, 1970), 265–74.

24. Robert Jay Lifton, *Revolutionary Immortality: Mao Tse-tung and the Chinese Cultural Revolution* (New York: Random House, 1968), 8, 69–70; idem, "Protean Man" and "The Young and Old: Notes on a New History," in *History and Human Survival,* 319, 321–22, 345, 355; see also Ryan, *Cradle of the Middle Class,* 176–77.

25. Demos, *Past, Present, and Personal,* 45–46; see also Locke, *Some Thoughts Concerning Education,* 151, 246–49; Wood, *Radicalism,* 194–95.

26. See Bushman, *Refinement,* 29; Clawson, *Constructing Brotherhood,* 52; Shklar, *Ordinary Vices,* 78; Don Sabo, "Pigskin, Patriarchy, and Pain," in Kimmel and Messner, eds., *Men's Lives,* 185–86.

27. Washington, "Rules of Civility" (1741), in Allen, ed., *George Washington,* 6–13; Bushman, *Refinement,* 402; David G. Smith, "Professional Responsibility and Political Participation," in *Participation in Politics,* ed. J. Roland Pennock and John W. Chapman (New York: Lieber-Atherton, 1975), 227; see also Mark E. Kann, *Middle Class Radicalism in Santa Monica* (Philadelphia: Temple University Press, 1986), 44–49; Charles Kesler, "Civility and Citizenship in the American Founding," in Banfield, ed., *Civility and Citizenship,* 60.

28. Mitchell Duneier, *Slim's Table: Race, Respectability, and Masculinity* (Chicago: University of Chicago Press, 1992), 110–13.

29. Barbara Myerhoff, *Number Our Days* (New York: Simon & Schuster, 1978), 180–83.

30. Ibid., 223–24, 266.

31. Gillette and Moore, *King Within,* 151–54; Garrison Keillor, *The Book of Guys* (New York: Penguin Books, 1993), 14; Carol Gilligan, *In a Different Voice: Psychological Theory and Women's Development* (Cambridge: Harvard University Press, 1982), chap. 3.

32. Bly, *Iron John,* 8, 22; Moore and Gillette, *King Within,* 7; Gerzon, *Choice of Heroes,* 2–3.

33. Eugene V. Debs, *Writings and Speeches of Eugene V. Debs,* ed. Arthur Schlesinger, Jr. (New York: Hermitage Press, 1948), 225.

34. Hartz, *Liberal Tradition in America,* 129; Wood, *Creation of the American Republic,* 605–6.

35. Duffield, "Sermon" (1783), in Sandoz, ed., *Political Sermons,* 780; Lienesch, *New Order of the Ages,* 179.

36. For studies of nineteenth-century manhood, see Rotundo, *American Manhood;* Kimmel, *Manhood in America;* Dubbert, *A Man's Place;* Leverenz, *Manhood and the American Renaissance;* Carnes and Griffin, eds., *Meanings for Manhood;* Pugh, *Sons of Liberty.*

37. See Kimmel, "Contemporary 'Crisis' of Masculinity," in Brod, *The Making of Masculinities,* 140–53; John W. Chambers, "Conscripting for Colossus," in *The Military in America: From the Colonial Era to the Present,* ed. Peter Karsten, new rev. ed. (New York: Free Press, 1986), 297–311.

38. William James, "The Moral Equivalent of War," in *International War: An Anthology,* ed. Melvin Small and J. David Singer, 2d ed. (Chicago: Dorsey Press, 1989), 328–36; Randolph S. Bourne, "A Moral Equivalent for Universal Military Service," in *War and the Intellectuals: Collected Essays, 1915–1919* (New York: Harper & Row, 1964), 142–47; Filene, *Him/Her/Self,* 97. For a recent proposal for national youth service, see

Benjamin Barber, *An Aristocracy of Everyone: The Politics of Education and the Future of America* (New York: Ballantine Books, 1992), chap. 7.

39. R. W. Connell, "Masculinity, Violence, and War," in Kimmel and Messner, eds., *Men's Lives*, 197; Moore and Gillette, *King Within*, 111; see also Murray Edelman, *The Symbolic Uses of Politics* (Urbana: University of Illinois Press, 1964), 76; Fliegelman, *Prodigals and Pilgrims*, 215.

40. Thomas Jefferson to Roger Weightman, June 24, 1826, in Peterson, ed., *The Portable Thomas Jefferson*, 584–85.

41. See Kerber, *Women of the Republic*, 224–25; May, *Enlightenment in America*, 225–26.

42. Rotundo, *American Manhood*, 17; Murray, "Desultory Thoughts" (1784), in Harris, ed., *Selected Writings*, 46, 48; Pateman, *Sexual Contract*; Hoff, *Law, Gender, and Injustice*, chap. 1.

43. Mather, "America's Appeal" (1775), in Sandoz, ed., *Political Sermons*, 483; Mayhew, "The Snare Broken" (1766), in Ibid., 248; Benjamin Franklin to Madame Helvétius, September 19, 1779, in Lemisch, ed., *Autobiography and Other Writings*, 314–315; Timothy Dwight, quoted in Bushman, *Refinement*, 194–95; Bloch, "Gendered Meanings of Virtue," 43; Parsons, "Essex Result" (1778), in Hyneman and Lutz, eds., *American Political Writings*, 1:497; Rush, "Thoughts upon Female Education" (1787), in Rudolph, ed., *Essays on Education*, 27–40; Franklin, "Celia Single" (1732), in Lemay, ed., *Writings*, 189–90; Jefferson to Barbé-Marbois, December 5, 1783, in Mayo, ed., *Jefferson Himself*, 43.

44. Webster, "Oration" (1802), in Hyneman and Lutz, eds., *American Political Writings*, 2:1234; Franklin, "On Constancy" (1734), in Lemay, ed., *Writings*, 225–26; idem, "On Drunkenness" (1733), in Ibid., 213–14; John Adams to Abigail Adams, June 3, 1778, in Adams, ed., *Familiar Letters*, 334; John Adams to Abigail Adams, August 25, 1776, in Ibid., 218–19; see also Fliegelman, *Declaring Independence*, 32, 130; Tyler, "The Contrast" (1790), in Lauter, ed., *The Heath Anthology*, 1:1102–42.

45. Foster, *The Coquette* (1797), in Lauter, ed., *The Heath Anthology*, 1:1150–68; Fliegelman, *Declaring Independence*, 38; Hamilton, *Federalist* No. 6, 54, 56–57; John Adams to Abigail Adams, April 14, 1776, in Mason and Baker, eds., *Free Government*, 119–20.

46. See Norton, *Liberty's Daughters*, esp. chap. 5; Kerber, *Women of the Republic*, 285; Kann, *On the Man Question*, chap. 9.

Bibliography

PRIMARY SOURCES

Adams, John. *The Political Writings of John Adams.* Edited by George Peek. Indianapolis: Bobbs-Merrill Co., 1954.

Adams, John, and Abigail Adams. *Familiar Letters of John Adams and His Wife Abigail Adams during the Revolution.* Edited by Charles Francis Adams. Freeport, N.Y.: Books for Libraries Press, 1970.

Adams, John, Abigail Adams, and Thomas Jefferson. *The Adams-Jefferson Letters: The Complete Correspondence between Thomas Jefferson and Abigail and John Adams.* Edited by Lester J. Cappon. 2 vols. Chapel Hill: University of North Carolina Press, 1959.

Anonymous. *An Essay in Defence of the Female Sex.* London: A. Roper & E. Wilkinson, 1696.

———. *A Farther Essay Relating to the Female Sex.* London: A. Roper & E. Wilkinson, 1696.

Astell, Mary. *The First English Feminist: Reflections upon Marriage and Other Writings by Mary Astell.* Edited by Bridget Hill. New York: St. Martin's Press, 1986.

Bailyn, Bernard, ed. *The Debate on the Constitution: Federalist and Antifederalist Speeches, Articles and Letters during the Struggle over Ratification.* 2 vols. New York: Library of America, 1993.

———, ed. *Pamphlets of the American Revolution, 1750–1776.* 2 vols. Cambridge: Harvard University Press, 1965.

Beccaria, Cesare. *On Crimes and Punishments and Other Writings.* Edited by Richard Bellamy. Translated by Richard Davies. Cambridge: Cambridge University Press, 1995.

Bolingbroke, Lord Henry St. John. *The Idea of a Patriot King.* In *The Works of Lord Bolingbroke.* 4 vols. Philadelphia: Carey & Hart, 1841.

Chudleigh, Lady Mary. *The Ladies Defence, or, the Bride-Woman's Counselor Answer'd.* London: John Deeve, 1701.

Cott, Nancy F., ed. *Roots of Bitterness: Documents of the Social History of American Women.* New York: Dutton, 1972.

Crèvecoeur, J. Hector St. John de. *Letters from an American Farmer.* New York: Penguin, 1981.

Debs, Eugene V. *Writings and Speeches of Eugene V. Debs.* Edited by Arthur Schlesinger, Jr. New York: Hermitage Press, 1948.

Fletcher, Andrew, of Saltoun. *A Discourse of Government with relation to Militias.* Edinburgh, 1698.

Franklin, Benjamin. *The Autobiography and Other Writings.* Edited by L. Jesse Lemisch. New York: New American Library, 1961.

———. *Writings.* Edited by J. A. Leon Lemay. New York: Library of America, 1987.

Gramsci, Antonio. *Selections from the Prison Notebooks.* Edited by Quintin Hoare and Geoffrey Nowell Smith. New York: International Publishers, 1971.

Greer, Germain, Susan Hastings, Jeslyn Medoff, and Melinda Sansone, eds. *Kissing the Rod.* New York: Farrar, Straus & Giroux, 1988.

Hamilton, Alexander. *A Biography in His Own Words.* Edited by Mary-Jo Kline. New York: Harper & Row, 1973.

Hamilton, Alexander, James Madison, and John Jay. *The Federalist Papers.* Edited by Clinton Rossiter. New York: New American Library, 1961.

Harrington, James. *The Commonwealth of Oceana.* London: J. Streater, 1656.

Hume, David. *A Treatise of Human Nature.* Edited by L. A. Selby-Bigge. Oxford: Oxford University Press, 1968.

Hyneman, Charles S., and Donald S. Lutz, eds. *American Political Writings during the Founding Era, 1760–1805.* 2 vols. Indianapolis: Liberty Press, 1983.

Jefferson, Thomas. *Jefferson Himself: The Personal Narrative of a Many-Sided American.* Edited by Bernard Mayo. Charlottesville: University Press of Virginia, 1970.

———. *The Political Writings of Thomas Jefferson.* Edited by Edward Dumbauld. Indianapolis: Bobbs-Merrill, 1955.

———. *The Portable Thomas Jefferson.* Edited by Merrill D. Peterson. New York: Viking Press, 1975.

Kammen, Michael, ed. *The Origins of the American Constitution: A Documentary History.* New York: Penguin Books, 1986.

Katz, Jonathan, ed. *Gay American History: Lesbians and Gay Men in the U.S.A.* New York: Harper & Row, 1976.

Ketcham, Ralph, ed. *The Anti-Federalist Papers and the Constitutional Convention Debates.* New York: New American Library, 1986.

Kimmel, Michael S., ed. *Mundus Foppensis (1691) and The Levellers (1703).* Augustan Reprint Society, no. 248. Los Angeles: William Andrews Clark Memorial Library, 1988.

Lauter, Paul, ed. *The Heath Anthology of American Literature.* 2 vols. 2d ed. Lexington, Mass.: D. C. Heath & Co., 1994.

Levy, Michael, ed. *Political Thought in America: An Anthology.* Homewood, Ill.: Dorsey, 1982.

Locke, John. *The Educational Writings of John Locke.* Edited by James Axtell. Cambridge: Cambridge University Press, 1968.

———. "Old England's Legal Constitution." In *The Life of John Locke,* edited by H. R. Fox Bourne. 2 vols. New York: Harper & Brothers, 1876.

———. *Two Treatises of Government.* Edited by Peter Laslett. Cambridge: Cambridge University Press, 1988.

Madison, James. *A Biography in His Own Words.* Edited by Merrill D. Peterson. New York: Harper & Row, 1974.

Manning, William. *The Key of Liberty.* Edited by Michael Merrill and Sean Wilentz. Cambridge: Harvard University Press, 1993.

Mason, Alpheus Thomas, and Gordon E. Baker, eds. *Free Government in the Making: Readings in American Political Thought.* 4th ed. New York: Oxford University Press, 1985.

Mason, George. *The Papers of George Mason, 1779–1786.* Edited by Robert A. Rutland. 3 vols. Chapel Hill: University of North Carolina Press, 1970.

McLaughlin, Jack, ed. *To His Excellency Thomas Jefferson: Letters to a President.* New York: Avon Books, 1991.

Millis, Walter, ed. *American Military Thought.* Indianapolis: Bobbs-Merrill, 1966.

Moynihan, Ruth Barnes, Cynthia Russett, and Laurie Crumpacker, eds. *Second to None: A Documentary History of American Women.* 2 vols. Lincoln: University of Nebraska Press, 1993.

Murray, Judith Sargent. *The Gleaner.* Schenectady, N.Y.: Union College Press, 1992.

———. *Selected Writings of Judith Sargent Murray.* Edited by Sharon M. Harris. New York: Oxford University Press, 1995.

Nussbaum, Felicity, ed. *Satires on Women.* Augustan Reprint Society, no. 180. Los Angeles: William Andrews Clark Memorial Library, 1976.

Paine, Thomas. *The Life and Major Writings of Thomas Paine.* Edited by Philip S. Foner. New York: Citadel Press, 1961.

———. "An Occasional Letter on the Female Sex." 1775. In *Against the Tide: Pro-Feminist Men in the United States, 1776–1990: A Documentary History,* edited by Michael S. Kimmel and Thomas F. Mosmiller. Boston: Beacon Press, 1992.

Ramsay, David. *The History of the American Revolution.* 1789. 2 vols. Indianapolis: Liberty Press, 1990.

Reform of Criminal Law in Pennsylvania: Selected Inquiries, 1787–1819. New York: Arno Press Reprint, 1972.

Rudolph, Frederick, ed. *Essays on Education in the Early Republic.* Cambridge: Harvard University Press, 1965.

Rush, Benjamin. *An Address to the Inhabitants of the British Settlements on the Slavery of Negroes in America.* 1773. New York: Arno Press Reprint, 1969.

———. *My Dearest Julia: The Love Letters of Dr. Benjamin Rush.* New York: Neale Watson Academic Publications, 1979.

———. *Vindication of the Address to the Inhabitants of the British Settlements, on the Slavery of Negroes in America in Answer to a Pamphlet entitled, "Slavery not Forbidden in Scripture; Or a Defence of the West-Indian Planters from the Aspersions thrown out against them by the Author of the Address."* 1773. New York: Arno Press Reprint, 1969.

Sandoz, Ellis, ed. *Political Sermons of the American Founding Era, 1730–1805.* Indianapolis: Liberty Press, 1991.

Sidney, Algernon. *Discourses Concerning Government.* 2d ed. London: John Darby, 1704.

Taylor, John. *Arator: Being a Series of Agricultural Essays, Practical and Political in Sixty-Four Numbers.* 1803. Edited by M. E. Bradford. Indianapolis: Liberty Press, 1977.

Toland, John. *The Militia Reform'd; or an Easy Scheme of Furnishing England with a Constant Land Force capable to prevent or to subdue any Forein Power, and to maintain perpetual Quiet at Home, without endangering the Publick Liberty.* London: John Darby, 1698.

Trenchard, John. *An Argument Shewing That a Standing Army Is Inconsistent with a Free Government, and Absolutely Destructive to the Constitution of the English Monarchy.* London, 1697.

Tyrrell, James. *Patriarcha non Monarcha: The Patriarch Unmonarch'd.* London: Richard Janeway, 1681.

Veit, Helen E., Kenneth R. Bowling, and Charlene Bangs Bickford, eds. *Creating the Bill of Rights: The Documentary Record from the First Federal Congress.* Baltimore: Johns Hopkins University Press, 1991.

Warren, Mercy Otis. *History of the Rise, Progress and Termination of the American Revolution, interspersed with Biographical, Political and Moral Observations.* 1805. Edited by Lester H. Cohen. 2 vols. Indianapolis: Liberty Press, 1988.

Washington, George. *Affectionately Yours, George Washington: A Self-Portrait in Letters of Friendship.* Edited by Thomas J. Fleming. New York: Norton, 1967.

———. *A Biography in His Own Words.* Edited by Ralph K. Andrist. New York: Harper & Row, 1972.

———. *George Washington: A Collection.* Edited by W. B. Allen. Indianapolis: Liberty Press, 1988.

SECONDARY SOURCES

Abramovitz, Mimi. *Regulating the Lives of Women: Social Welfare Policy from Colonial Times to the Present.* Boston: South End Press, 1988.

Adair, Douglass. *Fame and the Founding Fathers: Essays by Douglass Adair.* Edited by Trevor Colbourn. New York: Norton, 1974.

Appleby, Joyce. *Capitalism and a New Social Order: The Republican Visions of the 1790s.* New York: New York University Press, 1984.

———. *Liberalism and Republicanism in the Historical Imagination.* Cambridge: Harvard University Press, 1992.

Arendt, Hannah. *The Human Condition.* Chicago: University of Chicago Press, 1958.

Ariès, Phillipe. *Western Attitudes toward Death: From the Middle Ages to the Present.* Translated by Patricia Ranum. Baltimore: Johns Hopkins University Press, 1974.

Arnold, Marybeth Hamilton. "The Life of a Citizen in the Hands of a Woman: Sexual Assault in New York City, 1790 to 1820." In *Passion and Power: Sexuality in History*, edited by Kathy Peiss and Christina Simmons. Philadelphia: Temple University Press, 1989.

Bailyn, Bernard. *Education in the Forming of American Society*. New York: Vintage Books, 1960.

———. *Faces of the Revolution: Personalities and Themes in the Struggle for American Independence*. New York: Random House, 1992.

———. *The Ideological Origins of the American Revolution*. Cambridge: Harvard University Press, 1967.

Ball, Terence. *Reappraising Political Theory*. New York: Oxford University Press, 1994.

Ball, Terence, and J. G. A. Pocock, eds. *Conceptual Change and the Constitution*. Lawrence: University Press of Kansas, 1988.

Banfield, Edward C., ed. *Civility and Citizenship in Liberal Democratic Societies*. New York: Paragon House, 1992.

Barber, Benjamin. *An Aristocracy of Everyone: The Politics of Education and the Future of America*. New York: Ballantine Books, 1992.

Barker-Benfield, G. J. *The Culture of Sensibility: Sex and Society in Eighteenth-Century Britain*. Chicago: University of Chicago Press, 1992.

Becker, Carl. *The Declaration of Independence: A Study in the History of Political Ideas*. New York: Random House, 1970.

Blankenhorn, David, Steven Bayme, and Jean Bethke Elshtain, eds. *Rebuilding the Nest: A New Commitment to the American Family*. Milwaukee: Family Service of America, 1990.

Blewett, Mary H. *Men, Women, and Work: Class, Gender, and Protest in the New England Shoe Industry, 1780–1910*. Urbana: University of Illinois Press, 1988.

Bloch, Ruth H. "The Gendered Meanings of Virtue in Revolutionary America." *Signs: Journal of Women in Culture and Society* 13, 11 (1987): 37–58.

Bly, Robert. *Iron John: A Book about Men*. Reading, Mass.: Addison-Wesley, 1990.

Bourne, Randolph S. *War and the Intellectuals: Collected Essays, 1915–1919*. New York: Harper & Row, 1964.

Brennan, Teresa, and Carole Pateman. "'Mere Auxiliaries to the Commonwealth': Women and the Origins of Liberalism." *Political Studies* 27, 2 (June 1979): 183–200.

Buel, Joy Day, and Richard Buel, Jr. *The Way of Duty: A Woman and Her Family in Revolutionary America*. New York: Norton, 1984.

Bushman, Richard. *The Refinement of America: Persons, Houses, Cities*. New York: Random House, 1992.

Butler, Melissa. "Early Liberal Roots of Feminism: John Locke and the Attack on Patriarchy." *American Political Science Review* 72 (March 1978): 135–50.

Carnes, Mark C. *Secret Ritual and Manhood in Victorian America*. New Haven: Yale University Press, 1989.

Carnes, Mark C., and Clyde Griffin, eds. *Meanings for Manhood: Constructions of Masculinity in Victorian America.* Chicago: University of Chicago Press, 1990.

Chambers, John W. "Conscripting for Colossus." In *The Military in America: From the Colonial Era to the Present,* edited by Peter Karsten. New rev. ed. New York: Free Press, 1986.

Clawson, Mary Ann. *Constructing Brotherhood: Class, Gender, and Fraternalism.* Princeton: Princeton University Press, 1989.

Coffman, Edward M. *The Old Army: A Portrait of the American Army in Peacetime, 1784–1898.* New York: Oxford University Press, 1986.

Connell, R. W. *Gender and Power: Society, the Person and Sexual Politics.* Stanford: Stanford University Press, 1987.

———. *Masculinities.* Berkeley and Los Angeles: University of California Press, 1995.

Coontz, Stephanie. *The Social Origins of Private Life: A History of American Families 1600–1900.* London: Verso, 1988.

Cott, Nancy F., and Elizabeth H. Pleck, eds. *A Heritage of Her Own: Toward a New Social History of American Women.* New York: Simon & Schuster, 1979.

D'Emilio, John, and Estelle Freedman. *Intimate Matters: A History of Sexuality in America.* New York: Harper & Row, 1988.

Degler, Carl. *At Odds: Women and the Family in America from the Revolution to the Present.* Oxford: Oxford University Press, 1980.

Demos, John. *A Little Commonwealth: Family Life in Plymouth Colony.* Oxford: Oxford University Press, 1970.

———. *Past, Present, and Personal: The Family and the Life Course in American History.* New York: Oxford University Press, 1986.

Diggins, John P. *The Lost Soul of American Politics.* New York: Basic Books, 1984.

Di Stefano, Christine. *Configurations of Masculinity: A Feminist Perspective on Modern Political Theory.* Ithaca: Cornell University Press, 1991.

Dubbert, Joe L. *A Man's Place: Masculinity in Transition.* Englewood Cliffs, N.J.: Prentice-Hall, 1979.

Duneier, Mitchell. *Slim's Table: Race, Respectability, and Masculinity.* Chicago: University of Chicago Press, 1992.

Edelman, Murray. *Political Language: Words That Succeed and Policies That Fail.* New York: Academic Press, 1977.

———. *The Symbolic Uses of Politics.* Urbana: University of Illinois Press, 1964.

Ehrenreich, Barbara. *The Hearts of Men: American Dreams and the Flight from Commitment.* Garden City: Anchor/Doubleday, 1984.

Elazar, Daniel J., and Ellis Katz, eds. *American Models of Revolutionary Leadership: George Washington and Other Founders.* Lanham, Md.: University Press of America, 1992.

Filene, Peter G. *Him/Her/Self: Sex Roles in Modern America.* 2d ed. Baltimore: Johns Hopkins University Press, 1986.

Fitzgerald, Frances. *Cities on a Hill: A Journey through Contemporary American Cultures.* New York: Simon & Schuster, 1981.

Fliegelman, Jay. *Declaring Independence: Jefferson, Natural Language, and the Culture of Performance.* Stanford: Stanford University Press, 1993.

———. *Prodigals and Pilgrims: The American Revolution against Patriarchal Authority, 1750–1800.* Cambridge: Cambridge University Press, 1982.

Fowler, Robert Booth. *The Dance with Community: The Contemporary Debate in American Political Thought.* Lawrence: University Press of Kansas, 1991.

Fraser, Antonia. *The Weaker Vessel.* New York: Random House, 1984.

Gerzon, Mark. *A Choice of Heroes: The Changing Face of American Manhood.* Boston: Houghton Mifflin, 1982.

Gilligan, Carol. *In a Different Voice: Psychological Theory and Women's Development.* Cambridge: Harvard University Press, 1982.

Gilmore, David D. *Manhood in the Making: Cultural Concepts of Masculinity.* New Haven: Yale University Press, 1990.

Gray, J. Glenn. *The Warriors: Reflections on Men in Battle.* New York: Harper & Row, 1967.

Greven, Philip. *The Protestant Temperament: Patterns of Child-Rearing, Religious Experience, and Self in Early America.* New York: Knopf, 1977.

Gross, Robert A. *The Minutemen and Their World.* New York: Hill & Wang, 1976.

Grossberg, Michael. *Governing the Hearth: Law and the Family in Nineteenth-Century America.* Chapel Hill: University of North Carolina Press, 1985.

Gundersen, Joan R. "Independence, Citizenship, and the American Revolution." *Signs: Journal of Women in Culture and Society* 13, 11 (1987): 59–77.

Hall, Kermit. *The Magic Mirror: Law in American History.* New York: Oxford University Press, 1989.

Hartsock, Nancy. "The Barracks Community in Western Political Thought: Prolegomena to a Feminist Critique of War and Politics." In *Women and Men's Wars,* edited by Judith H. Stiehm. Oxford: Pergamon, 1983.

———. *Money, Sex, and Power: Toward a Feminist Historical Materialism.* New York: Longman, 1983.

Hartz, Louis. *The Liberal Tradition in America.* New York: Harcourt, Brace and World, 1955.

Hawes, Joseph M., ed. *Law and Order in American History.* Port Washington, N.Y.: Kennikat Press, 1979.

Higginbotham, Don. *The War of American Independence: Military Attitudes, Policies, and Practices, 1763–1789.* Boston: Northeastern University Press, 1983.

Hinton, R. W. K. "Husbands, Fathers and Conquerors." *Political Studies* 15, 3 (October 1967): 291–300.

Hoff, Joan. *Law, Gender, and Injustice: A Legal History of U.S. Women.* New York: New York University Press, 1991.

Hoffman, Ronald, and Peter Albert, eds. *Women in the Age of the American Revolution.* Charlottesville: University Press of Virginia, 1989.

Huntington, Samuel P. *The Soldier and the State: The Theory and Politics of Civil-Military Relations.* Cambridge: Harvard University Press, 1957.

James, William. "The Moral Equivalent of War." In *International War: An Anthology*, edited by Melvin Small and J. David Singer. 2d ed. Chicago: Dorsey Press, 1989.
Jónasdóttir, Anna G. *Why Women Are Oppressed.* Philadelphia: Temple University Press, 1994.
Juster, Susan. *Disorderly Women: Sexual Politics and Evangelicalism in Revolutionary New England.* Ithaca: Cornell University Press, 1994.
Kann, Mark E. *Middle Class Radicalism in Santa Monica.* Philadelphia: Temple University Press, 1986.
———. *On the Man Question: Gender and Civic Virtue in America.* Philadelphia: Temple University Press, 1991.
Keillor, Garrison. *The Book of Guys.* New York: Penguin Books, 1993.
Kerber, Linda K. *Women of the Republic: Intellect and Ideology in Revolutionary America.* Chapel Hill: University of North Carolina Press, 1980.
Kerber, Linda K., Nancy F. Cott, Lynn Hunt, Carroll Smith-Rosenberg, and Christine Stansell. "Forum: Beyond Roles, Beyond Spheres: Thinking about Gender in the Early Republic." *William and Mary Quarterly*, 3d ser., 64 (July 1989): 565–85.
Ketcham, Ralph. *Presidents above Party: The First American Presidency, 1789–1829.* Chapel Hill: University of North Carolina Press, 1984.
Kimmel, Michael S. "The Contemporary 'Crisis' of Masculinity in Historical Perspective." In *The Making of Masculinities: The New Men's Studies*, edited by Harry S. Brod. Boston: Allen & Unwin, 1987.
———. *Manhood in America: A Cultural History.* New York: Free Press, 1996.
Kimmel, Michael S., and Michael Messner, eds. *Men's Lives.* New York: Macmillan, 1989.
Lakoff, Sanford. "From the Common Good to the Public Interest." Paper presented to the Western Political Science Association annual meeting, Anaheim, California, March 1987.
Langguth, A. J. *Patriots: The Men Who Started the American Revolution.* New York: Simon & Schuster, 1988.
Lerner, Gerda. *The Creation of Patriarchy.* New York: Oxford University Press, 1986.
Leverenz, David. *Manhood and the American Renaissance.* Ithaca: Cornell University Press, 1989.
Lewis, Jan. "The Republican Wife: Virtue and Seduction in the Early Republic." *William and Mary Quarterly*, 3d ser., 44 (October 1987): 689–721.
Lienesch, Michael. *New Order of the Ages: Time, the Constitution, and the Making of Modern American Political Thought.* Princeton: Princeton University Press, 1988.
Lifton, Robert Jay. *The Future of Immortality and Other Essays for a Nuclear Age.* New York: Basic Books, 1987.
———. *History and Human Survival.* New York: Random House, 1970.
———. *Revolutionary Immortality: Mao Tse-tung and the Chinese Cultural Revolution.* New York: Random House, 1968.

Linderman, Gerald F. *Embattled Courage: The Experience of Combat in the American Civil War.* New York: Free Press, 1987.

Lloyd, Genevieve. *The Man of Reason: "Male" and "Female" in Western Philosophy.* 2d ed. Minneapolis: University of Minnesota Press, 1993.

Lockridge, Kenneth. *A New England Town: The First One Hundred Years.* New York: Norton, 1970.

———. *On the Sources of Patriarchal Rage: The Commonplace Books of William Byrd and Thomas Jefferson and the Gendering of Power in the Eighteenth Century.* New York: New York University Press, 1992.

Lofgren, Charles. *"Government from Reflection and Choice": Constitutional Essays on War, Foreign Relations, and Federalism.* New York: Oxford University Press, 1986.

Matthews, Glenna. *The Rise of Public Woman: Woman's Power and Women's Place in the United States, 1630–1970.* New York: Oxford University Press, 1992.

May, Henry F. *The Enlightenment in America.* Oxford: Oxford University Press, 1976.

McWilliams, Wilson Carey. *The Idea of Fraternity in America.* Berkeley and Los Angeles: University of California Press, 1973.

Meranze, Michael. *Laboratories of Virtue: Punishment, Revolution, and Authority in Philadelphia, 1760–1835.* Chapel Hill: University of North Carolina Press, 1996.

Mitchell, Reid. *The Vacant Chair: The Northern Soldier Leaves Home.* New York: Oxford University Press, 1993.

Mitford, Jessica. *The American Way of Death.* New York: Fawcett Crest, 1978.

Moore, Robert, and Douglas Gillette. *The King Within: Accessing the King in the Male Psyche.* New York: Avon Books, 1992.

Morgan, Edmund. "The Puritans and Sex." *New England Quarterly* 15 (1942): 591–607.

Myerhoff, Barbara. *Number Our Days.* New York: Simon & Schuster, 1978.

Myers, Minor, Jr. *Liberty without Anarchy: A History of the Society of the Cincinnati.* Charlottesville: University Press of Virginia, 1983.

Nash, Gary B. *Race, Class, and Politics: Essays on American and Colonial Society.* Urbana: University of Illinois Press, 1986.

Norton, Anne. *Republic of Signs: Liberal Theory and American Popular Culture.* Chicago: University of Chicago Press, 1993.

Norton, Mary Beth. *Founding Mothers and Fathers: Gendered Power and the Forming of American Society.* New York: Knopf, 1996.

———. *Liberty's Daughters: The Revolutionary Experience of American Women, 1750–1800.* Boston: Little, Brown, 1980.

O'Brien, Mary. *The Politics of Reproduction.* Boston: Routledge & Kegan Paul, 1981.

Pateman, Carole. *The Disorder of Women: Democracy, Feminism and Political Theory.* Stanford: Stanford University Press, 1989.

———. *The Sexual Contract.* Stanford: Stanford University Press, 1988.

Pateman, Carole and Elizabeth Gross, eds. *Feminist Challenges: Social and Political Theory.* Boston: Northeastern University Press, 1986.

Pitkin, Hanna Fenichel. *Fortune Is a Woman: Gender and Politics in the Thought of Niccolo Machiavelli.* Berkeley and Los Angeles: University of California Press, 1984.

Pugh, David G. *Sons of Liberty: The Masculine Mind in Nineteenth-Century America.* Westport, Conn.: Greenwood Press, 1983.

Robbins, Caroline. *The Eighteenth-Century Commonwealthman: Studies in the Transmission, Development and Circumstances of English Liberal Thought from the Restoration of Charles II until the War with the Thirteen Colonies.* Cambridge: Harvard University Press, 1961.

Rogin, Michael Paul. *Fathers and Children: Andrew Jackson and the Subjugation of the American Indian.* New York: Random House, 1975.

Rotundo, E. Anthony. *American Manhood: Transformations in Masculinity from the Revolution to the Modern Era.* New York: Basic Books, 1993.

———. "Patriarchs and Participants: A Historical Perspective on Fatherhood in the United States." In *Beyond Patriarchy: Essays by Men on Pleasure, Power, and Change,* edited by Michael Kaufman. New York: Oxford University Press, 1987.

Ryan, Mary P. *Cradle of the Middle Class: The Family in Oneida County, New York, 1790–1865.* Cambridge: Cambridge University Press, 1981.

———. *Womanhood in America: From Colonial Times to the Present.* 3d ed. New York: Franklin Watts, 1983.

Schloesser, Pauline. "Republican Motherhood, Modern Patriarchy, and the Question of Woman Citizenship in Post-Revolutionary America." Paper presented at the Annual Meeting of the American Political Science Association, Washington, D.C., August 29–September 1, 1991.

Schochet, Gordon J. *The Authoritarian Family and Political Attitudes in Seventeenth-Century England: Patriarchalism in Political Thought.* New Brunswick, N.J.: Transaction Books, 1988.

Schwoerer, Lois G. *"No Standing Armies!" The Anti-Army Ideology of Seventeenth-Century England.* Baltimore: Johns Hopkins University Press, 1974.

Shammas, Carol, Marylynn Salmon, and Michel Dahlin. *Inheritance in America: From Colonial Times to the Present.* New Brunswick: Rutgers University Press, 1987.

Shanley, Mary Lyndon. "Marriage Contract and Social Contract in Seventeenth-Century English Political Thought." *Western Political Quarterly* 32, 1 (March 1979): 79–91.

Shklar, Judith. *American Citizenship: The Quest for Inclusion.* Cambridge: Harvard University Press, 1991.

———. *Ordinary Vices.* Cambridge: Harvard University Press, 1984.

Shuffelton, Frank, ed. *A Mixed Race: Ethnicity in Early America.* New York: Oxford University Press, 1993.

Sloane, David C. *The Last Great Necessity: Cemeteries in American History.* Baltimore: Johns Hopkins University Press, 1991.

Smith, David G. "Professional Responsibility and Political Participation." In *Partici-*

pation in Politics, edited by J. Roland Pennock and John W. Chapman. New York: Lieber-Atherton, 1975.

Stansell, Christine. *City of Women: Sex and Class in New York: 1789–1860*. Urbana: University of Illinois Press, 1987.

Stiehm, Judith H. *Bring Me Men and Women: Mandated Change at the U.S. Air Force Academy*. Berkeley and Los Angeles: University of California Press, 1981.

———. "Government and the Family: Justice and Acceptance." In *Changing Images of the Family*, edited by Virginia Tufte and Barbara Myerhoff. New Haven: Yale University Press, 1979.

Stone, Lawrence. *The Family, Sex, and Marriage in England, 1500–1800*. New York: Harper & Row, 1977.

Tarcov, Nathan. *Locke's Education for Liberty*. Chicago: University of Chicago Press, 1984.

Theweleit, Klaus. *Male Fantasies*. Translated by Stephen Conway, Erica Carter, and Chris Turner. 2 vols. Minneapolis: University of Minnesota Press, 1987, 1989.

Thorne, Barrie. *Gender Play: Girls and Boys in School*. New Brunswick: Rutgers University Press, 1993.

Walker, Samuel. *Popular Justice: A History of American Criminal Justice*. New York: Oxford University Press, 1980.

Walzer, Michael. *Exodus and Revolution*. New York: Basic Books, 1985.

Weigley, Russell F. *History of the United States Army*. Enlarged ed. Bloomington: Indiana University Press, 1984.

Western, J. R. *The English Militia in the Eighteenth Century*. London: Routledge & Kegan Paul, 1965.

Williams, Raymond. *Marxism and Literature*. Oxford: Oxford University Press, 1977.

Wills, Garry. *Cincinnatus: George Washington and the Enlightenment*. Garden City, N.Y.: Doubleday, 1984.

Withington, Ann Fairfax. *Toward a More Perfect Union: Virtue and the Formation of American Republics*. New York: Oxford University Press, 1991.

Wolin, Sheldon, "The Idea of the State in America." In *The Problem of Authority in America*, edited by John P. Diggins and Mark E. Kann. Philadelphia: Temple University Press, 1981.

———. *The Presence of the Past: Essays on the State and the Constitution*. Baltimore: Johns Hopkins University Press, 1989.

Wood, Gordon S. *The Creation of the American Republic, 1776–1787*. New York: Norton, 1969.

———. *The Radicalism of the American Revolution*. New York: Knopf, 1992.

Yazawa. Melvin. *From Colonies to Commonwealth: Familial Ideology and the Beginnings of the American Republic*. Baltimore: Johns Hopkins University Press, 1985.

Index

Adair, Douglass, 34, 121
Adams, Abigail, 9, 25, 30, 41, 57, 88, 141, 153, 176
Adams, John, 30, 33, 48, 111, 133, 141-42, 144, 148-49, 153; and authority, 25, 46, 95, 176; and family spirit, 89-90, 102; and fraternal life, 125; and gender similarities, 175; and marriage, 83; and military service, 92; on mobs, 24, 57; and the natural aristocracy, 118; and the passion for distinction, 120; on property, 37, 87; and rape, 62; and women, 18-19, 32, 57, 60; and youth, 58, 88
Adams, Samuel, 19, 40, 69, 71
Adams, Zabdiel, 141
Addison, Alexander, 138
African-American males, 1, 15, 20, 77, 107, 158, 168. *See also* Slaves
Alexander the Great, 131
Alien and Sedition Acts, 95, 148
Allen, John, 34
Ames, Fisher, 22, 49, 98
Ames, Richard, 32
"Amicus Republicae," 77
André Major John, 73-74
Antifederalists, 42, 45, 108, 149, 159; and change, 94-95; and families, 102; and language, 49, 77; and the natural aristocracy, 116-19; and prerogative, 137; against standing armies, 72
Antimaritalism, 11, 22, 53, 60, 80, 158. *See also* Marriage
Appleby, Joyce, 14, 17, 25, 133, 159
Arendt, Hannah, 49
Ariès, Phillipe, 163
Arnold, Benedict, 124
Arnold, Marybeth Hamilton, 62
Articles of Confederation, 45, 77, 94, 135, 138
Astell, Mary, 9, 53
Atwater, Jeremiah, 76
Auspitz, Katherine, 133
Authority, 28-29, 106, 113, 131, 140; defiance to, 24-25, 100, 107; and individualism, 22; and kindness, 81, 87-88, 148; and language, 153-54; skepticism of, 8, 46, 103-4, 115, 133, 159, 173. *See also* Heroes; Leadership

Bachelors, 3, 21, 35, 52, 83-84, 88, 96, 98, 101, 111, 127, 130, 143, 157, 160, 171, 175; English precedents, 53-56; against manhood, 55-56, 79; punishments for, 61; ridiculing of, 56; stigmatizing as children, 58-59, 76-78; and sedition, 53-54; as slaves to passion, 53, 81
Backwoodsmen, 42, 65-66, 107, 159
Bacon, Francis, 79, 134
Bailyn, Bernard, 1, 24, 59, 93, 159
Baldwin, Simeon, 48, 77, 123
Ball, Terence, 25
Barker-Benfield, G. J., 13
Barlow, Joel, 21, 32, 57, 63, 83, 101, 142
Battle of the sexes, 7, 32
Beccaria, Cesare, 73-74
Behn, Aphra, 53
Bill of Rights, 42, 94, 139
Bland, Richard, 132
Bloch, Ruth, 17, 61, 98
Bly, Robert, 163
Bolingbroke, Lord, 131, 145
Boston Tea Party, 33, 132
Bourne, Randolph, 172
Boy culture, 156-57
Bradford, William, 62-64, 87
Brennan, Teresa, 130
"Brutus," 102, 116, 149
Bryan, Samuel, 117-18
Burr, Aaron, 113
Bushman, Richard, 12, 110-11, 168
Byrd, William, 84

Caesar, Augustus, 131
Caesar, Julius, 131

"Caractacus," 71
Carnes, Mark, 160
Carroll, Charles, 60
"Cato," 42, 100
Chastellux, Marquis de, 81
Cincinnati, Society of the, 46, 71-72, 102, 119, 126-27
Citizenship: earned, 29-31, 33; and family status, 7, 79-80, 87, 96-100, 120, 128, 130, 155, 171, 175-76; and gender, 1-2, 16-18, 39, 99-100; limits of, 100-104; male exclusions from, 52, 76-77; and passivity, 170-73; and property, 1, 38-39; truncated, 102-4. *See also* Women
"Civic Rusticus," 77
Civility, 14, 16, 54, 58, 90-91, 109-12, 115, 120, 151, 155, 167-69, 174, 176-77
Clark, George Rogers, 77, 106
Clawson, Mary Ann, 125
Clinton, DeWitt, 125-26
Commoners, 23-24, 104, 163. *See also* Gentlemen
Common Sense, 3, 30
Connell, R. W., 28, 134, 157
"Constant Customer, A" 42
Constitutional Convention, 38, 45, 97, 135, 143, 145, 153
Continental Congress, 107, 132
Coontz, Stephanie, 84
Cooper, Samuel, 34, 138
Coquette, 6-7, 176
Coram, Robert, 87
Cosway, Maria, 23
Cott, Nancy F., 6, 11, 104
Coverture, 38
Coxe, Tench, 77, 148
Crèvecoeur, J. Hector St. John de, 20, 44-45, 65
Criminal justice system, 52. *See also* Punishment
Dana, James, 20
Daughters of Liberty, 31
Dawson, John, 72
Debs, Eugene, 170
Declaration of Independence, 173
Democratic disorders, 1, 14, 25-26, 31, 43, 49, 52, 72, 79-80, 98, 103, 105, 109, 130-31, 155, 173
Democratic Societies, 126-27
Demos, John, 7, 84, 167
"DeWitt, John," 72, 94
Dickinson, John, 40, 74, 88
Diggins, John, 14, 159
Di Stefano, Christine, 19
Downer, Silas, 34, 82
Dubbert, Joe, 17
Duffield, George, 36, 121-22
Dulany, Daniel, 38, 131
Duneier, Mitchell, 168-69
Dwight, Theodore, 66
Dwight, Timothy, 12

Edelman, Murray, 147
Edwards, Jonathan Jr., 64
Effeminacy, 3, 12-13, 16-17, 19, 22, 28, 31, 53, 69, 76, 105-7, 120, 134, 143, 156, 172
Elizabeth I, Queen, 145
Emerson, William, 46, 121
Emmons, Nathanael, 86, 88-89, 149
Evangelicalism, 2, 14
Evans, Israel, 138, 149

Factionalism, 42-43, 46, 49, 51, 105, 110, 126-27, 150, 159
Fame, 29, 34, 45, 50, 119-24, 131, 151. *See also* Infamy
Families, 8, 36; dynasties, 7, 23, 33, 36, 39, 79-81, 85-87, 92-93, 100, 102-3, 121, 164-67, 169; versus individualism, 84-85, 97, 159; and parochialism, 100-104; and political corruption, 102; and politics, 98-99, 165; surrogate, 166-67. *See also* Fatherhood; Marriage; Sons; Women
Fatherhood, 84-85; and citizenship, 96-100; educating youth, 87-91; and family welfare, 7, 84-87, 91-93; flawed, 101; and friendship, 9, 11; limits of, 8-12; and obsolescence, 94-95; and politics, 140; and self-sacrifice, 2, 89, 92. *See also* Sons
Fathers, 49; civic, 8, 137-41, 150, 164-65; father figures, 47, 130, 138-39, 148-49, 167; forefathers, 31, 33-36, 146, 173; honoring of, 164
"Federal Farmer," 72, 116
Federalist Papers, 18
Federalists, 159; and change, 94-95; and families, 98-99, 102; and language, 48, 138; and leadership, 99, 122, 135-37; and maturity, 77; and the natural aristocracy, 116-19
Ferrars, Sir George, 56
Filene, Peter, 17, 162
Filmer, Sir Robert, 164-65
Fitch, Thomas, 33, 131
Fletcher, Andrew, 55

Fliegelman, Jay, 8, 25, 84, 88, 164
Fobes, Peres, 42, 49, 112, 122, 138, 149
Ford, Timothy, 20
Foster, Hannah Webster, 6, 21, 176
Franklin, Benjamin, 30, 73, 87, 101, 106, 124, 126, 142; and bachelors, 56-59; and citizenship, 97-98; on civility, 90; and economic opportunity, 6; and fraternity, 125, 159; on gender similarities, 21, 23, 174-75; and Indians, 65; and lust, 59; on marriage, 7, 35, 81-83; and the press, 114; on property, 36, 86; reputation of, 117-18, 123; and soldiers, 70-71; and vagrants, 65
Fraternity, 40-43, 105-7, 120, 125-27, 167; as fellow feeling, 106, 128, 149-50, 152; and future generations, 44-45; and individualism, 14, 43, 159-60, 169; interclass, 110-11, 128; international, 106, 151; limits of, 128-29; and nationality, 108-9, 127-29
Freemasonry, 46, 125-26, 160

Galloway, Grace, 11
Gates, General Horatio, 124
Gender turbulence, 2, 15, 26-27, 159-63, 173-74
Gentlemen, 23-24, 46, 54, 102-4, 110-12, 117, 163. *See also* Commoners
George III, King, 131-32, 140
Gerry, Elbridge, 57
Gerzon, Mark, 157, 161
Gettysburg Address, 47
Gilligan, Carol, 170
Gilmore, David, 161
Goode, William, 157
Goodrich, Elizur, 115, 141
Gould, Robert, 53
Grammar of Manhood, 1, 3, 29, 124, 155, 176; and hegemony, 50-51; idiom of childishness, 77-78, 156-58; against individualism, 159-63; rules of, 35, 39, 43, 47, 50; uses of, 30, 52, 72, 76-77, 79-80, 104-5, 120, 130-31, 139, 153-54
Gramsci, Antonio, 28
Gray, J. Glenn, 166
Great Awakening, 6
Greene, Nathanael, 133
Gregory, John, 6
Greven, Philip, 17, 31, 106
Griswold, Stanley, 3, 34-35, 140
Gross, Robert, 39, 57, 71, 92
Gundersen, Joan, 16-17

Haines, David, 164
Hall, Kermit, 69
Hamilton, Alexander, 60, 73, 75, 77, 94, 98-100, 109, 111, 113, 127-28, 145, 148; and fame, 122, 124; and foreign policy, 151-52; and leadership, 133, 135-36, 138, 147; on marriage, 80; on men's nature, 21, 23, 107; and the natural aristocracy, 116, 119; and necessity, 45-46, 135-37; and standing armies, 72
Harrington, James, 9, 165
Hartsock, Nancy, 16, 49
Hartz, Louis, 1, 15, 170-71
Hegemony, 1, 3-4, 26, 28, 139, 155, 170, 173, 177; and masculinity, 28-29, 31, 50, 76-77, 82, 134, 157, 171; and patriarchy, 137-43; in peacetime, 143-50
Henry, Patrick, 30, 90, 94, 137, 144
Henry VIII, King, 145
Heroes, 34, 46, 155, 167, 176-77; characteristics of, 141-42, 148-49; and law, 133-34, 137, 143-46; need for, 129-31, 140-42, 170-73; and prerogative, 136; and public opinion, 143-46; and public trust, 148-50; against women, 79, 133-35. *See also* Leadership
Heroines, 130-31
Higginbotham, Don, 69, 71, 108
Hill, Jeremiah, 48
Hinton, R. W. K., 12
Hitchcock, Gad, 137, 141, 145
Hobbes, Thomas, 18, 32
Hoff, Joan, 1, 17, 100, 159, 174
Holcombe, Henry, 139
Howard, Martin, 113
Howard, Simeon, 70, 92
Howe, General William, 19, 41, 124, 134, 147
Howell, David, 129
"Humble, John," 72
Hume, David, 54
Hutchinson, Thomas, 33

"Impartial Citizen, An," 84
"Impartial Examiner," 72
Indian males, 1, 15, 37, 65-66, 77, 107, 158
Individualism, 14, 22, 43, 84-85, 97, 159-63, 169-72
Infamy, 119, 123-24, 134
Instruction schemes, 142-43
Iredell, James, 98
Itinerants, 64-65
Izard, Alice, 80

James, William, 172
Jay, John, 98, 108, 135, 141, 151
Jay Treaty, 151
Jefferson, Thomas, 22-23, 30, 102, 108, 113, 127, 144, 173-75; and citizenship, 97; on civility, 90, 110; and families, 34, 82, 88-90, 93; and foreign policy, 151, 153; and fraternity, 40-41, 126-27; on the French Revolution, 44-45, 95; and generational change, 93-95; and Indian males, 65; and Louisiana Purchase, 6, 134, 137; and lust, 59-60; and marriage, 60, 83; and misogyny, 11, 21, 32; and the natural aristocracy, 116, 118-19; and prerogative, 46, 133-34, 145, 153; on property, 36-37, 85-86; and sociability, 74, 109; on Shays's Rebellion, 44-45, 95; on slavery, 67-69; on women's domesticity, 43
Jeffersonians, 15
Johnson, Lyndon, 158
Johnston, Zachariah, 99
Jónasdóttir, Anna, 18, 32
Juster, Susan, 6, 17

Keillor, Garrison, 169-70
Kendal, Samuel, 138
Kent, James, 106
Kerber, Linda, 1, 17, 19, 100
Ketcham, Ralph, 132
Kimmel, Michael, 12, 17
Knox, General Henry, 126

Lakoff, Sanford, 159
Langdon, Samuel, 138-39
Langguth, A. J., 69
Lathrop, Joseph, 101
Laurens, Henry, 96, 124
Laurens, John, 96, 113
Leadership, 46, 112, 128, 155, 173, 175-77; active, 132; characteristics of, 141, 150; and fame, 122, 124; and foreign policy, 151-54; and law, 128, 143-46; legitimacy, 31, 47, 99, 119-20; need for, 44, 103-6, 131; and political fatherhood, 137-39; prerogative, 47, 146, 150, 157, 170-71; and public opinion, 111-12, 143-46; and symbolic politics, 147-50. *See also* Fathers; Heroes; Manhood; Natural aristocracy; Prerogative
Lee, General Charles, 77, 113
Leland, John, 32
Lerner, Gerda, 32
Leverenz, David, 158
Lewis, Jan, 17
Liberalism, 14; conservative core of, 3, 163, 171; and gender, 17, 26-27
Libertines, 6-7, 13, 15, 20, 51, 53, 58, 60, 62, 64, 88, 105, 107, 131. *See also* Antimaritalism; Bachelor; Rape; Sex
Lienesch, Michael, 39, 95, 103, 137, 171-72
Lifton, Robert Jay, 166-67
Lincoln, Abraham, 47
Linderman, Gerald, 162
Livingston, Robert, 116, 142
Lloyd, Genevieve, 18
Locke, John, 8-9, 11, 18, 32, 36, 54, 145, 165
Lockridge, Kenneth, 10-11
Lownes, Caleb, 39

Machiavelli, Niccolo, 16, 134
Madison, Bishop James, 49
Madison, James, 38, 58, 94, 110, 112, 117, 121, 155; and Bill of Rights, 42, 94, 139; and citizenship, 98; and foreign policy, 152-53; and fraternal unity, 42, 108, 128, 150; and leadership, 122, 135-36, 138, 141-43, 145-46; and necessity, 45, 135-36
Male bonding: citizens and leaders, 99, 115, 149-50; fathers and sons, 32-35, 39, 50, 89-90, 96; fraternal bonds, 40-43, 104, 108, 160; intergenerational tensions, 93-96; limits of, 109
Males: disorderly, 2-3, 21-28, 31, 42-44, 51-52, 65-66, 69, 71-72, 109-10, 156, 170-71, 175-77; order in the ranks of, 2, 23-24, 31, 50, 76, 104-5, 118, 134, 154-55, 158, 167, 171-73; and reason, 18, 23; rivalry, 21, 28; and sociability, 40, 107, 109, 160
Manhood, 2-3, 6, 123; aristocratic, 12-13, 15-16, 29, 52, 110-12, 121, 161; the better sort, 4, 25, 46, 102, 104-6, 110-13, 115, 119-20, 122, 124, 128, 130, 141, 155, 157; black exceptions to, 68; and blood, 44-47, 50-51; and citizenship, 2-3, 16, 18, 20; consensual norms of, 15-16, 28-29, 31, 40-41, 46, 52, 72, 76, 96, 128, 158, 163, 167; and deference, 42, 47, 50, 139-40, 143, 150, 155, 160; and family rule, 5, 7-8, 10, 26-27, 50, 81-82; and family status, 4, 15-16, 84, 87; and fraternity, 39-43, 50, 52; heroic, 4, 50, 103, 129, 133-37, 139, 144-46, 148; and immortality, 29, 33, 35, 45, 81, 84, 88, 114, 121, 163-67, 169; versus individualism, 159-63; international norms of, 161; and leadership, 42,

44-47, 50; and liberty, 30-31, 33-35, 38-41, 43; and military service, 30-31, 69-73, 160-61; and nationhood, 47-50; in opposition to slavery, 20, 31, 76; in opposition to womanhood, 1-3, 16-22, 31, 50, 76, 162, 174; in opposition to youth, 20-21, 58-59, 76; and procreation, 21-22, 31-32, 35-37, 44, 47-51, 96, 103, 105, 135, 139, 142-43, 153-55, 159, 162-67, 171-73, 175-77; and property, 36-37; republican, 13-16, 29, 52, 82, 121, 161; and reputation, 112-15; and respectability, 152-54; self-made, 14-16, 29, 52, 76, 86, 109, 121, 158, 161; and self-restraint, 30-31, 50, 158; and self-sacrifice, 45-47, 50, 89, 97, 159-61, 169-70, 172; and space, 36-39, 47, 50, 52, 88; and time, 35, 39, 47, 50, 52, 88; unifying threads of, 162-63; and womanhood, 19, 21, 23, 174-77. *See also* Effeminacy
Manning, William, 71, 118-19, 126-27
Mao Tse-tung, 167
Marriage, 80-84; and adultery, 60-61, 66, 81, 131; and citizenship, 96-100; companionate ideals of, 8-10, 13-14, 80-81; and divorce, 8, 84; as duty, 2, 5-6, 61; and fulfillment, 61, 80-81; incentives to, 54, 56, 83; and individualism, 14; and male sex right, 63, 100, 105; and property, 6; taming effect of, 6-8, 16, 21, 27, 79-80, 82-84, 175-76. *See also* Antimaritalism
Mason, George, 14, 84-85, 90, 92, 97, 109, 113
Mason, John Mitchell, 144
Mason, Sally, 88
Mather, Cotton, 162
Mather, Moses, 34, 40
Maxey, Jonathan, 49
May, Henry, 127
Mayhew, Jonathan, 22, 33
McClintock, Samuel, 106, 138
McDonald, Forrest, 110
McWilliams, Wilson Carey, 41, 159
Militia, 39, 47, 83, 92, 100-102; and corruption, 71; versus standing armies, 55, 70-71
Miller, Samuel, 48
Milton, John, 81
Miscegenation, 42, 65-67
Misogyny, 11, 14, 19, 27, 105, 174
Mitchell, Reid, 140
Mohl, Raymond, 65
Monroe, James, 108
Moore, Robert and Douglas Gillette, 161, 163, 169
Moore, Zephaniah Swift, 138, 141
Morris, Gouverneur, 122, 124
Murray, Judith Sargent, 5-6, 10, 13, 29, 35, 105, 112, 114, 120; and bachelors, 61; and education, 57; and language, 49; and marriage, 80-81; and political patriarchy, 138; and women, 16, 49-50, 130, 174
Myerhoff, Barbara, 168-69

Nash, Gary, 101
Natural aristocracy, 115-19, 123
Newburgh Addresses, 46
Norton, Mary Beth, 61, 84, 113, 140
Noyes, Mary Fish, 6, 81-82

O'Brien, Mary, 165-66
"Officer of the Late Continental Army," 91
"Old State Soldier," 48
Order of Odd Fellows, 167
Osgood, David, 127
Otis, James, Jr., 9, 24, 30, 40, 74

Paine, Thomas, 3, 107, 151; gender metaphors, 20; and generational change, 95-96; on liberty, 30, 91, 93; and property, 85; versus redcoats, 70; and self-restraint, 30; and war, 40-41, 92; and women, 9, 60, 130, 134
Parsons, Theophilus, 18, 114
Pateman, Carole, 17-18, 21, 27, 32, 130, 164, 174
Patriarchal rage, 11, 27
Patriarchy, 81-82, 96, 99-100, 105, 120, 155, 157, 161, 165-67, 167, 173-77; black exceptions to, 68; corruption of, 52, 140; defense of, 19, 47, 51, 79-80; destabilization of, 8-11, 22; and hegemony, 137-43; language of, 139-40; revolt against, 137; traditional, 2, 5-8, 15-16, 27, 29, 52, 82, 130, 134-35
Paupers, 65
Payson, Phillips, 70, 109, 122, 137
Pendleton, Edmund, 97
Penn, William, 63
Perkins, John, 12, 111
"Philanthrop," 140
Philips, Josiah, 137
Pickering, Timothy, 99
Pinckney, Charles, 115
Pinckney, Charles Cotesworth, 86
Pitkin, Hanna, 16
Pitt, William, 154
Plato, 94, 131, 134

Pleck, Joseph, 157
"Plough Jogger," 88
Plutarch, 131
Pocock, J. G. A., 25
"Preceptor," 92, 110
Prerogative, 170; English history of, 145; in foreign policy, 153-54; manly, 45, 151; patriarchal, 2, 27, 166; political, 29, 46-47, 121, 129, 131-37, 145-46, 157; royal and parliamentary, 27, 131-32. *See also* Heroes; Leadership
Primogeniture, 85-86
Proclamation of Neutrality, 121, 134-35, 143, 153
Prynne, William, 55
Pugh, David, 17
Punishments, 73-75; banishment, 75, 107; capital, 63-64, 68, 73; corporal, 64; emasculation, 24, 73-74; humiliation, 74-75, 107; imprisonment, 63, 74; isolation, 74; rehabilitation, 74-75

Quarrier, Samuel, 74
Quincy, Josiah, 62

Race war, 68-69
Ramsay, David, 20, 24, 41, 62, 77, 86, 99, 106-8, 121, 124, 132
Randolph, Edmund, 77, 112, 128, 135, 145
Rape, 55, 62-63, 66, 69-70
Redcoats, 54-56, 62, 69-70, 82
Reed, Joseph, 132
Refinement, 12, 110-12, 120
"Republican," 153
Republicanism, 14, 26-27
Reynolds, Maria, 60
Rice, David, 66
Robbins, Caroline, 14
Robinson, John, 7
Rogin, Michael, 17, 162
Rotation Schemes, 142
Rotundo, E. Anthony, 5, 17, 156, 159, 174
Rush, Benjamin, 59, 61, 68, 71, 98, 101; and capital punishment, 73-75
Rush, Jacob, 60

Saar, Doreen Alvarez, 65-66
Sabo, Don, 168
Sandys, Sir Edwin, 56
Schmitt, Gary, 46
Schochet, Gordon, 9
Schuyler, Elizabeth, 80
Separate spheres, 11
Sex: black hypersexuality, 67-68; as conquest, 58; and crime, 62-64; dangers of, 19, 53, 59, 61; incest, 66; and marriage, 6, 54, 64, 83-84; and natality, 51; premarital, 57, 60; same-sex relationships, 63-64; and self-discipline, 62-64; and soldiers, 55; subversiveness of, 5-6, 27; and women, 51. *See also* Rape
Sexual contract, 17, 174
Shaftesbury, Third Earl of (Anthony Ashley Cooper), 54
Shays's Rebellion, 44-46, 95, 126
Sherman, Roger, 142
Sherwood, Samuel, 40
Shklar, Judith, 17, 20, 38, 146-47
Shuffelton, Frank, 67
Shute, Daniel, 34, 122
Sidney, Algernon, 8
Silliman, Mary Fish Noyes. *See* Noyes, Mary Fish
Slaveholders, 66-69
Slavery, 6, 42, 67, 156
Slaves, 37, 66-69, 71. *See also* African-American males
Smalley, John, 140
Smith, Melancton, 102, 116
Smith-Rosenberg, Carroll, 17
Sons, 90, 161; autonomy of, 93-94; education of, 54, 87-91; and inheritance, 85-87; and military service, 92-93
Stamp Act, 22, 24, 40
Standing armies, 54-55, 70-72, 75. *See also* Militia
Stansell, Christine, 17-18
Stevens, John, 112, 120, 123
Stiles, Ezra, 44
Stockton, Annis Boudinot, 10, 115, 138
Stockton, Julia, 61
Stone, Lawrence, 9
Stone, Timothy, 138
Symbolic politics, 147-50

Taylor, John, 20, 37, 67-69
Thacher, Peter, 88
Thatcher, Oxenbridge, 40, 132
Thayer, John, 148
Thorne, Barrie, 156-57
Toland, John, 55-56
Trenchard, John, 54-55
Tucker, John, 47, 141

Tyler, Royall, 13, 57, 103-4
Tyrrell, James, 8

Ulrich, Laurel Thatcher, 7, 71
Universal Military Training, 160
U.S. Constitution, 31, 42, 48, 72, 91, 94, 98-99, 109, 117-18, 121, 126, 129, 133-36, 138, 141, 153, 170-73
U.S. House of Representatives, 98
U.S. presidency, 98-99; and foreign policy, 153-54
U.S. Senate, 38, 98, 100

Wadsworth, Jeremiah, 143, 147
Wait, Thomas, 117
Wales, Samuel, 112, 144
Warren, Joseph, 41
Warren, Mercy Otis, 19, 33, 91, 106, 120, 124, 126; and language, 48-49; and prerogative, 132, 146; and soldiers, 69-70
Warren, Winslow, 89
Washington, George, 31, 48, 73, 76, 77, 94, 119, 125, 127; and agriculture, 36; and civility, 91, 109, 111, 127, 168; against disorder, 24-25, 46; and economic opportunity, 6; and fame, 121-22, 124; and families, 32-33, 83, 93; as a father figure, 138-39; and foreign policy, 134-35, 151, 153; and the frontier, 65-66; and leadership, 130, 132-33, 135, 142, 144, 147-48, 170; and marriage, 81; and militias, 71, 101; and property, 37; and reputation, 13, 46, 113-14, 117-19; and self-discipline, 30-31; and sex, 57-58, 60, 83; and soldiers, 45; on Shays's Rebellion, 44; and war, 40-41
Washington, Lund, 113
Washington, Martha, 83
Webster, Noah, 21, 23, 27, 43, 49, 60, 77, 84, 87, 109-10, 112, 127, 149, 175; and the natural aristocracy, 115, 118, 138, 142
Webster, Pelatiah, 108, 115
Weigley, Russell, 71
West, Samuel, 97
Whiskey rebels, 75, 148
Williams, Daniel, 68
Williams, Raymond, 28
Williams, Samuel, 19, 84
Wills, Garry, 37, 121
Wilson, James, 38, 99, 116, 138
Wilson, Woodrow, 172-73
Winthrop, James, 42, 52
Winthrop, John, 64
Witherspoon, John, 2, 40-41, 67, 106
Withington, Ann Fairfax, 105, 107
Wolin, Sheldon, 33
Wollstonecraft, Mary, 174
Women: and citizenship, 99-100, 130-31, 153; domineering, 6-7, 16-17, 81; and disorder, 7, 10, 16-17, 19-22, 47, 51, 81, 100, 175-77; and education, 81-82, 174; as family members, 7, 15-16, 39, 43, 61; and historical agency, 10, 22; and historical continuity, 166; and patriotism, 26, 51, 174; political exclusion of, 1, 3, 18-19, 26-27, 31-32, 38-39, 43, 50, 100, 105, 155, 174; in the public sphere, 18, 27, 49-50; and reason, 18, 174; rights of, 9, 156, 158, 174; and sex, 51, 59-60; and slavery, 66; Spartan, 35
Wood, Gordon, 14, 23, 115, 126, 137, 171
Workman, Benjamin, 72
Wortman, Tunis, 67, 114

Yazawa, Melvin, 87
Young Men's Christian Association, 167

About the Author

Mark E. Kann, Professor of Political Science at the University of Southern California, holds the USC Associates Chair in Social Science. He has taught in the Gender Studies Program and the American Studies and Ethnicity Program as well as in the Department of Political Science. He is the recipient of numerous teaching awards.

Professor Kann has authored and edited seven books and dozens of academic articles. His prior book was *On the Man Question: Gender and Civic Virtue in America* (1991).

In addition to teaching and research, Kann has been editor of the interdisciplinary journal *Humanities in Society*, written monthly political commentary for the Los Angeles *Herald Examiner*, and served as Associate Dean of Graduate Studies at the University of Southern California. He received his Ph.D. from the University of Wisconsin-Madison in 1975.